W9-ACE-090

Case Studies in Contemporary Criticism

A Companion to
JAMES JOYCE's

Ulysses

Case Studies in Contemporary Criticism
SERIES EDITOR: Ross C Murfin

Case Studies in Contemporary Criticism

SERIES EDITOR: Ross C Murfin, *Southern Methodist University*

A Companion to JAMES JOYCE's *Ulysses*

Biographical and Historical Contexts, Critical History, and Essays from Five Contemporary Critical Perspectives

EDITED BY

Margot Norris

University of California, Irvine

Bedford Books

BOSTON NEW YORK

For Bedford Books
President and Publisher: Charles H. Christensen
General Manager and Associate Publisher: Joan E. Feinberg
Managing Editor: Elizabeth M. Schaaf
Developmental Editor: John Sullivan
Production Editors: Ellen C. Thibault, Deborah Baker
Copyeditor: Lisa Wehrle
Text Design: Sandra Rigney, The Book Department
Cover Design: Richard Emery Design, Inc.
Cover Art: Photograph of the O'Connell Bridge, Dublin, ca. 1902.
Courtesy of the National Library of Ireland.
Composition: Pine Tree Composition, Inc.
Printing and Binding: Haddon Craftsmen, Inc.

Library of Congress Catalog Card Number: 97–74966

2   1   0   9   8
f   e   d   c   b   a

For information, write: Bedford Books, 75 Arlington Street, Boston,
MA 02116 (617–426–7440)

ISBN: 0–312–11598–9 (paperback)
ISBN: 0–312–21067–1 (hardcover)

Acknowledgments

Jacques Derrida, "Ulysses Gramophone." In *James Joyce: The Augmented Ninth.*
Edited by Bernard Benstock, 27–54. Syracuse, NY: Syracuse University Press, 1988.
Wolfgang Iser. "Patterns of Communication in Joyce's *Ulysses*." In *The Implied
Reader: Patterns of Communication in Prose Fiction from Bunyan to Beckett.* 1974.
Reprinted by permission of the Johns Hopkins University Press.

About the Series

Volumes in the Case Studies in Contemporary Criticism series provide college students with an entrée into the current critical and theoretical ferment in literary studies. Each volume presents critical essays that discuss a classic literary work from different theoretical perspectives, together with the editors' introductions to both the literary work and the critics' theoretical perspectives. Other volumes in the series include the complete text of the classic work under study. This volume, however, does not reprint the text of *Ulysses*, due to its substantial length and ready availability.

The volume editor of each Case Study has written an introduction to the work's biographical and historical contexts, surveyed the critical responses to the work since its initial publication, and when necessary, selected and prepared an authoritative text of the classic work. Thus situated biographically, historically, and critically, the work is examined in five critical essays, each representing a theoretical perspective of importance to contemporary literary studies. These essays, prepared especially for undergraduates by exemplary critics, show theory in praxis; whether written by established scholars or exceptional young critics, they demonstrate how current theoretical approaches can generate compelling readings of great literature.

As series editor, I have prepared introductions, with bibliographies, to the theoretical perspectives represented in the five critical essays. Each introduction presents the principal concepts of a particular theory in their historical context and discusses the major figures and key works that have influenced their formulation. It is my hope that these introductions will reveal to students that effective criticism is informed by a set of coherent assumptions, and will encourage them to recognize and examine their own assumptions about literature. After each introduction, a selective bibliography presents a partially annotated list of important works from the literature of the particular theoretical perspective, including the most recent and readily available editions and translations of the works cited in the introduction. Finally, I have compiled a glossary of key terms that recur in these volumes and in the discourse of contemporary theory and criticism. We hope that the Case Studies in Contemporary Criticism series will reaffirm the richness of its literary works, even as it introduces invigorating new ways to mine their apparently inexhaustible wealth.

Ross C Murfin
Series Editor
Southern Methodist University

About This Volume

This *Companion to James Joyce's "Ulysses": A Case Study in Contemporary Criticism* differs from the other volumes in the Case Studies series because it does not reprint the text of the work under consideration. The length of *Ulysses*—one of the "big" books among the classics, with 644 pages in the Gabler edition—makes its inclusion impractical. Instead, this volume—with its various introductory discussions of Joyce, *Ulysses*, and contemporary criticism and its critical essays about the novel—can usefully supplement whatever edition of the work is being read.

There is, in effect, no "definitive" edition of *Ulysses*. Joyce's text had a difficult birth: typed by friends when paid typists objected to its obscenity, published by a kindly bookseller who permitted the author to make endless changes and corrections, and printed by French printers daunted by highly experimental prose in a foreign language. *Ulysses* was an editing nightmare from the start. Editorial controversy revisited the book twice—first in the 1980s when argument surrounded the unveiling of a new "corrected text" by Hans Walter Gabler (now known as "the Gabler edition") that was published in 1986 by Vintage Books, a division of Random House. I discuss these editorial difficulties briefly in "A Critical History of *Ulysses*" later in this volume, noting that the Gabler edition enjoys wide use among Joyce critics, including the authors whose original essays appear here. More recently, a new text edited by Danis Rose called *Ulysses: A Reader's Edition* (1997) has aroused argument over its alterations of Joyce's spelling, punctuation, and some words.

The essays by Jacques Derrida and Wolfgang Iser reprinted here cite the 1968 London Penguin edition and the 1937 London Bodley Head edition, respectively. The differences between these earlier editions and the Gabler edition are extensive and significant enough to warrant leaving *Ulysses* citations in the Derrida and Iser essays in their original form. The argument and interpretation of Derrida, in particular, might have been affected by changing his citations to the Gabler edition.

Because of its enormous complexity and difficulty, *Ulysses* poses special challenges both to the novice reader and to an introductory volume like this that attempts to help with the initiation. In response I have tried to give a very basic introduction to the novel's organization and narrative in my discussion of its critical history, complete with the Homeric "titles" for the episodes because these are not part of the text of *Ulysses* itself. I also have attached an expanded bibliography of *Ulysses* that includes many introductory guidebooks and episode-by-episode analyses, which I hope undergraduate students and first-time readers will find valuable.

Ulysses yields a new and rich possibility of meaning to virtually any critical approach applied to it. Theorists developing new approaches are frequently challenged to explore the implications of their assumptions and the usefulness of their methods by testing them against this experimental text. Thus have I enjoyed the unique opportunity to demonstrate deconstructive and reader-response approaches to *Ulysses* by going to their theoretical source in the works of Jacques Derrida and Wolfgang Iser. Inventors and pioneers of deconstruction and reader-response criticism, respectively, Derrida and Iser demonstrate how *Ulysses* illuminates theory at the same time that theory illuminates *Ulysses*. Jacques Derrida has graciously permitted me to reprint a portion of the essay that he presented at the Ninth International James Joyce Symposium in Frankfurt in June 1984. The piece, translated by Tina Kendall with emendations and some notes by Shari Benstock, was published in 1988 in *James Joyce: The Augmented Ninth*, edited by Bernard Benstock. Wolfgang Iser prepared a shortened and simplified version of his essay, "Patterns of Communication in Joyce's *Ulysses*," for this volume. This piece was taken from his seminal study of reader-response theory, *The Implied Reader*. There is much to appreciate in the work of Derrida and Iser: groundbreaking theory, an original and significant contribution to Joyce studies, and their generosity as colleagues and teachers of theory at the University of California, Irvine. The other three essays on *Ulysses* demonstrating feminist, psychoanalytical, and Marxist approaches to the novel were especially prepared for this volume by Vicki Mahaffey, Kimberly Devlin, and Patrick McGee. They reflect the innovative and theoretically sophisticated work these young scholars have contributed to the study of Joyce over the years, as well as their enthusiastic commitment to teach Joyce effectively to undergraduates. I am also grateful to the Case Study series editor, Ross Murfin, for entrusting me with this project, and for providing the essays with insightful critical contexts. Ellen Thibault, Deborah Baker, Lisa Wehrle, and John Sullivan deserve my thanks for their expert editorial work on behalf of Bedford Books.

My own students, both undergraduate and graduate, deserve my warmest gratitude for continually renewing my understanding and appreciation of Joyce's *Ulysses* and for reminding me of the challenges that first-time readers of the novel confront. They have shared with me for a quarter of a century now the strange effect this radically innovative novel has on its readers. First affronting us as an elite artifact, it eventually becomes a living experience—a lifestyle, almost—that knits its readers into sympathetic communities. My wish is that this volume helps bring a new generation of students and readers into our charmed circle.

Margot Norris
University of California, Irvine

Contents

A Companion to
James Joyce's *Ulysses*
A Case Study in Contemporary Criticism

Case Studies in Contemporary Criticism

A Companion to
JAMES JOYCE's

Ulysses

Introduction:
Biographical and
Historical Contexts

After the extraordinary complexity that James Joyce brought to the telling of life stories in his fiction, any account of Joyce's own life must feel the burden of biography's limitations, biases, and conventionalities. Writing Joyce's biography is complicated further by the problem of maintaining crucial distinctions between his life and his writing. Besides the many autobiographical details that shape Joyce's *A Portrait of the Artist as a Young Man* (1916), hundreds of real people, places, and events are represented in the texts of *Dubliners* (1914), and *Ulysses* (1922). Joyce told his friend Frank Budgen, "I want . . . to give a picture of Dublin so complete that if the city one day suddenly disappeared from the earth it could be reconstructed out of my book" (Budgen 67). This verisimilitude obliges biography writers to resist dual temptations in the case of Joyce: the temptation to read his life *into* his fiction, and the temptation to read his life *out of* his fiction.

Fortunately, we have a range of excellent biographies of Joyce whose emphases balance each other. Richard Ellmann's monumental *James Joyce*, published in 1959 and revised in 1982, offers a compendious and copiously documented record of Joyce's life and work that is generally regarded as definitive, although it clearly follows the heroic contours of the *Künstlerroman*, the novel genre that portrays artistic development. In contrast to Ellmann's Irish artist with immortal longings for greatness, Peter Costello's 1992 *James Joyce: The Years of Growth 1882–1915* draws Joyce's youth in the more prosaic historical rhythms of Irish life suggested by *Stephen Hero* (1944), Joyce's incomplete first version of *Portrait*. Morris Beja's 1992 *James Joyce: A Literary Life* pays special attention to the interplay of his writing and his life to offer the most illuminating blend of biography and criticism we now have. Other biographies of Joyce range from such early works as Herbert Gorman's 1939 *James Joyce*, an "authorized" version commissioned by Joyce in 1930, to Brenda Maddox's scholarly but "unauthorized" *Nora: The Real Life of Molly Bloom* (1988). The latter gives a feminist account of the Joyces' domestic, social, and sexual lives that angered some of Joyce's descendants upon its 1988 publication.

The following account of Joyce's life attempts to emphasize those aspects of the biography and its historical setting most relevant to the scope and complexity of *Ulysses*.

James Joyce was born in Rathgar, a suburb of Dublin, on February 2, 1882, and died in Zurich, Switzerland, on January 13, 1941. His life span, which coincided with that of Virginia Woolf (1882–1941), began in Victorian Ireland and ended in a Europe whose maps were being redrawn by World War II. In his father's time, Ireland's quasi-colonial status gave the country representation in the British Parliament, but very little control over its own affairs. The potato famines of the 1840s had caused many Irish tenant farmers to default on rents and to suffer evictions from their land, which led to strong pressures for agrarian reform and Home Rule in the later nineteenth century. Charles Stewart Parnell (1846–1891), a member of the Protestant Anglo-Irish Ascendancy, or landowning ruling class, became leader of the Home Rule party and allied himself with the more revolutionary Land League. However, his hopes for achieving Irish home rule through parliamentary negotiations with Prime Minister William Ewart Gladstone's government were not realized. He was politically rejected by the electorate when his role in the divorce of his mistress, Kitty O'Shea, and their subsequent marriage aroused the condemnation of the Catholic hierarchy. This was the political climate into which James Joyce was born in 1882, nine years before Parnell died of a heart broken by political betrayal, as it was popularly construed. In *A Portrait of the Artist as a Young Man,* Joyce dramatized how his family enshrined the legend of the martyred Parnell, now deemed Ireland's "uncrowned king."

Joyce's father, John Stanislaus Joyce, came from a well-to-do Cork family related to the Irish patriot, Daniel O'Connell, called "the Liberator." He attended Queen's College in Cork to study medicine but never achieved the degree. Under the aegis of a family coat of arms, he considered himself "a gentleman" in class terms. John Joyce was a boisterous, funny, volatile man of "absolutely unreliable temper," according to his son Stanislaus (35), but with a good tenor voice and a flair for mimicry and storytelling that made him highly popular with the hard-drinking friends that he cultivated after coming to Dublin in 1874 or 1875. In 1880 John Joyce married an even-tempered, cultured woman named Mary Jane (May) Murray, whose family he reviled. He eventually lost his only real job as a tax collector and never developed a career. He attributed this failing (perhaps not entirely unjustly) to political conspiracies and reprisals aimed at him for his support of Parnell (Costello 118). With his wife pregnant nearly every year, John Joyce produced children and mortgages in tandem as he sought to stave off debts to moneylenders that were eroding his inheritance. He failed, and by James's twelfth year in 1894, John Joyce had ten surviving children, eleven mortgages, and no remaining property (Ellmann 21).

As the eldest surviving child, James Joyce keenly felt the decline from the affluence of his infancy—which allowed him briefly to attend a distinguished Jesuit boarding school—to a mean, poverty-stricken adolescence clouded by the death of a much-loved younger brother, George, from typhoid fever. Of James's many siblings, Stanislaus—the brother next in age—became his closest companion and confidante. The many street addresses of Joyce's youth attest to the frequent evictions or threats of eviction that kept the large family on the move to poorer and more urban residences. After forty-four-year-old May Joyce died in 1903 of cancer, the many Joyce children, neglected by an improvident father, fell into desperate disorder and hardship.

Joyce's mother came from a family that valued erudition. Joyce's parents, ambitious for their sons even when their fortunes declined, secured for James what his friend Oliver St. John Gogarty later called "'a miserable background and sumptuous education'" (Maddox 35). The Jesuit schools Joyce attended—Clongowes Wood College (1888–1891), Belvedere College, Dublin (1893–1898), and University College, Dublin (1898–1902)—taught him the Latin classics, trained him in rigorous scholastic thinking, and subjected him to the intellectual authority of the Catholic Church in matters of taste and morality. Patrick Parrinder describes the insular effects of this education: "Virtually every development in European philosophy since the Renaissance was condemned *a priori*, being the product of heretics, atheists, Protestants or Jews" (19). These schools taught Joyce the canons of the British public school curriculum (including cricket as the favored sport) while increasingly pressing the claims of an Irish cultural nationalism. The young Joyce found the latter—especially the recovery of the Gaelic language, occultism, and folklore—parochial and backward-looking. At University College, Dublin, founded by John Henry Newman in 1854, Joyce chose the modern language course of study, regarded as "the Ladies' Course" according to Peter Costello (159).

Joyce supplemented his studies with visits to the Capel Street Library in Dublin, whose new books introduced him to the brilliant Continental literature then published abroad. This reading provided an alternative to the imperialistic inflections of the English poetic tradition as Joyce would later represent it in *Ulysses*. In his essay "Drama and Life," delivered to the university Literary and Historical Society in 1900, he defined the progressive principles of a new realism in Continental drama: "Life we must accept as we see it before our eyes, men and women as we meet them in the real world, not as we apprehend them in the world of faery" (*Critical Writings* 45). These words announce the uncompromising realism that became a crucial aspect of *Ulysses*. Before leaving the university, Joyce had achieved a precocious cosmopolitanism, reading Ibsen's plays in Dano-Norwegian and Dante in the original, translating the plays of Gerhart Hauptmann, and publishing an essay on Ibsen's *When We Dead Awaken* (1899) in the prestigious London *Fortnightly Review*.

"Joyce made a powerful impression on his fellow-students," Patrick Parrinder notes. "For all his celebrated aloofness he wrote, debated, joked, conversed, and plunged into the mêlée as a precocious intellectual and champion of unpopular causes" (21). Joyce moved in an original and witty circle that he supplemented with his father's political and drinking cronies. This allowed him to populate the Dublin of his fictions with lively, verbally gifted, professionally thwarted male characters, whose fates he entwined with colonial politics. Many of Joyce's university colleagues moved on to distinguished, and tragic, careers in Ireland: George Clancy (Davin) was murdered while serving as Mayor of Limerick during the period known as the Troubles; Thomas Cosgrave (Lynch) drowned in the Thames in 1926, a possible suicide; Francis Sheehy-Skeffington (McCann), Joyce's pacifist, socialist, feminist friend, was murdered while trying to prevent looting during the 1916 Easter uprising in Dublin; Thomas Kettle, elected to Parliament on a Home Rule platform, was killed in the Battle of the

Somme in World War I. Only J. F. Byrne (Cranly), Constantine Curran, and Oliver St. John Gogarty (Mulligan) survived to a comfortable maturity: Curran as Registrar of the High Court, and Gogarty as a successful physician, poet, and senator in the Free State. In Joyce's youth, these figures roamed a city small enough in social and political scale to be contained in a large book. Fredric Jameson described this Dublin as "not exactly the full-blown capitalist metropolis, but like the Paris of Flaubert, still regressive, still distantly akin to the village, still un- and underdeveloped enough to be representable" (135).

The cultural life of that "ambitious and intense" city (Ellmann 98) was dominated by an Anglo-Irish intelligentsia whose chief figures included the novelist George Moore, the theosophist George Russell (pseudonym AE), Lady Augusta Gregory (one of the founders of the Abbey Theatre), and the eminent poet W. B. Yeats. Although Joyce represents Dublin's cultural elite as spurning Stephen Dedalus in *Ulysses*, Ireland's leading literati actually gave Joyce considerable help, offering him publication opportunities, hospitality, letters of introduction and recommendation, and outright subsidies. When upon matriculation Joyce decided to study at the Faculty of Medicine in Paris, Lady Gregory gave money for his passage; Yeats met him in London, dined him, lodged him, and introduced him to Arthur Symons, who later arranged to publish Joyce's poems, *Chamber Music* (1907); dramatist John Synge visited him in Paris.

Joyce's Paris sojourn was neither academically nor artistically successful, and it came to a premature end when his mother's terminal illness obliged him to return to Ireland in 1903. Joyce spent the year following his mother's death in desultory activity, writing and trying to publish, taking singing lessons, teaching school. He lived with various relatives, borrowed money, and stayed briefly with Gogarty at the Martello Tower in Sandycove, which became the setting for the opening of *Ulysses*. Joyce was salvaged from this spiritual vagrancy by the unlikely agency (given the ineptitude in romance that drove him to prostitutes in his teens) of love. On June 16, 1904—a day he was to memorialize as the date of the events of *Ulysses*—Joyce went walking with a young Galway woman named Nora Barnacle, who worked at Finn's Hotel in Dublin. A complex intimacy ensued in which the young woman showed her wit and unruffled self-possession as her lover tried to shock her with his various irreverences and apostasies. The relationship culminated in an ill-planned elopement to the Continent that soon found the penniless couple chasing an elusive Berlitz position, which eventually materialized in the Adriatic seaports of

Pola, where they lived for six months, and Trieste. There the couple began a marriage without the benefit of legal sanction that fulfilled the waggish prophecy of Joyce's father, who on hearing Nora's name, joked, "Barnacle? She'll never leave him" (Maddox 9).

As a city, Trieste was a perfect place for what William Johnsen has called "the moment of modernism, when Joyce modernised himself" (6). A largely Italian city under lax Austrian rule since the fourteenth century, Trieste culturally blended East and West in its colorful population of Italians, Austrians, Slovenes, Hungarians, Greeks, Turks, and Jews. This cosmopolitanism blended with traits that made the city similar to Dublin, including a small-town familiarity and much political ferment sparked by the Irredentist movement agitating for the city's freedom from Austrian rule. Joyce took a lively philosophical and ideological interest in the city's socialist and anarchist activity.

As interesting and exciting as Trieste proved to be, Joyce's newly established home life was plagued by cultural isolation and lack of money. The isolation was especially difficult for Nora, who did not speak the language and who soon faced the upheaval of pregnancy and the birth of a new baby, George (Giorgio), in 1905. The birth of a son posed a legal dilemma that Joyce, whose decision not to marry was a rebellion against religious and governmental authority, may have solved with a ruse. To register Giorgio as legitimate without entirely abandoning his principle, Joyce may have married Nora in a civil ceremony in Trieste under an assumed name. The Joyces' domestic situation was soon simultaneously eased and complicated when Joyce's brother Stanislaus joined the young family. For the next decade Stanislaus became the family's mainstay—acting as bank, factotum, superego, muse, and critic for his brother. Meanwhile, Joyce's teaching at the Berlitz school gave him valuable contact with a diverse European clientele including the Austrian-Italian novelist Ettore Schmitz, also known as Italo Svevo. The teaching job was sufficiently flexible that it allowed him time to work on his own writing.

Joyce wrote on two fronts simultaneously: an autobiographical novel entitled *Stephen Hero* that grew to a thousand unpublishable pages and a collection of short stories, *Dubliners*, written in the spare, precise, objective style of Gustave Flaubert's *contes*. Like its successor, the later *Bildungsroman A Portrait of the Artist as a Young Man*, *Stephen Hero* described a young Irishman's university social world and intellectual progress, but in a style less tight, smooth, and aesthetically mannered. The stories of *Dubliners*, on the other hand, already exhibited the polished language Joyce needed to have his countrymen take "one good look at themselves in my nicely polished looking-glass" (Ellmann 222).

Joyce spent much time in 1905 and 1906 negotiating with a publisher, Grant Richards, who, after signing a contract to publish *Dubliners*, requested many changes and deletions in the stories to protect himself and his printer from prosecution for libel and obscenity. Joyce refused and, dismayed and disrupted in his writing, abruptly relocated his wife and infant son to Rome in 1906 to work in the correspondence department of a bank. The family found the city uncongenial and dangerous, and after Joyce had been mugged and robbed by some drinking companions, they returned to Trieste the following year. The sojourn, however, was not totally unproductive: while in Rome, Nora conceived another child, while Joyce conceived ideas for two highly significant pieces of future writing: a story called "The Dead," which eventually became the extravagant finale of *Dubliners*, and a sketch about a Dubliner named Mr. Hunter, which eventually turned into the novel *Ulysses*.

During his next two years in Trieste, Joyce settled down to the business of being a serious writer. Aided by his pupil Roberto Prezioso he began to write articles for the paper *Il Piccolo della Sera*. Later another pupil, Attilio Tomaro, gave him the opportunity to deliver lectures at the Università Popolare. His topic was Ireland under British rule, aimed at a general Triestine audience interested in cities under imperial rule. His negotiations with the publisher Elkin Matthews at last resulted in his first publication at the age of twenty-five: the volume of lovely, lyrical poems called *Chamber Music*. Offers to set the lyrics to music excited and energized Joyce. He began translating Synge's *Riders to the Sea* into Italian and recasting *Stephen Hero* into the clean, taut prose he had been perfecting in *Dubliners*. This period of professional optimism was marred by some severe personal difficulties. Joyce suffered the first of many bouts of eye inflammation, or iritis, and was hospitalized for rheumatic fever at the same time Nora delivered their second child in the pauper's ward. The little girl was named Lucia, meaning *light*, perhaps as a talisman against her father's troubled eyesight (though she herself was born with a disfiguring cast in her eye). But Joyce's writing progressed, and by the time he decided to return to Ireland for a visit with his son Giorgio, he made contact with Maunsel and Company to arrange the publication of *Dubliners*.

Between 1909 and 1912 Joyce made three ill-fated trips to Ireland, which were to be his last despite the wealth of experience they provided for the writing of *Ulysses*. Brenda Maddox believes that the first trip was troubled in advance by Joyce's fears of censure for his son's illegitimacy, which made him defensive and easily offended (87). As a result, when his former classmate Thomas Cosgrave (Lynch in *Portrait*) confided that he had been intimate with Nora before Joyce met her, Joyce fell into a delirium of rage, jealousy, and abjection that he spewed out in a series of brutal letters to Nora. Before Nora replied, Joyce's friend J. F. Byrne (Cranly in *Portrait*) calmed him by declaring the accusation a "blasted lie" (Maddox 92), an exoneration quickly corroborated by Stanislaus, who had once heard Cosgrave complain of being rejected by Nora. Byrne's deliverance of Joyce from his imagined fears of betrayal occurred at 7 Eccles Street in Dublin, the address commemorated as the home of Leopold and Molly Bloom in *Ulysses*. His immense relief at having averted a conjugal crisis was quickly transformed into an erotic obsession that became a series of obscene letters and importunities addressed to Nora. These letters, with an even more explicit set produced during Joyce's second trip to Ireland, comprised the "masturbatory correspondence" (Maddox 103) that so shocked readers when they appeared among the *Selected Letters* edited by Richard Ellmann in 1975. But apart from their private function in bridging the sexual privations of a traumatic marital separation, they served Joyce's apprenticeship in pornographic writing exhibited later in the polymorphously perverse fantasies of the "Circe" and "Penelope" chapters of *Ulysses*.

Joyce returned to Trieste from his first trip to Dublin in September 1909 with one of his sisters, Eva, who inspired another turnaround trip with her delight at the novelty of cinema in Trieste. Backed by several Italian entrepreneurs, Joyce returned to Dublin the next month to open a cinema there. After many problems and added expenses, Cinematograph Volta opened in December 1909. Although the venture soon failed and had to be sold without profit, the conspicuous cinematographic effects in Joyce's later writing attest to his early interest in film. Many years later Joyce discussed the possibility of filming *Ulysses* with the great Russian director, Serge Eisenstein. (A black-and-white film of *Ulysses* was eventually made in 1967 by Joseph Strick.)

Upon Joyce's second return from Dublin, another sister, Eileen, joined the colony of six other family members to form what Brenda Maddox describes as a genial commune:

> It was in many ways a lively place. Giorgio and Lucia made everyone laugh. There was much singing around the rented piano. . . . Nora, Eileen, and Eva did the cooking together. Nora roasted

chickens stuffed with mashed potatoes, sauteed onion, and a touch of cinnamon, her specialty. . . . Right in the midst of all their activity in the kitchen sat Joyce. He liked to work there, where the light was best, and would sit there reading, with his feet propped up on the table, or writing, with his papers spread across it. (110)

These were much happier years for Nora, whose successful adjustment to the cultural sophistication of Trieste was abetted by its superb opera, which became one of her lifelong passions. In 1912 Nora took Lucia on her first visit home to Ireland. She was soon joined by Joyce and Giorgio, and the family made a sentimental visit to Ireland's western coast. They visited Nora's family in Galway, the Oughterard cemetery (where Michael Furey—based on Nora's adolescent beau, Michael Bodkin—is buried in "The Dead"), and the Aran Isles. Back in Dublin, Joyce faced increasing resistance from George Roberts, the director of Maunsel and Company, to the publication of *Dubliners.* The controversy ended with Roberts threatening to sue Joyce for delivering a libelous manuscript for publication. Joyce desperately tried to rescue the edition by offering to buy it himself. He was too late: the printer, John Falconer, fearing prosecution for libel and obscenity, had burned the pages and broken the type. Joyce salvaged only the one copy of proofs and the title page, which became the basis of the 1914 edition, and wrote a vengeful poem, "Gas from a Burner," on the back of his violated contract as he returned to Trieste.

While the James Joyces were visiting Ireland, in Trieste brother Stanislaus was unable to prevent yet another eviction for unpaid back rent. The Joyces thus returned to a new and different Triestine address, at which they remained for three years until World War I forced them to evacuate to Switzerland. Soon after his return to Trieste, Joyce resumed work on *Portrait* and began to explore publication options with friends and patrons, including W. B. Yeats. He recast his earlier story of a sensitive Dublin boy into an ironic new version, creating an imitative style that allowed the narrative to enact and parody the boy's mental and artistic development in a corresponding poetic language. These efforts were accompanied by other new and strange projects. Joyce, who was now teaching English at the commercial high school as well as to an enlarged body of private pupils, began to develop a silent and voyeuristic passion for one of the beautiful young women he tutored, whom Ellmann identified as Amalia Popper (342). He transformed his erotic feelings and fantasies into the strange Swinburnean poetic document that was later published as *Giacomo Joyce*

(1914). At the same time, Joyce began making notes for *Exiles* (1918), a play possibly inspired by jealousy and titillation at the idea that his former student and benefactor, Roberto Prezioso, harbored a triangular attraction to Nora and Joyce himself (Maddox 115). These interiorized romantic excitations and adventures find their way into the complicated erotic texture of the Blooms' marital dynamics and imaginings in *Ulysses.*

By the end of 1913 Joyce's luck was turned by the historical tides of modern literary history. That winter American poet Ezra Pound heard of Joyce's talent and publication difficulties from Yeats, with whom Pound was staying at Stone Cottage in England. Pound, who was to help numerous experimental writers of the period get funded and published, wrote Joyce, encouraging him to send some pieces to two literary journals with which he was connected. "The latter can pay a little, the former practically can not pay at all, we do it for larks and to have a place for markedly modern stuff," Pound wrote to Joyce (Ellmann 349). At the same time, Grant Richards reopened negotiations to publish *Dubliners.* Pound's overture catapulted Joyce at last into publication and public notice. Better than any other writer of the time, Pound understood the difficulty of financing modernistic writing whose formal traits—simple, direct language enriched by resonant international erudition and cultural allusion—made it difficult to market to a general public. His own efforts included intensive fund-raising from a network of affluent friends and supporters of the modern arts.

But a more enduring solution was what Sally Dennison has called "alternative publishing" (3), of which Pound wrote "80% of such literature of my generation (from 1910 to 1930) as has any solid value, has been published only via specially founded 'amateur' publishing houses" (*Pound/Joyce* 247). These publishing ventures included the "little magazines," of which Hoffman, Allen, and Ulrich wrote, "Little magazines are willing to lose money, to court ridicule, to ignore public taste, willing to do almost anything—steal, beg, or undress in public—rather than sacrifice their right to print good material" (2). Joyce sent Pound *Dubliners* and the first chapters of *Portrait* in response to his letter, and one of these "little magazines," *The Egoist,* agreed to begin publishing *Portrait* in serial form. Joyce was especially fortunate that one of the editors of *The Egoist,* which had begun as a feminist journal called *The New Freewoman,* was a politically sensitive, intellectually open-minded, and culturally altruistic young woman named Harriet Shaw Weaver. Weaver eventually became Joyce's patron, making it possible for him to write the most elaborate experimental fiction in twentieth-century literature.

The years 1914 and 1915 were among the most eventful, if disheartening, of Joyce's life, with World War I disrupting the long-awaited onset of success. *The Egoist* was publishing *Portrait* to mixed, but nonetheless encouraging, reviews. Grant Richards, intrigued by this reception, wrote a new contract for *Dubliners* and brought the volume out in June 1914. In August 1914, Great Britain declared war on Austria-Hungary, putting Joyce, who was formally a British subject, in an awkward and dangerous position. "His enemy had been England; now he, as a British subject, was the enemy. Most confusing," Peter Costello writes (314). The uncertainty of the mails made serialization difficult. Joyce's pupils dispersed, and Stanislaus was arrested while on holiday near Trieste and interned by the Austrians for much of the war. Joyce's sister Eileen married one of her brother's pupils, the Czech bank manager Frantisek Schaureck, who many years later was to embezzle funds and commit suicide. In May 1915 Italy declared war on Austria, and the Joyces decided that they must move to safer territory. Joyce's aristocratic pupils, who fortuitously included the sons of the Austrian governor, helped his family secure exit visas. In June 1915, the Joyces moved to Zurich in neutral Switzerland.

In spite of the stress of these two years, Joyce had now completed *A Portrait of the Artist as a Young Man* and begun writing the first three chapters of *Ulysses*. These opening chapters, commonly called the "Telemachiad," reflect Joyce's life during the year after his mother's death. They reverse the triumphant ending of *Portrait* by resuming the story of Stephen Dedalus with his defeated return from flight and exile. *Ulysses*, a modern psychological reenactment of the events of Homer's *Odyssey*, was to interweave the life of the young artist with that of a Jewish-Irish couple, Leopold and Molly Bloom, on a single day in 1904 Dublin. The "style of scrupulous meanness" (*Selected Letters* 83) that Joyce had perfected in *Dubliners* and *Portrait* was abandoned for a richly textured and ever-changing narrative reflecting states of individual consciousness mingled with a variety of public and cultural discourses.

Joyce's move to Zurich at this time was a fortuitous benefit because the city had become an asylum for avant-garde art and theater. Now increasingly recognized as an important new author, Joyce made many friends, including several Greeks with whom he could discuss the *Odyssey*. He met the painter Frank Budgen, who became one of the closest friends of his adulthood. Joyce frequented the Club des

Étrangers, and occasionally visited the headquarters of the Dadaists Tristan Tzara and Hans Arp at the Café Voltaire. He saw all of August Strindberg's plays, became interested in the works of Frank Wedekind, made friends with the actors Claud and Daisy Sykes, and tried to find ways to have *Exiles* produced. Joyce helped found a company called the English Players in the hopes it might eventually stage *Exiles*. They rounded up a cast of professional and amateur actors for their first play, Oscar Wilde's *The Importance of Being Earnest* (1895), a production that subsequently involved Joyce in ridiculous litigation with an English actor named Henry Carr over the price of tickets and a pair of trousers. Tom Stoppard eventually made this incident the absurd center of *Travesties* (1974), his play about the Dada-like convergence of Joyce, Tzara, and Lenin in Zurich during the war.

Joyce worked steadily on *Ulysses*, but in 1917 his writing was interrupted dramatically by attacks of glaucoma, which required an iridectomy and convalescence in Locarno. During his three months in Locarno, Joyce befriended a young, tubercular physician named Gertrude Kaempffer to whom he began to make erotic overtures. She steadfastly declined, but Joyce's brief arousal may have become memorialized in the name of Gerty MacDowell in the "Nausicaa" chapter of *Ulysses*. The following year in Zurich, he initiated another such overture to a young woman with a limp named Marthe Fleischmann. This relationship went much further and in time involved an epistolary exchange that brought Joyce into a violent confrontation with Marthe Fleischmann's guardian. Along with Gertrude Kaempffer, Marthe Fleischmann seems to have contributed her name and characteristics to Leopold Bloom's extramarital dalliances with Gerty MacDowell and Martha Clifford in *Ulysses*. These erotic forays seem not to have ruffled the Joyce marriage.

In 1918, *Little Review*, a little magazine published by the American partners Jane Heap and Margaret Anderson, offered to serialize *Ulysses*. Joyce's writing became easier at this time because two separate, anonymous patrons came forward with generous subsidies that allowed him to abandon teaching for the writing of *Ulysses*. The first of these turned out to be Harriet Shaw Weaver, who donated a large war bond on which Joyce could draw interest. Weaver, who later in life became a member of the Communist Party, felt uncomfortable living on unearned income while Joyce labored incessantly on writing that failed to earn him a living. She eventually endowed Joyce with a bequest that later sustained his family during their years in Paris and beyond. The second patron was later revealed as the wealthy daughter of John D. Rockefeller, Edith McCormick, a philanthropist living in Zurich who supported musicians and artists. She was heavily under the influence of the psychoanalyst Carl Jung. When she abruptly canceled her funding at the end of the war, without offering an explanation, some speculated that it was because Joyce had refused to let Jung psychoanalyze him.

When the war ended in November 1918, the Joyce clan slowly reassembled in Trieste. Eileen and Frantisek Schaureck and their two infant daughters took a large apartment and were soon joined by Stanislaus, at last released from his internment in Austria. Joyce, who had been finishing "Scylla and Charybdis," "Wandering Rocks," "Cyclops," and "Sirens" in Zurich, hesitated for many months before moving Nora and the children back to Trieste, where they were to join Eileen's extended household. During this last period in Zurich, he was trying to find a publisher for *Ulysses*; he was refused by, among others, Leonard and Virginia Woolf's Hogarth Press. Discomfort with the book's indecency, as well as the inadequacy of their hand presses to produce such a large and complex book, may have figured in the Woolfs' refusal. At this same time the Austrian writer Stefan Zweig became fascinated with the psychological complexities of Joyce's play *Exiles* and managed to facilitate its production on the Munich stage in 1919. Unfortunately it opened to largely poor reviews that hastened its closing. The Joyces finally moved back to Trieste, where Joyce worked on the "Nausicaa" and "Oxen of the Sun" chapters of *Ulysses*. But the clan's flat was overcrowded with eleven people, counting the cook and nanny, and the Joyces came not to like postwar Trieste. In May 1919, Joyce at last met Ezra Pound in person in Lago di Garda, where Pound's wife was recuperating from an illness. Pound suggested that Joyce move to Paris. The Joyces arrived in Paris in July 1920, planning to stay only for a few weeks on their way to London. They stayed for twenty years.

Pound helped the family find a tiny apartment on loan from a friend and lined up people to help the always needy Joyces get settled. After commandeering extra beds, furniture, favors, and loans from the literary agent Jenny Serruys, Joyce continued writing the difficult, experimental "Circe" chapter of *Ulysses*. Pound also asked friends to receive the Joyces, and at a party hosted by the poet André Spire, Joyce met two booksellers who were life companions as well as business partners: Adrienne Monnier and Sylvia Beach. Sylvia Beach's Left Bank bookstore, Shakespeare and Company, had become a commercial salon for English language writers where they could pick up mail, read literary magazines, and borrow newly published books from the excellent lending library. Joyce soon joined the writers André Gide, Gertrude Stein, F. Scott Fitzgerald, the musician George Antheil, and many others as one of Sylvia Beach's "bunnies"—"from the word *abonné*: subscriber" (Beach 22). As he had done in Trieste and Zurich, Joyce found good friends and excellent drinking companions in Paris. In time these included Robert McAlmon (husband of the poet H.D.'s companion, "Bryher" Ellerman), Wyndham Lewis, Ernest Hemingway, Valéry Larbaud, Arthur Power (an Irishman who later published his conversations with Joyce), and the avant-garde novelist Djuna Barnes. He met other famous contemporaries, including T. S. Eliot and Marcel Proust. The supper meeting with Proust, after a Stravinsky-Diaghilev ballet, did not go well. According to witnesses, the two novelists chiefly exchanged symptoms—"Joyce said, 'I've headaches every day. My eyes are terrible.' Proust replied 'My poor stomach.'" (Ellmann 508)—and discussed truffles.

Within the year the censorship difficulties of Margaret Anderson and Jane Heap, whose *Little Review* was sued and financially ruined by the New York Society for the Suppression of Vice for serializing *Ulysses*, convinced Joyce that he would not find a commercial publisher for the book. When Sylvia Beach asked Joyce if he would let Shakespeare and Company "have the honor of bringing out your *Ulysses*," he reportedly accepted "immediately and joyfully" (Beach 47). The French printer Maurice Darantière of Dijon agreed to undertake printing the work and, to finance the venture, a prospectus was circulated asking for advance subscriptions. "Ezra Pound made a sensation when he deposited on my table one day a subscription blank with the signature of W. B. Yeats on it. Ernest Hemingway was down for several copies of the book" (Beach 51). But many difficulties delayed the publication process. The French printers had trouble with the unconventional English; Joyce reworked nearly a third of the text with corrections and emendations; the typists were shocked by "Circe." After the husband of one typist threw the pages into the fire, Sylvia Beach's sister, Cyprian, followed by other friends and volunteers, typed "Circe." Joyce suffered another massive iritis emergency while writing "Penelope," but by October 1921, he completed "Ithaca," and *Ulysses* was finished. Always intensely superstitious about his birthday, Joyce desperately wanted the book out by his fortieth, on February 2, 1922. Darantière drove his staff to heroic efforts and had two copies ready to send by mail on February 1. To deliver them on time, he gave them to the conductor of the Dijon-Paris express train, who handed them to

Sylvia Beach when the train pulled into the Paris station at 7 A.M. A ten-minute taxi ride delivered the first copy of *Ulysses* to Joyce's flat; Beach exhibited the second copy to admiring crowds at Shakespeare and Company all day.

Soon after the publication of the book, Nora decided she wanted to visit Ireland again, a plan that greatly perturbed Joyce because, in the wake of a controversial treaty with Great Britain signed in 1921, Ireland was now a Free State on the verge of civil war. The treaty provisions divided Ireland into a republican Catholic south and a British Protestant north and required that the Irish parliament pledge allegiance to the Crown. These provisions created division and conflict within the army factions. Nora planned to travel at Easter, the anniversary of the 1916 Easter uprising in Dublin. When they reached Galway, Nora and her teenage children did indeed get a firsthand glimpse of the Troubles, as this period of upheaval came to be called. Troops that Giorgio contemptuously thought of as "Zulus" taunted the seventeen-year-old, soldiers invaded their boarding house bedroom to set up artillery for firing on Irregulars below, and the train car in which they fled back to Dublin was shot at by both sides. These frightening experiences only confirmed Joyce's cynicism about Irish politics.

By the time the family returned, however, they discovered that they were famous. Brenda Maddox describes the effects of *Ulysses* on Joyce: "If *A Portrait* had made Joyce's reputation, *Ulysses* turned him into a celebrity. People clambered on chairs to get a look at him. They sent notes in restaurants asking him to join them, they rang his doorbell. Journalists crowded in at parties" (211). Joyce's time was now divided between concerns about the advertisement, reviews, editions, and translations of *Ulysses*, and the conception and design of a new, even more outrageously experimental book that was for many years known only as "Work in Progress." Joyce kept the title of this new book, *Finnegans Wake* (1939), secret from everyone but Nora. He began this new work by collecting and sorting many kilos of old stories and unused notes left over from *Ulysses*, recording conversations he heard and overheard, and writing down his dreams. Joyce planned *Finnegans Wake* as a night book, or dream book, exploring unconscious thoughts, wishes, and fears to balance the wakeful day book of *Ulysses*. Dreams, irrationality, and unconscious states had been a chief preoccupation of the Dadaists and Surrealists, whose work he had first encountered in Zurich. During the two years after the publication of *Ulysses*, Joyce's concentration was fragmented by trips to the Côte d'Azur and Bognor Regis in Sussex and enervated by iritis and dental problems. He nevertheless managed to sketch the first eight chapters of *Finnegans Wake* before the end of 1923.

The 1920s in Paris were a heady, troubled time for Joyce. At the center of modern art in its heyday, he nonetheless felt himself awash in complex and contradictory critical currents. At the very time the genius of *Ulysses* became gradually indisputable, the avant-gardism of *Finnegans Wake* met increasing skepticism. In August 1922, Joyce at last met his great benefactor, Harriet Shaw Weaver, and Maddox suspects she was as disturbed by Joyce's profligacy as she was later alarmed by his drinking. "Within hours she witnessed 'her' money flying in all directions—to waiters, porters, taxi drivers. He tipped proudly and wildly" (213). Although during the years of composing *Finnegans Wake*, Joyce made Weaver his literary confidante, the stylistic extravagance and linguistic impenetrability of the text brought her, at times, close to apostasy: "It seems to me you are wasting your genius," she wrote him in 1927 (Ellmann 590). But she never abandoned her support of him or his family.

Other friends did not remain blindly loyal to this new project. Pound defected with candor and humor. "Nothing so far as I make out, nothing short of divine vision or a new cure for the clapp [sic] can possibly be worth all the circumambient peripherization," he wrote Joyce in November 1926 (Ellmann 584). Wyndham Lewis criticized Joyce in his book *Time and Western Man* (1927). His attack was vicious because it was ad hominem; Ellmann describes it as Lewis treating Joyce "as an Irish *parvenu*" (595). Stanislaus Joyce, his brother's strongest supporter in the early days, was perhaps most unkind, calling *Finnegans Wake* "the beginning of softening of the brain" (Ellmann 577).

Fortunately, new friends and admirers emerged to replace the defectors. The twenty-three-year-old Samuel Beckett turned up in Paris to pay his respects and stayed to serve as translator, scribe, and unpaid secretary to the near-blind Joyce. Eugene and Maria Jolas put their new avant-garde journal *transition* at his disposal to print installments of "Work in Progress." In 1929, a dozen of Joyce's friends including Beckett and William Carlos Williams published a book defending *Finnegans Wake* against the published attacks of Lewis, Rebecca West, and Sean O'Faolain. Published by Shakespeare and Company, the essays in *Our Exagmination Round His Factification for Incamination of Work in Progress* (after a line in *Finnegans Wake*) used Eugene Jolas's call for a "revolution of the word" to place Joyce's poetic experiments in the context of the philosophical avant-garde of the 1920s. An even more dramatic show of support was marshalled by the

plight of *Ulysses* in America. Because the United States was not a signa-
tory to the Bern convention that ratified international copyright law,
Ulysses was not protected by copyright in the United States. An entre-
preneurial magazine publisher named Samuel Roth exploited this legal
vulnerability to produce pirated installments of *Ulysses* in his magazine
Two Worlds Monthly. Unable to get a rapid judicial injunction against
this piracy, Joyce organized an international petition to protest his
legal plight. The 167 signatories of this protest constituted a veritable
who's who of modern literature.

The personal lives of the Joyces during the 1920s were marked by
stability, fame, and luxury, on the one hand, and by medical problems
and family worries on the other. Nora was finally able to furnish a
wonderful apartment in the Square Robiac, where she could cook and
entertain. The Joyces hosted lively social evenings at home as alterna-
tives to their regular, expensive dining at the restaurant Les Trianons.
They dressed like dandies. Holidays were spent in Holland, Sussex,
Austria, and many other resort areas, often to allow Joyce to recuper-
ate from his frequent eye operations.

Stanislaus at last became engaged in his early forties, but his marriage to Nelly Lichtensteiger was postponed for a time because he had
to help the shattered Eileen Schaureck after her husband's suicide.
Nora was diagnosed with cancer that was cured with a hysterectomy.
The Joyce children were growing up talented and affectionate but
increasingly showed the strains of their nomadic upbringing. They
had learned many languages (German, French, and English, in addition to their native "house" language, Italian) and attended many
schools. They were bright and interesting, but ill-trained for any pro-
fession outside the realm of art. Giorgio had an excellent voice, and
Lucia a gift for dance; neither had the discipline and emotional
stamina needed to sustain a career. Giorgio began to attach himself to
a married socialite named Helen Fleischman, who was eleven years
older than his twenty years and the mother of a son. Joyce became ob-
sessed with promoting the career of an Irish opera singer named John
Sullivan, claiming the connection would help him foster Giorgio's
singing career. Lucia gave up her dancing and became increasingly un-
focused, aimless, and erratic in her behavior. In 1930, Giorgio and
Helen Kastor Fleischman married, with Joyce delighted at his acquisi-
tion of an extended Jewish family. His son's marriage increased pressure to legitimate his own children. To secure the inheritance rights of
Giorgio's progeny, Joyce married Nora in July 1931, in London, in
the glare of much unwanted publicity. (The earlier Triestine marriage

under an assumed name would not have served legal purposes.) In the following year Joyce wrote the poem "Ecce Puer" to express how the birth of his grandson, Stephen James Joyce, consoled him for the death of his own father.

During the 1930s, Joyce labored on *Finnegans Wake* while his vision deteriorated into near blindness and his daughter's symptoms worsened into full-blown madness. He also provoked an estrangement from the two women who had been his most loyal and trusted supporters, Sylvia Beach and Harriet Shaw Weaver. Beach, exhausted by Joyce's importunings for services and money, was angry and bitter when Joyce, through friends, pressured her into reducing the inflated asking price by which she hoped to repel bids to sell her interest in *Ulysses*. She eventually reverted the rights to Joyce, but the "separation was a painful one" (Banta and Silverman, 162). Joyce needed an American publisher to stop Roth's piracy of *Ulysses* in the United States. Bennett Cerf of Random House offered him a contract and hired an attorney, Morris Ernst, to argue the case of *Ulysses* in an obscenity trial before Judge John M. Woolsey of the United States District Court in New York. On December 6, 1933, a favorable decision was handed down, and Joyce was soon featured in *Time* magazine. Joyce's friendship with Sylvia Beach was destroyed by these professional complications.

Joyce's friendship with Harriet Shaw Weaver was destroyed later in the decade by familial complications. Beginning soon after her parents' marriage, Lucia Joyce's adolescent idiosyncrasies metamorphosed into a serious mental illness. A series of obsessional or contrived romances with young men, including Alexander Calder and Samuel Beckett, aggravated rather than relieved her symptoms. On Joyce's fiftieth birthday, February 2, 1932, Lucia threw a chair at her mother and became so violent that she was carried off to a mental clinic by her brother. During the next several years, as her behavior became increasingly bizarre and dangerous, she was bundled from doctor to doctor, treatment to treatment. She spent time at the posh sanitarium, Prangins, near Geneva, where Zelda Fitzgerald was also treated, and in Zurich saw Carl Jung. Joyce's friends and family members across several countries—including his widowed sister, Eileen Schaureck, Maria Jolas, and Harriet Shaw Weaver—were pressed into service as nurses and jailers to keep Lucia from turning on gas jets and setting fires. Joyce, frantic and helpless in the face of Lucia's catastrophic decline, blamed her difficulties on doctors and keepers, including the saintly Miss Weaver. Lucia was hospitalized permanently in the mid-1930s and spent the last thirty years of her life at St. Andrew's Hospital in Northampton, England, where she died in 1982.

Joyce continued to work on *Finnegans Wake* during this tragic time and managed to produce some of his sunniest, most playful writing, including "The Mime of Mick, Nick, and the Maggies," his pantomime of children's games, dances, songs, and riddles in Book II of *Finnegans Wake*. Nora complained that Joyce kept her awake nights by laughing at his own writing; she reported she had to tell him, "Now, Jim, stop writing or stop laughing" (Maddox 324). The funny writing may have served as a shoring of fragments against an increasingly horrifying world in which there was little to laugh about. Lucia's illness was to be followed some years later by the growing illness of Giorgio's wife, whose manic-depressive condition worsened with a failing marriage. Samuel Beckett was stabbed in Paris and seriously wounded. With Hitler's annexation of Austria in 1938, the Joyces became worried about the safety of Jewish family and friends. Joyce finished *Finnegans Wake* as signs of impending war alarmed Europe. Joyce's daughter-in-law Helen was miraculously well enough to throw a lavish celebration for the book's publication on Joyce's fifty-seventh birthday, February 2, 1939. But by Christmas of that year, Joyce and Nora, like many of their friends, had left Paris. They were desperately worried about their family: a daughter and daughter-in-law both hospitalized for psychosis, a nearly blind paterfamilias, a dazed son, and a rather lost young grandson. They stayed for a time in a village in Burgundy, while their loyal friend Paul Léon returned to their abandoned Paris flat to rescue Joyce's papers. Léon was later arrested during a Gestapo roundup of Parisian Jews and was killed on a forced march in 1942.

The Joyces returned to Zurich at the outbreak of World War II, as they had done at the outbreak of World War I. Lucia had been denied a visa to leave France, and unable to get access to their London funds, the Joyces had an anxious scramble to raise money for the entry deposit required of refugees by Switzerland. They arrived in Zurich in mid-December 1940; less than a month later, Joyce was dead. The stomach pains he had suffered for years had been unrecognized as the symptoms of an ulcer, whose perforation required emergency surgery on January 10. Joyce survived the surgery, but peritonitis followed, and he died on January 13, 1941. He was buried two days later in Fluntern Cemetery in Zurich. Nora Joyce lived on in Zurich for another decade, dying there in 1951.

Margot Norris

WORKS CITED

Banta, Melissa, and Oscar A. Silverman, eds. *James Joyce's Letters to Sylvia Beach, 1921–1940*. Bloomington: Indiana UP, 1987.

Beach, Sylvia. *Shakespeare & Company*. Lincoln: U of Nebraska P, 1991.

Beja, Morris. *James Joyce: A Literary Life*. Columbus: Ohio State UP, 1992.

Budgen, Frank. *James Joyce and the Making of "Ulysses."* Bloomington: Indiana UP, 1973.

Costello, Peter. *James Joyce: The Years of Growth 1882–1915*. London: Kyle Cathie, 1992.

Dennison, Sally. *(Alternative) Literary Publishing*. Iowa City: U of Iowa P, 1984.

Ellmann, Richard. *James Joyce*. Rev. ed. New York: Oxford UP, 1982.

Gorman, Herbert. *James Joyce*. New York: Rinehart, 1948.

Hoffman, Frederick J., Charles Allen, Carolyn F. Ulrich. *The Little Magazine*. Princeton: Princeton UP, 1947.

Jameson, Fredric. "*Ulysses* in History." *James Joyce and Modern Literature*. Ed. W. J. McCormack and Alistair Stead. London: Routledge, 1982. 126–41.

Johnsen, William A. "Joyce's *Dubliners* and the Futility of Modernism." *James Joyce and Modern Literature*. London: Routledge, 1982.

Joyce, James. *The Critical Writings of James Joyce*. Ed. Ellsworth Mason and Richard Ellmann. Ithaca: Cornell UP, 1989.

———. *Selected Letters*. Ed. Richard Ellmann. New York: Viking, 1975.

Joyce, Stanislaus. *My Brother's Keeper*. New York: Viking, 1958.

Maddox, Brenda. *Nora: The Real Life of Molly Bloom*. Boston: Houghton, 1988.

Manganiello, Dominic. *Joyce's Politics*. London: Routledge, 1980.

Parrinder, Patrick. *James Joyce*. Cambridge: Cambridge UP, 1984.

Pound/Joyce: The Letters of Ezra Pound to James Joyce. Ed. Forrest Read. New York: New Directions, 1967.

A Critical History of
Ulysses

I

Perhaps every novice reader of *Ulysses* is doomed to reenact the frustrations of its first generation of readers, who found the great novel—considered by some the greatest novel written in English—obscured by a pyrotechnic display of stylistic devices, arcane erudition, and an immense symbolic superstructure. Yet Joyce himself provided help with the technical difficulties even before the book's publication. In 1920 he sent his Italian translator Carlo Linati a complex scheme of Homeric and other parallels, with the following explanation:

> I think that in view of the enormous bulk and the more than enormous complexity of my damned monster-novel it would be better to send him a sort of summary—key—skeleton—scheme (for home use only). . . . It is the epic of two races (Israel-Ireland) and at the same time the cycle of the human body as well as a little story of a day (life). The character of Ulysses has fascinated me ever since boyhood. . . . My intention is not only to render the myth *sub specie temporis nostri* but also to allow each adventure (that is, every hour, every organ, every art being interconnected and interrelated in the somatic scheme of the whole) to condition and even to create its own technique. (*Selected Letters* 271)

Although this description also buries the realism of the plot ("a little story of a day") under a mass of allusion and allegory, Joyce here clarifies his intention to have novel, style, myth, and symbolism work together organically.

When Joyce advised his aunt Josephine Murray (an excellent example of a common reader) that she should buy a copy of Charles Lamb's *Adventures of Ulysses* (1808) for help with *Ulysses* (*Selected Letters* 293), he was by no means condescending. Lamb's redacted version of Homer's *Odyssey* had introduced him to the classic at age twelve, and he continued to receive his Homer in translation (Butcher and Lang), scholarship (Samuel Butler), and interpretations that shaped his use of the myth (for example, Victor Bérard [*Les Phéniciens et l'Odyssée*, 1902–1903], whose theory on the Semitic origins of the *Odyssey* contributed to Joyce's decision to make his Ulysses a Jew [Seidel]). By exploring life in modern day Dublin through a classical text, Joyce situated himself at the heart of the early-twentieth-century Anglo-American literary movement known as Modernism. Like T. S. Eliot's great poem *The Waste Land* (published in 1922, the same year as *Ulysses*) Joyce's novel was imbued with a revisionary classicism that began to revitalize modern thinking in the late nineteenth century. This classical pulse quickened in archaeology with Heinrich Schliemann's discovery of the historical Troy and coursed through the diverse fields of philosophy (Friedrich Nietzsche's "The Birth of Tragedy," 1872), anthropology (Jessie Weston's *From Ritual to Romance*, 1920; Sir James Frazer's *The Golden Bough*, 1890), and psychoanalysis (Freud's classical typologies, such as the Oedipus complex). Joyce's contemporaries freely invested their writing with classical reference and mythology—Ezra Pound in "Homage to Sextus Propertius," W. B. Yeats in "Leda and the Swan," H.D. in "Eurydice," "Helen," and "Cassandra," Rainer Maria Rilke in "Sonnets to Orpheus," and Eugene O'Neill in *Mourning Becomes Electra*, to name only a few. In his 1923 essay, "*Ulysses*, Order, and Myth," T. S. Eliot pays tribute to Joyce's *Ulysses*—"I hold this book to be the most important expression which the present age has found" (175)—and attributes its greatness to what he called "the mythical method" (178). For Eliot the function of myth in the novel is nothing less than to restore meaning to the chaos of the modern world. "It is simply a way of controlling, of ordering, of giving a shape and a significance to the immense panorama of futility and anarchy which is contemporary history. . . . It is, I seriously believe, a step toward making the modern world possible for art" (177).

Hugh Kenner reminds us that Joyce had access not to a single Homer, but to many Homers. He suggests that the Homers that Joyce privileged served less the aims of transcendence, as Eliot would have it, than those of novelization. Kenner writes of Samuel Butler's Homer (whom Butler identified, in his *The Authoress of the "Odyssey,"* 1897, as a woman): "Butler's was simply the first creative mind— Joyce's was the second—to take the archaeologist's Homer seriously: to consider what it might mean to believe that the *Odyssey* was composed by a real person in touch with the living details of real cities, real harbors, real bowls and cups and pins and spoons, real kings, real warriors, real houses" ("Homer's Sticks and Stones" 293). In other words, *Ulysses* may have served to domesticate the *Odyssey* as much as to mythologize the modern world. Kenner's is one of many attempts to confound what Michael Groden describes as the two predominant sides of "*Ulysses*' many dualisms—the 'novelistic' story and the 'symbolistic' pattern of parallels and correspondences" (4). Harry Levin also argues that *Ulysses* is best read with myth and map, that is, the *Odyssey* in one hand and *Thom's Dublin Directory* in the other. *Ulysses* retains such meticulous historical grounding that it is difficult to tell its historical realism from its fictional realism: "the Gold Cup races were run off at Ascot. At New York, when the *General Slocum* exploded in the East River, five hundred lives were lost. From the Orient came news of Russo-Japanese conflict over Port Arthur. . . . At the Gaiety Theatre Mrs. Bandman Palmer was appearing in *Leah*. . . . Clery's was advertising a summer sale; sandwich-men, bearing the more or less consecutive letters of H. E. L. Y. S., filed through the streets" (Levin 69). Years later, Phillip Herring did research in Gibraltar that rescued Molly Bloom from her overmythification as earth goddess by filling in the mysterious parentage and sketchy childhood of a "historical Molly Bloom" (*Joyce's Uncertainty Principle* 117–40) as though she had been a living personage rather than a fictional creation.

Before turning to a more systematic account of *Ulysses* criticism over the last seventy years, it may be helpful to summarize the novel briefly in a way that glosses at least some of the Homeric parallels, sketches in the major outlines of the plot, and indicates some of the stylistic strategies and experiments in the text. Its chief Greek intertext is the *Odyssey*, Homer's epic poem that recounts the adventures of Odysseus, king of Ithaca, as he attempts to return home after fighting in the Trojan War. His journey is delayed for twenty years by many obstacles, including storms and shipwrecks; seduction by goddesses; the narcosis of lotus-eaters; encounters with cannibals, one-eyed giants, and sirens; a journey to the underworld; and navigation past treacherously moving rocks, monsters, and maelstroms. During Odysseus' long absence, his wife Penelope staves off insolent suitors for her hand and for Odysseus' vacant throne by weaving and unweaving a shroud, while her nearly grown son Telemachus searches for his father. Upon his return, Odysseus kills the suitors in a bloody battle and reunites with his family and his people.

Joyce's *Ulysses* is divided into three sections, conventionally called "The Telemachiad," "The Wanderings of Odysseus," and "Nostos" or "The Homecoming." These three sections are comprised of eighteen chapters or *episodes*, as they are commonly called, named after Homeric parallels Joyce assigned to each chapter in schema he drew up as guides to the novel for his friends Stuart Gilbert and Carlo Linati:

I. Telemachiad

1: Telemachus
2: Nestor
3: Proteus

II. The Wanderings of Odysseus

4: Calypso
5: Lotus-Eaters
6: Hades
7: Aeolus
8: Lestrygonians
9: Scylla and Charybdis
10: Wandering Rocks
11: Sirens
12: Cyclops
13: Nausicaa
14: Oxen of the Sun
15: Circe

III. Nostos

16: Eumaeus
17: Ithaca
18: Penelope

The novel is set in Dublin on June 16, 1904, and traces the activities, convergences, and thoughts of three people: Stephen Dedalus (Telemachus), Leopold Bloom (Odysseus), and Molly Bloom (Penelope)—amid the busy commercial, cultural, and political life of a modern city.

"The Telemachiad" describes the morning activities of Stephen Dedalus, the protagonist of *A Portrait of the Artist as a Young Man* (1916), who has returned from Paris to attend his dying mother. After breakfast with a friend (Buck Mulligan) and a British visitor (Haines) in the Martello Tower in Sandycove ("Telemachus"), Stephen goes on to teach at the school of the anti-Semitic Mr. Deasy ("Nestor"). He then walks toward Dublin along Sandymound strand, lost in philosophical meditations revealed through the technique of "stream-of-consciousness," which Joyce credited to Édouard Dujardin's 1888 novel *Les Lauriers sont coupés* ("Proteus"). Like Telemachus in the *Odyssey*, whose home and security are threatened by suitors in his father's absence, Stephen's state is one of dispossession: his birthright squandered by his father and his place as an Irish poet usurped by Trinity and Oxford students with better claims as "gentlemen," he is forced to collude in inculcating imperialistic ideologies (Roman history and English poetry) into the minds of Irish scions. Having refused to pray at his mother's deathbed, he is racked by guilt like another literary mourning and dispossessed son, Hamlet.

The second section of *Ulysses,* "The Wanderings of Odysseus," begins at the home of the Irish-Jewish couple Leopold and Molly Bloom at 7 Eccles Street in Dublin. Bloom's enactment of Odysseus' amorous and dangerous adventures take chiefly psychological and social form. He serves his wife breakfast in bed and cooks himself a pork kidney ("Calypso"), picks up a clandestine pornographic letter at the post office on his way to the Turkish baths ("Lotus-Eaters"), and attends a funeral at the cemetery in Glasnevin ("Hades"). There he enacts Odysseus' journey to the underworld by confronting the general topic of death in its most intimate form by thinking of his father's suicide and the mysterious death of his newborn son eleven years before. Bloom's job as an advertising canvasser takes him to Dublin newspaper offices ("Aeolus") and, after a modest lunch at Davy Byrne's eatery ("Lestrygonians"), to the National Library, where Stephen Dedalus is informally lecturing on Shakespeare. "Aeolus" metaphorically enacts its Homeric parallel (Aeolus was lord of the winds) with windy rhetoric and mimics its newspaper setting by writing in the typographic layout of newspaper columns and headlines: "SOPHIST WALLOPS HAUGHTY HELEN SQUARE ON PROBOSCIS. SPARTANS GNASH MOLARS. ITHACANS VOW PEN IS CHAMP" (*U* 7.1032). Stephen's attempt at the library to establish his artistic credentials among influential literati requires him to steer a tricky course between the conceptual predilections and artistic investments of his interlocutors, like Odysseus trying to maneuver his ship between a six-headed monster ("Scylla") and a deadly whirlpool ("Charybdis").

After a chapter depicting all of Dublin on the move ("Wandering Rocks"), Bloom sees his wife's impresario, Hugh "Blazes" Boylan, drinking and flirting before keeping what Bloom fears (correctly) will be an adulterous tryst with Molly at 7 Eccles Street. Odysseus' temptation by the music of the Sirens (which he hears tied to his mast) is thematically recapitulated as flirtation and operatic performance, and stylistically by writing that resembles an orchestral fugue ("Sirens"). Stopping in Barney Kiernan's pub to meet friends, Bloom is assaulted by a fiercely nationalistic and anti-Semitic citizen, who, prejudiced and xenophobic like the one-eyed Cyclops throwing rocks, tosses a biscuit tin after him ("Cyclops"). The gigantism of "Cyclops" is stylistically represented as hyperbolic and inflated rhetoric.

Calming himself on Sandymount strand, where three young women are minding three little boys, Bloom catches sight of the underclothes of one of the girls and becomes incited to masturbation. The episode narrates the romantic fantasies of Gerty Mac-Dowell ("Nausicaa") in the prose of ladies' magazines, advertising, and sentimental novelettes. Bloom stops at the Holles Street Maternity Hospital to inquire about the prolonged labor of a friend, Mrs. Purefoy, and ends up joining a group of roistering medical students ("Oxen of the Sun"). Their brutish humor regarding human reproduction signifies the "crime against fecundity" committed by Odysseus' men when they slaughtered the sacred oxen of the sun god. "Oxen of the Sun" stylistically recapitulates the embryonic gestation of English prose style in pastiches ranging from Anglo-Saxon to modern slang. Worried about the drunken Stephen Dedalus carousing with the medicals, Bloom paternally decides to follow him and his friends to Nighttown, the Dublin red-light district ("Circe"). There, in Bella Cohen's brothel, Bloom turns metaphorically into a pig (Circe turns Odysseus' men into swine) as masochistic fantasies are triggered by his day's casual pornographic reading (*Sweets of Sin*) and fears of cuckoldry. This episode of magical enchantment and disenchantment is narrated through the transmogrifications of Expressionist drama. "Circe" ends with Stephen breaking a lamp while striking at a hallucinated image of his mother with his stick and with Bloom narrowly saving him from arrest for getting into a fight with two British soldiers.

In "Eumaeus" Bloom takes Stephen to a cabman's shelter (analogous to the safe hut of the swineherd Eumaeus in the *Odyssey*) where they hear the incredible yarns of a sailor who identifies himself as W. B. Murphy. This chapter, about disguises and trust, prepares the way for the return home ("Nostos") to the "Ithaca" of Bloom's house at 7 Eccles Street. There Bloom offers Stephen cocoa, friendship, and a home, which he declines, in a chapter structured in the factitious question-and-answer format of the Catholic catechism. After Stephen wanders off into the night, Bloom returns to his wife's bed of adultery having worked through the "antagonistic sentiments" of "Envy, jealousy, abnegation, equanimity" (*U* 17.2155), like Odysseus who alone knows the secret of his marriage bed. Penelope ends the book with the long, unpunctuated sentences of Molly Bloom's thoughts in bed: her suitors (old boyfriends, Boylan, fantasized lovers including Stephen) slain as her own marital equanimity returns her to thoughts of her husband's romantic courtship and first lovemaking. "Then he asked me would I yes to say yes my mountain flower and first I put my arms around him yes and drew him down to me so he could feel my breasts all perfume yes and his heart was going like mad and yes I said yes I will Yes" (*U* 18.1605).

II

Because *Ulysses* was serialized in the *Little Review*, criticism of the text preceded its single-volume publication in 1922. The book's reception throughout the 1920s and 1930s was strongly colored by controversy about its form (or rather its "formlessness") and its putatively obscene content. The strongest early objections to the book came from British writers and critics, who read its vulgarity as a mark of the author's class inferiority and found its form nowhere visible within the British novel tradition. Stanley Sultan reports that "Alfred Noyes, England's 'unofficial poet laureate,' spoke on *Ulysses* before the Royal Society of Literature. 'There is no foulness conceivable to the mind of madman or ape that has not been poured into its imbecile pages,' he said" (3). Virginia Woolf wrote in her diary, "I finished *Ulysses* and think it a mis-fire. Genius it has, I think; but of the inferior water. The book is diffuse. It is brackish. It is pretentious. It is underbred, not only in the obvious sense, but in the literary sense" (48). Even his fellow Irishman, George Moore, supposedly said of *Ulysses*, "How can one plow through such stuff? I read a little here and there, but, oh my God, how bored I got! Probably Joyce thinks that because he prints all the dirty little words he is a great novelist. . . . Joyce, Joyce, why he's nobody—from the Dublin docks: no family, no breeding" (qtd. in Ellmann, *James Joyce* 529). Edmund Gosse, a translator of Ibsen, who at Yeats's request had secured a subsidy from the Royal Literary Fund for Joyce during the war, stridently urged Louis Gillet in 1924 to refuse to review *Ulysses* in *Revue des Deux-Mondes.* "You could only expose the worthlessness and impudence of his writing," he insisted, calling Joyce "a literary charlatan of the extremest order" and "a sort of Marquis de Sade, but does not write so well." He called *Ulysses* "an anarchical production, infamous in taste, in style, in everything" and deplored its "perfectly cynical appeal to sheer indecency" (qtd. in Ellmann, *James Joyce* 528).

These pedigreed hostilities to *Ulysses* stimulated the urgency and occasional defensiveness of many of the early tributes to the work's genius. Ezra Pound's praise was blunt and unequivocal: "All men should 'Unite to give praise to *Ulysses*'; those who will not, may content themselves with a place in the lower intellectual orders," he wrote in the opening of his famous "Paris Letter" published in *The Dial* in June 1922 (*Pound/Joyce* 194). He brushed aside the obscenity issue as a monstrous hypocrisy. "And the book is banned in America, where every child of seven has ample opportunity to drink in the details of the Arbuckle case" (200), he wrote, referring to the lurid rape and manslaughter trial of the silent film star Fatty Arbuckle. He praised the novel's perfectly crafted form and language by placing it squarely in the tradition of Gustave Flaubert. "Joyce has taken up the art of writing where Flaubert left it. . . . *Ulysses* has more form than any novel of Flaubert's" (194). This restoration of Joyce to a Continental novel tradition became the most effective strategy for justifying its form. Joyce's friend and admirer, the novelist Valéry Larbaud, recognized Dujardin's influence on Joyce's stream of consciousness technique and employed it in his own 1923 novel *Amants, heureux amants.* Another friend of Joyce, Stuart Gilbert, countered the charges of formlessness levied against the novel by stressing (with the help of the Homeric schema supplied by Joyce) the novel's complex mythic and structural organization (ix).[1]

[1] In 1972, Richard Ellmann's *Ulysses on the Liffey* revisited the novel's structure with an aesthetically nuanced scheme modeled on the schema Joyce had given Gilbert and Linati (see p. 24).

A year later, the American critic Edmund Wilson related Joyce's writing to the poetics of French Symbolism and French fiction and described the structure of *Ulysses* as "symphonic rather than narrative" (209). Wilson's essay, which Jeffrey Segall calls "a crucial document in the history of Joyce criticism" (94), introduced *Ulysses* sympathetically to an intellectual American audience attuned to the ideological debates about modern literature between humanists and Marxists throughout the 1930s.[2] Joyce would be criticized and defended by both sides during this period, most strongly in 1934 at the First International Writers' Congress in Moscow, where Karl Radek sharply attacked *Ulysses* for lacking a social conscience, while Wieland Herzfelde defended the significance of its representational innovations. Other commentaries on the social value of Joyce's work, positive and negative, were written during the 1930s by Paul Elmer More and Alick West. Joyce reportedly complained to Eugene Jolas about the harsh Marxist criticisms of his work by noting "I don't know why they attack me. Nobody in any of my books is worth more than a thousand pounds" (Ellmann, *James Joyce* 5).

By 1941—the year of Joyce's death—his academic respectability was consolidated in America when Harry Levin, a Harvard professor of comparative literature, published the first U.S. full-length critical study of Joyce's work. Levin's *James Joyce: A Critical Introduction* maintained Larbaud's and Wilson's powerful strategy of reading *Ulysses* through the philosophical preoccupations of Continental fiction. Levin used Thomas Mann's "dialectical pattern of *Künstler* versus *Bürger*" (66) to argue that "Joyce's work commemorates the long-standing quarrel between the bourgeois and the bohemian" (133).[3] Informed by the ideological debates of his colleagues in the 1930s, Levin read *Ulysses'* protest against a Philistine culture as a doomed gesture of liberalism.

<hr/>

[2] In addition to the social preoccupations of criticism in the 1930s, the arts—particularly the highly experimental visual arts—provided a more aesthetic lens for the reading of *Ulysses*. In 1932 Joseph Beach wrote an article, "Post-Impressionism: Joyce," and the psychoanalyst Carl Jung described in his essay, "*Ulysses*: A Monologue," the "new consciousness" produced by cubistic practices in the novel.

[3] The practice of reading Joyce intertextually by exploring literary, artistic, and philosophical influences in *Ulysses* has become a long-standing tradition in Joyce criticism. Studies on the influence of Aquinas (William Noon), Shakespeare (William Schutte), and Catholicism (J. Mitchell Morse) all appeared in the 1950s, and Virginia Mosely's study of Joyce and the Bible was published in the 1960s. In later decades, these intertextual approaches were sophisticated with more complex philosophical arguments by such critics as Robert Boyle and Beryl Schlossman on Joyce's Catholicism and

In reaction to the vexed ideological debates of the 1930s, the so-called New Criticism that came into fashion in the 1940s and 1950s inaugurated critical practices of close reading and textual analysis that put the external determinants of biography and history aside. During this period, *Ulysses* received rigorous scholarly scrutiny that neutralized earlier complaints of vulgarity and lack of discipline by focusing on the work's poetic craft and verbal texture. Richard M. Kain's 1947 book-length study of the novel, *Fabulous Voyager: James Joyce's "Ulysses,"* inaugurated meticulous attention to the naturalistic detail and stylistic precision of the text. Close reading, carefully glossed allusions, and heavy symbolic allegory made *Ulysses* readily accessible to common readers in William York Tindall's 1959 *A Reader's Guide to James Joyce.* Such other well-known writers of the New Criticism as R. P. Blackmur and William Empson also wrote essays on *Ulysses* during this time.

The publication of Hugh Kenner's *Dublin's Joyce* in 1956 was a major critical event in Joyce studies. The strategies of this book, refined and elaborated during the next four decades, consisted of meticulously close reading supplemented by noting significant interventions that are operative in the text by their *absence*: the subtle effects and changes produced by intonation, idiom, and other qualities of voice; the irony produced by unstated incongruities, significant errors, omissions, and silences ("we ought to observe how much silence pervades such of their conversation as we do hear" [Kenner, *Ulysses* 51]). For the next several decades, Kenner refined his complex close readings of the Joycean text at the same time that he consolidated his influence as the premier critic of Modernism. He published his ambitious study of modernist poetics, *The Pound Era*, in 1971. In his 1978 work, *Joyce's Voices*, he articulated the "Uncle Charles Principle": *"the narrative idiom need not be the narrator's"* (18). His 1980 edition of *Ulysses* elaborated the myriad ways the text stimulates the reader's interpretive creativity with the questions it embeds.

Mary Reynolds on Joyce and Dante. More broadly conceived studies of philosophical influence on Joyce's text were written by Jackson Cope and Theoharis Constantine Theoharis, and in 1982 Umberto Eco published *The Aesthetics of Chaosmos: The Middle Ages of James Joyce.* In 1987 Phillip Herring's *Joyce's Uncertainty Principle* inflected Joyce's philosophy with theories of relativity and uncertainty in modern science. The influence of Continental drama, fiction, and opera on *Ulysses* were explored by Bjorn Tysdahl (Ibsen), Richard Cross (Flaubert), Peter Egri (Mann), Breon Mitchell (the German novel), and Timothy Martin (Wagner). In 1976 Michael Seidel reexamined Joyce's poetic and philosophical inspiration by the *Odyssey* in *Epic Geography: James Joyce's "Ulysses."* More recently, Martha Black's study of Joyce and Shaw and Scott Klein's on Joyce and Wyndham Lewis continue this tradition.

While New Criticism dominated American literary practice, British criticism extended an Arnoldian tradition of promoting high culture and moral seriousness into midcentury, largely through the influential thinking of F. R. Leavis. Leavis expelled Joyce from his *The Great Tradition* for failing to write, like D. H. Lawrence, from a "depth of religious experience." He complained that

> there is no organic principle determining, informing, and controlling into a vital whole, the elaborate analogical structure, the extraordinary variety of technical devices, the attempts at an exhaustive rendering of consciousness, for which *Ulysses* is remarkable, and which got it accepted by a cosmopolitan literary world as a new start. It is rather, I think, a dead end. (25–26)

Leavis, unprepared for the revolution in critical theory that would come to dominate literary study for the last quarter of the twentieth century, could not have been more wrong. He failed to see that it was precisely the absence of an "organic principle" in *Ulysses*—indeed, the text's questioning the concept and validity of an "organic principle"— that for the next thirty years made *Ulysses'* open form create the multiplicity of interpretive possibilities that transformed it into a poetic chameleon, a text for all critical seasons.

The need to find the vision or telos behind the novel's technical complexity stirred critical creativity in the 1960s. S. L. Goldberg's 1961 *The Classical Temper: A Study of James Joyce's "Ulysses"* answered Leavis most directly by elevating the novel to a high moral plane on the basis of the "classical temper" of its humanistic objectivity. In the following year, Robert Martin Adams' *Surface and Symbol: The Consistency of James Joyce's "Ulysses"* (1962) probed Joyce's strategy in a controversial, but fascinating, analysis of the interplay between the novel's factual and fictional materials and their narrative and symbolic effects. A few years later Arnold Goldman's 1966 *The Joyce Paradox: Form and Freedom in His Fiction* addressed the problem of the text's propensity to produce conflicting readings with an ambitious argument that related its interpretive openness to the paradoxes inherent in all of Joyce's texts. The *Ulysses* critics of the 1960s defeated the early charges against the text's formlessness with mounting evidence of precise craft[4]

---

[4]A. Walton Litz's *The Art of James Joyce* (1961) inaugurated a tradition of genetic research into Joyce's composition practices that eventually informed editorial principle and expertise while contributing a scholarly underpinning to Joyce's design. This work

at the same time that they deflected pressure to link its technical virtuosity to a single origin, function, or purpose.

The 1970s and 1980s brought an explosion of criticism and scholarship to the study of *Ulysses* that was increasingly colored by the mounting translations and importations of French and German critical theory into the American academy. The influence of Continental theory produced two important effects on the study of Joycean texts. First, poststructuralism and deconstruction stressed the metaphysics of language by exploring its performativity, its freeplay, its rhetorical productivity, and its self-referentiality. This highly theoretical approach to language validated Joyce's avant-garde linguistic experiments (which had first been celebrated in the 1930s) with greater technical and logical insight. Although some examples of this approach appeared as early as 1972—Sally Purcell's translation of Hélène Cixous's *The Exile of James Joyce*, for example—most deconstructive approaches to Joyce appeared later in the decade and initially focused on *Finnegans Wake*, such as Margot Norris's 1976 *The Decentered Universe of "Finnegans Wake."* In addition, Continental theory encompassed methods and insights from a variety of disciplines—especially linguistics, philosophy, psychoanalysis, and anthropology. As a result, criticism assumed a highly interdisciplinary focus during the 1970s and 1980s, as exemplified in Colin MacCabe's *James Joyce and the Revolution of the Word* (1978), which used structuralist, psychoanalytic, and Marxist theories to argue for the philosophically revolutionary potential of Joyce's most radical formal experiments.

One of the earliest effects of Continental theory was found in linguistically informed attention to the nature of narrative, which

---

was continued in the 1970s by Phillip Herring, who edited the British Museum notesheets for the last seven chapters of *Ulysses*, and Michael Groden, whose 1977 *"Ulysses" in Progress* used a meticulously researched composition history to represent the novel as a palimpsest of Joyce's creative development. Groden identifies Joyce's three experimental compositional phases as the interior monologue, the parodies and imitative styles, and the final strategy of compositional self-reflection. The 1960s also saw the first readers' guides and research tools for *Ulysses*. Stanley Sultan, Harry Blamires, and Clive Hart's studies were designed to help readers with the generic and narrative progress of the novel. Weldon Thornton's *Allusions in "Ulysses": An Annotated List* appeared in 1968 and was the first reference guide to offer annotations for the numerous allusions in the work. This text was followed in 1974 by an even more comprehensive guide: Don Gifford and Robert Seidman's *Notes for Joyce*, which were issued in a revised and expanded version as *"Ulysses" Annotated* in 1988.

produced increasingly sophisticated speech act theory, rhetorical analysis, and reception theory. One of the earliest narratological approaches was David Hayman's *"Ulysses": The Mechanics of Meaning* (1970), which analyzed the book's techniques, structures, and styles to postulate the influential notion that point of view in *Ulysses* may be controlled by an "Arranger," rather than a narrator or groups of narrators.

A decade later, Karen Lawrence's 1981 *The Odyssey of Style in "Ulysses"* argued that the increasingly radical narrative and stylistic experiments of the later episodes in the novel function self-reflexively, to make style itself a performative activity in the novel. Two other studies appeared in the 1980s oriented, like Lawrence's, toward effects on the reader of *Ulysses*. Brook Thomas's 1982 *James Joyce's "Ulysses": A Book of Many Happy Returns* used the premises of reader-response criticism—including the notion that the text constructs the reader—to focus on the self-revealing textual consciousness at work in the novel's telling. John Paul Riquelme's *Teller and Tale in Joyce's Fiction: Oscillating Perspectives* (1983) challenged the notion of Joyce's impersonal narration in *Ulysses*. On a more technical level of language, Roy Gottfried's *The Art of Joyce's Syntax in "Ulysses"* (1980) argued that Joyce creates deliberate tensions between order and freedom in the text by transgressing traditional rules of syntax. Finally, in the mid-1980s two important collections of essays on Joyce's language at last brought together the work of the eminent Swiss Joyce scholar, Fritz Senn. Senn's *Nichts Gegen Joyce: Joyce Versus Nothing*, published in Zurich in 1983, includes several important essays on *Ulysses*, including "Dynamics of Corrective Unrest" in which Senn argues that the novel is "probably the first consistently autocorrective work of literature" (121). A year later, John Paul Riquelme edited Senn's *Joyce's Dislocutions: Essays on Reading as Translation*, in which Senn uses the trope of translation to explore Joyce's creation of shifting and multivalent meanings through a polyglot's sense of language.

The disciplinary diversity of critical theory, which explored literary language through the lenses of various "human sciences," expressed itself in a Joycean criticism increasingly inflected by methodologies drawn from other fields. The interiorized nature of *Ulysses*, whose language portrays and exposes a complex variety of psychic states and mechanisms, made Joyce's work a particularly rich subject for psychoanalytic criticism. Mark Shechner's 1974 *Joyce in Nighttown: A Psychoanalytic Inquiry into "Ulysses"* appeared as the first significant Freudian study of the novel, tracing the psychoanalytic strategies that transformed biographical material into fictional complications in the text.[5] In 1980 Sheldon Brivic's *Joyce Between Freud and Jung* offered a psychoanalytically balanced and eclectic overview of Joyce's fictional development with attention to *Ulysses*. More than a decade later, psychoanalytic criticism—under the influence of Jacques Lacan, who was himself influenced by Joyce—significantly turned its focus toward the performative nature of writing and textuality. Mature explorations of the role of language in the construction of the subject as a self-divided creation of cultural discourses emerged in the 1990s, notably in Kimberly Devlin's analysis of the "uncanny" Joycean text in her 1991 *Wandering and Return in "Finnegans Wake": An Integrative Approach to Joyce's Fictions*. A year earlier, Suzette Henke's *James Joyce and the Politics of Desire* used the psychoanalytic theories of Freud, Jacques Lacan, and Julia Kristeva to explore gendered gestures of textual performativity in Joyce's works. This same attention to psychoanalytically performative language may be found in the essays by Joseph Boone, Marilyn Brownstein, and Ellen Carol Jones in Susan Stanford Friedman's 1993 collection of essays, *Joyce: The Return of the Repressed*.

Politics in a broad sense—including Marxist criticism, Frankfurt School criticism, cultural study, postcolonial criticism, and feminism— began to dominate *Ulysses* studies in the late 1980s and early 1990s.[6] The inaugural text for this trend was Dominic Manganiello's 1980 *Joyce's Politics*, whose focus on the biographical restoration of Joyce's interest in political theories and issues laid the groundwork for the later studies of postcolonialism and culture study in *Ulysses*. Franco Moretti's 1983 *Signs Taken for Wonders* contains a provocative essay, "The Long Goodbye: *Ulysses* and the End of Liberal Capitalism," that argues for the homology between the novel and Britain's capitalist crisis in the early twentieth century. Cheryl Herr's *Joyce's Anatomy of Culture* (1986) looks specifically at the ideologies Joyce imported into his texts by using Irish popular discourses, particularly the newspaper, the sermon, and the music-hall stage. Herr's analysis of "Circe" is

---

[5]Three works that are not explicitly psychoanalytical but that nonetheless focus on the function of metamorphosis and transformation in *Ulysses* are books by Elliott Gose, John Gordon, and Lindsey Tucker. Tucker's work focuses specifically on the body and alimentation as tropes of creativity in *Ulysses*.

[6]During the 1970s, Bernard Benstock, John Garvin, and C. H. Peake all contributed studies of Joyce's relationship to Ireland. Patrick Parrinder's 1984 study for advanced students contains excellent chapters on five chapters in *Ulysses*, with many interesting glosses on the political issues they raise.

greatly enriched by her discovery of intriguing source materials from the popular culture of turn-of-the-century Ireland. Patrick McGee's 1988 *Paperspace: Style as Ideology in Joyce's "Ulysses"* resists the textualist impulse to treat Joyce's radical stylistic experiments in the novel as autonomous in favor of restoring them to the realm of the historical and the social.

Following Seamus Deane's 1985 *Celtic Revivals: Essays in Modern Irish Literature*, the Irish Field Day Theatre Company sponsored a book of three essays by noted Marxist critics Terry Eagleton, Fredric Jameson, and Edward Said called *Nationalism, Colonialism, and Literature* (1990); Eagleton and Jameson's essays contain specific reference to *Ulysses*. Jeffrey Segall uses *Ulysses* to cast "a beam under which we may scrutinize a period in American cultural history when polemics dominated literary debate" (8) in his 1993 *Joyce in America: Cultural Politics and the Trials of "Ulysses."* Enda Duffy's 1994 *The Subaltern "Ulysses"* makes even greater revolutionary claims for the novel: "I want to reclaim *Ulysses* in these terms for Irish readers as *the* text of Ireland's independence . . . a novel preoccupied . . . with both the means by which oppressed communities fight their way out of abjection and the potential pitfalls of anticolonial struggles" (1). Vincent Cheng's 1995 *Joyce, Race, and Empire* contains chapters on *Ulysses* that focus particularly on the "ethnography of Irishness and . . . perspectives of racial and ethnic otherness in the novel" (xvi). Finally, at the other spectrum of politics, James McMichael is concerned with how the novel educates and enlarges our sense of human responsibility to others through its ethics of reading (*"Ulysses" and Justice*, 1991).

Feminist approaches to *Ulysses* reflect many of the ideological shifts and theoretical inflections that invigorated the sophistication of feminist criticism in the 1970s and 1980s. Moving away from querulous complaints that Joyce failed to make women sufficiently strong, heroic, independent, or intellectual (in the work of Sandra Gilbert, Susan Gubar, Carolyn Heilbrun, and other American feminist critics), later feminist criticism complicated both misogynistic and gyneolatrous readings of Molly Bloom with historical considerations. In Winter 1981, the *James Joyce Quarterly* published Mary Power's essay, "The Discovery of *Ruby*," which located and identified the novel *Ruby. A Novel. Founded on the Life of a Circus Girl* as the source of the text Molly Bloom reads in bed in *Ulysses*. Power's discovery led to an important reconsideration of the role of pornography in the novel and stressed the importance of historical research for achieving an accurate grasp of the text's sexual politics. Bonnie Kime Scott's 1984 *Joyce and*

Feminism corrected general misperceptions about Joyce's attitudes and experiences with respect to historical feminism and his relationship with women in his familial and professional life. Both Scott's book and Suzette Henke and Elaine Unkeless's 1982 *Women in Joyce* contain discussions of *Ulysses*. Richard Brown's 1985 *James Joyce and Sexuality* supplies a broad historical context for Joyce's engagement with the philosophical, scientific, and social sexologies prominent in early twentieth-century thought. Mary Lowe-Evans is more pointedly indebted to the approaches of new historicism in excavating the discourses of population control that shape many ideological issues in the Joycean text. Her 1989 *Crimes Against Fecundity: Joyce and Population Control* contains an important chapter on "Oxen of the Sun."

The figure of Molly Bloom alone has generated an impressive body of scholarship. David Hayman's "The Empirical Molly" in Staley and Benstock's *Approaches to "Ulysses"* (1970), and Phillip Herring's "Toward an Historical Molly Bloom" (1978) treat Molly as a complex character, on a par with Stephen Dedalus and Leopold Bloom. James Van Dyck Card's 1984 *An Anatomy of "Penelope"* displays Molly's contradictions as products of careful author intention, given the archival evidence of manuscripts, typescripts, and proofs. Richard Pearce's collection of essays, *Molly Blooms: A Polylogue on "Penelope" and Cultural Studies* contains provocative sections on "Molly and the Male Gaze," "Molly in Performance," "Negotiating Colonialism," "Molly as Consumer," and "Molly as Body and Embodied." Another excellent selection of essays on Molly Bloom, "Feminist Readings of Joyce," appeared in the 1989 special issue of *Modern Fiction Studies,* guest edited by Ellen Carol Jones.

A series of books that in the late 1980s and early 1990s explored problems of authority in the Joycean text fruitfully use gender issues as a trope for problems of legitimacy and power. Although her discussion of *Ulysses* merely caps her exploration of the British novel tradition, Christine van Boheemen's 1987 *The Novel as Family Romance: Language, Gender, and Authority from Fielding to Joyce* contributes an influential exploration of gender in the novel with an approach theoretically inflected by Continental deconstruction. Vicki Mahaffey's 1988 *Reauthorizing Joyce* uses Molly Bloom and "Penelope" to typologize a multiple and collective alternative to the more oppressive authorities associated with other figures, styles, and institutions in *Ulysses*. Frances Restuccia's 1989 *Joyce and the Law of the Father* uses chiefly psychoanalytic theories, in which resistance is typologized by the trope of the perverse (sadism, fetishism, the phallic mother, prohibition, and so forth), to explore the fate of authority in the Joycean text. Jean-Michel Rabaté's 1991 *James Joyce, Authorized Reader* likewise uses Derridian and Lacanian premises to explore the figure of paternity in delineating problems of authorization in the compact between author and reader. Even though deconstructive criticism gravitated more readily toward *Finnegans Wake* than the earlier works, Derek Attridge and Daniel Ferrer's 1984 *Post-structuralist Joyce* includes two interesting essays on *Ulysses*: André Topia's "The Matrix and the Echo: Intertextuality in *Ulysses*" and Daniel Ferrer's psychoanalytically explored "Circe, Regret, and Regression." Derek Attridge's 1988 *Peculiar Language: Literature as Difference from the Renaissance to James Joyce* conducts a Derridian exploration of the language of *Ulysses* in its chapter 6, "Literature as Deviation: Syntax, Style, and the Body in *Ulysses*." Robert Scholes' 1992 *In Search of James Joyce* contains a series of important essays on *Ulysses*, including "*Ulysses*: A Structuralist Perspective," and a fascinating chapter on "Circe" and modern painting, entitled "In the Brothel of Modernism: Picasso and Joyce."

The flood of new studies on *Ulysses* is not abating in the 1990s. They include some works on teaching *Ulysses* that augment the large number of introductory studies, chapter-by-chapter discussions, and collections of essays[7] that have accumulated over the years. In 1993, the Modern Language Association published Kathleen McCormick and Erwin Steinberg's *Approaches to Teaching Joyce's "Ulysses"*, which attempts to introduce students to background materials and various theoretical approaches to the text. In 1996 Robert Newman published a collection of essays on teaching *through* or *with Ulysses* under the title *Pedagogy, Praxis, "Ulysses": Using Joyce's Text to Transform the Classroom*.

This summary of the critical history of *Ulysses* is inevitably incomplete. New introductory guides like Vincent Sherry's and other research tools continue to augment the large number of older directories and companion studies with important new material on *Ulysses*. Fortunately, there are a series of excellent bibliographical aids available for finding much additional *Ulysses* scholarship that is here omitted, although these are inevitably limited by their publication dates. The

---

[7]Among the most useful introductory guides for students are the episode-by-episode discussions of Harry Blamires and Suzette Henke (*Joyce's Moraculous Sindbook*) and the collection of essays focused on each episode edited by Clive Hart and David Hayman. Single volume introductory discussions of the novel are found in Clive Hart, Vincent Sherry, and Patrick McCarthy. The studies of Stanley Sultan and Daniel Schwarz are somewhat more complex. Some other excellent collections of essays are edited by Thomas Staley (*"Ulysses": Fifty Years*, which contains Hugh Kenner's provocative essay on "Molly's Masterstroke") and by Staley and Bernard Benstock.

most comprehensive of these, if not the most recent, is Thomas Jackson Rice's *James Joyce: A Guide to Research* (1982). Thomas Staley's user-friendly *An Annotated Critical Bibliography of James Joyce* (1989) is more up to date. Sidney Feshbach and William Herman offer a compact "History of Joyce Criticism and Scholarship" in Zack Bowen and James F. Carens's 1984 *A Companion to Joyce Studies*. And recently, the *James Joyce Quarterly* 32 (Winter 1995) published a thirty-year index listing the contents of the journal's first thirty volumes that is beautifully organized and indexed for easy retrieval of virtually anything published on *Ulysses* in its pages.

The future of *Ulysses* scholarship will be enriched by two landmark publishing events of 1978 and 1984. The first was the astonishing production of *The James Joyce Archive*, an event whose significance Phillip Herring described as "galactic" (Review 86). Sixty-three oversized volumes collect a facsimile of virtually Joyce's entire workshop, which includes most of the available notes and notebooks, holograph drafts, manuscripts, typescripts, and text proofs for his published work. Using *The James Joyce Archive*, Joyce scholars can now check the evolution of the chapters of *Ulysses* from early notes through successive drafts and galley proofs in the comfort of their own university libraries.

The second seismic event in the field of *Ulysses* scholarship was the 1984 publication of a critical and synoptic edition of *Ulysses*, edited by Hans Walter Gabler with Wolfhard Steppe and Claus Melchior. In 1986, Random House published a trade edition of Gabler's text that called itself "The Corrected Text," which made the work available in paperback. Gabler, who was assisted in this editorial enterprise by an international advisory committee that included Richard Ellmann, Clive Hart, A. Walton Litz, and Michael Groden, confronted an unusual array of editorial problems created by the chaotic exigencies of the process leading up to the publication of the 1922 edition. In his introduction, Gabler carefully laid out the editorial premises and procedures he adopted for making difficult decisions on what to retain or change in the 1984 critical and synoptic edition. This exposure of his editorial process provided the information that led to an attack by John Kidd, initially in an essay with the somewhat scurrilous title of "The Scandal of *Ulysses*." The Gabler edition thus became a point of intense controversy that spilled far beyond the confines of the Joyce community.

But while the Gabler edition's flaws have been quite thoroughly explored in Sandulescu and Hart's 1986 *Assessing the 1984 "Ulysses"*, the text has endured with considerable popularity among large numbers of scholars, students, and readers, who appear to trust the judgments behind its corrections. Furthermore, Michael Groden's "Afterword" to the 1993 Bodley Head publication of the Gabler edition of *Ulysses* pointed out that Gabler's presentation of his editing procedures has "lifted the general public, students, literary critics, and scholars—the vast majority of whom are not themselves editors—to a heightened awareness of textual editing" (647). Jerome McGann theorizes the implications of the impossibility of producing a definitive text in his 1985 article *"Ulysses* as a Postmodern Text: The Gabler Edition" in *Criticism.* The Fall 1990 issue of the *James Joyce Quarterly* carried pieces by Michael Groden ("A Response to John Kidd's 'An Inquiry into *Ulysses: The Corrected Text'*" 81–110) and John Kidd ("Gabler's Errors in Context: A Reply to Michael Groden on Editing *Ulysses*") stating and discussing the editorial points in dispute.

The future of *Ulysses* study holds an entirely different and brave new world of editing in its cards. A number of scholars, among whom Michael Groden appears to be in the vanguard, are now at work exploring the possibilities of an electronic hypertext of *Ulysses*—a text enhanced with simultaneous annotations, illustrations, and criticism—made possible by computer technology. At the moment when *Ulysses* scholarship is about to undergo a millennial revolution, Joyce's wonderful novel demonstrates once again its unquenchable vigor as a text for all times and for all critical and scholarly seasons.

Margot Norris

WORKS CITED

Adams, Robert Martin. *Surface and Symbol: The Consistency of James Joyce's "Ulysses."* New York: Oxford UP, 1962.

Attridge, Derek. *Peculiar Language: Literature as Difference from the Renaissance to James Joyce.* Ithaca: Cornell UP, 1988.

Attridge, Derek, and Daniel Ferrer. *Post-Structuralist Joyce: Essays from the French.* Cambridge: Cambridge UP, 1984.

Barrow, Craig Wallace. *Montage in James Joyce's "Ulysses."* Potomac, MD: Studia Humanitatis, 1980.

Beach, Joseph Warren. "Post-Impressionism: Joyce." *The Twentieth-Century Novel: Studies in Technique.* New York: Appleton, 1932.

Benstock, Bernard. *James Joyce: The Undiscover'd Country.* New York: Barnes, 1977.

Benstock, Shari, and Bernard Benstock. *Who's He When He's at Home: A James Joyce Directory.* Urbana: U of Illinois P, 1980.

Black, Martha Fodaski. *Shaw and Joyce: The Last Word in Stolentelling.* Gainesville: U of Florida P, 1995.

Blackmur, R. P. "The Jew in Search of a Son: Joyce's *Ulysses.*" *Eleven Essays in the European Novel.* New York: Harcourt, 1964.

Blamires, Harry. *The Bloomsday Book: A Guide Through Joyce's "Ulysses."* London: Methuen, 1966.

Boheemen, Christine van. *The Novel as Family Romance: Language, Gender, and Authority from Fielding to Joyce.* Ithaca: Cornell UP, 1987.

Bowen, Zack. *Musical Allusions in the Works of James Joyce: Early Poetry through "Ulysses."* Albany: SUNY P, 1974.

Bowen, Zack, and James F. Carens, eds. *A Companion to Joyce Studies.* Westport, CT: Greenwood, 1984.

Boyle, Robert, S. J. *James Joyce's Pauline Vision: A Catholic Exposition.* Carbondale: Southern Illinois UP, 1978.

Brivic, Sheldon R. *Joyce between Freud and Jung.* Port Washington, NY: Kennikat, 1980.

Brown, Richard. *James Joyce and Sexuality.* Cambridge: Cambridge UP, 1985.

Card, James Van Dyck. *An Anatomy of "Penelope."* Rutherford, NJ: Farleigh Dickinson UP, 1984.

Cheng, Vincent J. *Joyce, Race, and Empire.* Cambridge: Cambridge UP, 1995.

Cixous, Hélène. *The Exile of James Joyce.* Trans. Sally A. J. Purcell. New York: Lewis, 1972.

Cope, Jackson I. *Joyce's Cities: Archaeologies of the Soul.* Baltimore: Johns Hopkins UP, 1981.

Cross, Richard K. *Flaubert and Joyce: The Rite of Fiction.* Princeton: Princeton UP, 1971.

Deane, Seamus. *Celtic Revivals: Essays in Modern Irish Literature, 1880–1980.* London: Faber, 1985.

Dent, R. W. *Colloquial Language in "Ulysses": A Reference Tool.* Newark: U of Delaware P, 1994.

Devlin, Kimberly J. *Wandering and Return in "Finnegans Wake": An Integrative Approach to Joyce's Fictions.* Princeton: Princeton UP, 1991.

Duffy, Enda. *The Subaltern "Ulysses."* Minneapolis: U of Minnesota P, 1994.

Eagleton, Terry, Fredric Jameson, and Edward W. Said. *Nationalism,*

Colonialism, and Literature. Minneapolis: U of Minnesota P, 1990.

Eco, Umberto. *The Aesthetics of Chaosmos: The Middle Ages of James Joyce.* Trans. Ellen Esrock. Tulsa: University of Tulsa P, 1982.

Egri, Peter. *Avantguardism and Modernity: A Comparison of James Joyce's "Ulysses" with Thomas Mann's "Der Zauberberg" and "Lotte in Weimar."* Trans. Paul Aston. Tulsa: University of Tulsa P, 1972.

Eliot, T. S. "*Ulysses,* Order, and Myth." *Selected Prose of T. S. Eliot.* Ed. Frank Kermode. New York: Harcourt, 1975. 175–78.

Ellmann, Richard. *James Joyce.* Rev. ed. New York: Oxford UP, 1982.

———. Ulysses *on the Liffey.* New York: Oxford UP, 1972.

Empson, William. "The Theme of *Ulysses.*" *Kenyon Review* 18 (1956): 26–52.

French, Marilyn. *The Book as World: James Joyce's "Ulysses."* Cambridge: Harvard UP, 1976.

Friedman, Susan Stanford, ed. *Joyce: The Return of the Repressed.* Ithaca: Cornell UP, 1993.

Garvin, John. *James Joyce's Disunited Kingdom and the Irish Dimension.* Dublin: Gill, 1976.

Gifford, Don, with Robert J. Seidman. *"Ulysses" Annotated: Notes for James Joyce's 'Ulysses.'* Rev. ed. Berkeley: U of California P, 1988.

Gilbert, Stuart. *James Joyce's "Ulysses": A Study.* London: Faber, 1930.

Gillespie, Michael Patrick. *Inverted Volumes Improperly Arranged: James Joyce and His Trieste Library.* Ann Arbor: UMI Research P, 1983.

Goldberg, S. L. *The Classical Temper: A Study of James Joyce's "Ulysses."* London: Chatto, 1961.

Goldman, Arnold. *The Joyce Paradox: Form and Freedom in His Fiction.* Evanston: Northwestern UP, 1966.

Gordon, John. *James Joyce's Metamorphoses.* Dublin: Gill, 1981.

Gose, Elliott B. *The Transformation Process in Joyce's "Ulysses."* Toronto: U of Toronto P, 1980.

Gottfried, Roy K. *The Art of Joyce's Syntax in "Ulysses."* Athens: U of Georgia P, 1980.

Groden, Michael. Afterword. *Ulysses.* By James Joyce. Ed. Hans Walter Gabler. London: Bodley Head, 1993. New York: Vintage, 1996.

———. "A Response to John Kidd's 'An Inquiry Into *Ulysses: The Corrected Text.*'" *James Joyce Quarterly* 28 (Fall 1990): 81–110.

———. *"Ulysses" in Progress.* Princeton: Princeton UP, 1977.

Hart, Clive. *James Joyce's "Ulysses."* Sydney: Sydney UP, 1968.

Hart, Clive, and David Hayman, eds. *James Joyce's "Ulysses": Critical Essays.* Berkeley: U of California P, 1974.

Hart, Clive, and A. M. Leo Knuth. *A Topographical Guide to James Joyce's "Ulysses."* 2 vols. Colchester, Eng.: Wake Newslitter, 1975.

Hayman, David. "The Empirical Molly." *Approaches to "Ulysses": Ten Essays.* Ed. Thomas F. Staley and Bernard Benstock. Pittsburgh: U of Pittsburgh P, 1970. 103–35.

———. *"Ulysses": The Mechanics of Meaning.* Englewood Cliffs: Prentice-Hall, 1970.

Henke, Suzette A. *James Joyce and the Politics of Desire.* New York: Routledge, 1990.

———. *Joyce's Moraculous Sindbook: A Study of "Ulysses."* Columbus: Ohio State UP, 1978.

Henke, Suzette A., and Elaine Unkeless, eds. *Women in Joyce.* Urbana: U of Illinois P, 1982.

Herr, Cheryl. *Joyce's Anatomy of Culture.* Urbana: U of Illinois P, 1986.

Herring, Phillip F., ed. *Joyce's "Ulysses" Notesheets in the British Museum.* Charlottesville: UP of Virginia, 1972.

———. *Joyce's Uncertainty Principle.* Princeton: Princeton UP, 1987.

———. Rev. of *The James Joyce Archive. James Joyce Quarterly* 19 (Fall 1981): 85–97.

———. "Toward an Historical Molly Bloom." *English Literary History* 45(1978): 501–21.

The James Joyce Archive. Ed. Michael Groden, et al. New York: Garland, 1978–.

Jones, Ellen Carol, guest co-ed. *Modern Fiction Studies* 35 (Autumn 1989). "Feminist Readings of Joyce" issue.

Joyce, James. *Selected Letters.* Ed. Richard Ellmann. New York: Viking, 1975.

———. *Ulysses.* Ed. Hans Walter Gabler, with Wolfhard Steppe and Claus Melchior. New York: Vintage, 1986.

Jung, Carl G. "*Ulysses:* A Monologue." *The Spirit in Man, Art, and Literature.* Trans. R. F. C. Hull. Princeton: Princeton UP, 1966.

Kain, Richard M. *Fabulous Voyager: James Joyce's "Ulysses."* Chicago: U of Chicago P, 1947.

Kelly, Dermot. *Narrative Strategies in Joyce's "Ulysses."* Ann Arbor: UMI Research P, 1988.

Kenner, Hugh. *Dublin's Joyce.* Bloomington: Indiana UP, 1956.

——. "Homer's Sticks and Stones." *James Joyce Quarterly* 6(Summer 1969): 285–98.

——. *Joyce's Voices.* Berkeley: U of California P, 1978.

——. *The Pound Era.* Berkeley: U of California P, 1971.

——. *Ulysses: Revised Edition.* Baltimore: Johns Hopkins UP, 1987.

Kidd, John. "Gabler's Errors in Context: A Reply to Michael Groden on Editing *Ulysses*." *James Joyce Quarterly* 28(Fall 1990): 111–51.

——. "The Scandal of *Ulysses*." *The New York Review of Books.* 30 June 1988: 32.

Klein, Scott W. *The Fictions of James Joyce and Wyndham Lewis: Monsters of Nature and Design.* Cambridge: Cambridge UP, 1994.

Lawrence, Karen. *The Odyssey of Style in "Ulysses."* Princeton: Princeton UP, 1981.

Leavis, F. R. *The Great Tradition.* London: Chatto, 1960.

Levin, Harry. *James Joyce: A Critical Introduction.* Norfolk, CT: New Directions, 1941.

Litz, A. Walton. *The Art of James Joyce: Method and Design in "Ulysses" and "Finnegans Wake."* London: Oxford UP, 1961.

Lowe-Evans, Mary. *Crimes Against Fecundity: Joyce and Population Control.* Syracuse: Syracuse UP, 1989.

MacCabe, Colin. *James Joyce and the Revolution of the Word.* London: Macmillan, 1978.

Maddox, James H. *Joyce's "Ulysses" and the Assault upon Character.* New Brunswick: Rutgers UP, 1978.

Mahaffey, Vicki. *Reauthorizing Joyce.* New York: Cambridge UP, 1988.

Manganiello, Dominic. *Joyce's Politics.* London: Routledge, 1980.

Martin, Timothy. *Joyce and Wagner: A Study of Influence.* Cambridge: Cambridge UP, 1991.

McCarthy, Patrick A. *"Ulysses": Portals of Discovery.* Boston: Twayne, 1990.

McCormick, Kathleen, and Erwin R. Steinberg, eds. *Approaches to Teaching Joyce's "Ulysses."* New York: MLA, 1993.

McGann, Jerome J. "*Ulysses* as a Postmodern Text: The Gabler Edition." *Criticism* 27 (1985): 283–306.

McGee, Patrick. *Paperspace: Style as Ideology in Joyce's "Ulysses."* Lincoln: U of Nebraska P, 1988.

McMichael, James. *"Ulysses" and Justice.* Princeton: Princeton UP, 1991.

Mitchell, Breon. *James Joyce and the German Novel, 1922–33.* Athens: Ohio UP, 1976.

More, Paul Elmer. "James Joyce." *On Being Human.* Princeton: Princeton UP, 1936.

Moretti, Franco. *Signs Taken for Wonders: Essays in the Sociology of Literary Forms.* Trans. Susan Fischer, David Forgacs, and David Miller. London: Verso, 1983.

Morse, J. Mitchell. *The Sympathetic Alien: James Joyce and Catholicism.* New York: New York UP, 1959.

Mosely, Virginia. *Joyce and the Bible.* De Kalb: Northern Illinois UP, 1967.

Newman, Robert, ed. *Pedagogy, Praxis, "Ulysses": Using Joyce's Text to Transform the Classroom.* Ann Arbor: U of Michigan P, 1996.

Noon, William T., *Joyce and Aquinas.* New Haven: Yale UP, 1957.

Norris, Margot. *The Decentered Universe of "Finnegans Wake."* Baltimore: Johns Hopkins UP, 1976.

Parrinder, Patrick. *James Joyce.* Cambridge: Cambridge UP, 1984.

Peake, C. H. *James Joyce: The Citizen and the Artist.* Stanford: Stanford UP, 1977.

Pearce, Richard, ed. *Molly Blooms: A Polylogue on "Penelope" and Cultural Studies.* Madison: U of Wisconsin P, 1994.

Pound/Joyce: The Letters of Ezra Pound to James Joyce. Ed. Forrest Read. New York: New Directions, 1967.

Power, Mary. "The Discovery of *Ruby.*" *James Joyce Quarterly* 18(Winter 1981): 115–21.

Rabaté, Jean-Michel. *James Joyce, Authorized Reader.* Trans. Baltimore: Johns Hopkins UP, 1991. Trans. of *James Joyce, Portrait de l'auteur en autre lecteur.* 1984.

Raleigh, John Henry. *The Chronicle of Leopold and Molly Bloom: "Ulysses" as Narrative.* Berkeley: U of California P, 1977.

Restuccia, Frances L. *Joyce and the Law of the Father.* New Haven: Yale UP, 1989.

Reynolds, Mary T. *Joyce and Dante: The Shaping Imagination.* Princeton: Princeton UP, 1981.

Rice, Thomas Jackson. *James Joyce: A Guide to Research.* New York: Garland, 1982.

Riquelme, John Paul. *Teller and Tale in Joyce's Fiction: Oscillating Perspectives.* Baltimore: Johns Hopkins UP, 1983.

Sandulescu, Constantin-George. *The Joycean Monologue.* Colchester, Eng.: Wake Newslitter, 1979.

Sandulescu, C. George, and Clive Hart, eds. *Assessing the 1984 "Ulysses."* Totowa, NJ: Barnes, 1986.

Schlossman, Beryl. *Joyce's Catholic Comedy of Language.* Madison: University of Wisconsin P, 1985.

Schneider, Ulrich. *Die Funktion der Zitate im "Ulysses" von James Joyce.* Bonn: Bouvier, 1970.

Scholes, Robert. *In Search of James Joyce.* Urbana: U of Illinois P, 1992.

Schutte, William M. *Joyce and Shakespeare: A Study in the Meaning of "Ulysses."* New Haven: Yale UP, 1957.

Schwarz, Daniel R. *Reading Joyce's "Ulysses."* London: Macmillan, 1987.

Scott, Bonnie Kime. *Joyce and Feminism.* Bloomington: Indiana UP, 1984.

Segall, Jeffrey. *Joyce in America: Cultural Politics and the Trials of "Ulysses."* Berkeley: University of California P, 1993.

Seidel, Michael. *Epic Geography: James Joyce's "Ulysses."* Princeton: Princeton UP, 1976.

Senn, Fritz. *Joyce's Dislocutions: Essays on Reading as Translation.* Ed. John Paul Riquelme. Baltimore: Johns Hopkins UP, 1984.

———. *Nichts Gegen Joyce: Joyce Versus Nothing.* Zurich: Haffmans Verlag, 1983.

Shechner, Mark. *Joyce in Nighttown: A Psychoanalytic Inquiry into "Ulysses."* Berkeley: U of California P, 1974.

Sherry, Vincent. *James Joyce "Ulysses."* New York: Cambridge UP, 1994.

Staley, Thomas F. *An Annotated Critical Bibliography of James Joyce.* New York: St. Martin's, 1989.

———, ed. *"Ulysses": Fifty Years.* Bloomington: Indiana UP, 1974.

Staley, Thomas F., and Bernard Benstock, eds. *Approaches to "Ulysses": Ten Essays.* Pittsburgh: U of Pittsburgh P, 1970.

Steinberg, Erwin. *The Stream of Consciousness and Beyond in "Ulysses."* Pittsburgh: U of Pittsburgh P, 1973.

Sultan, Stanley. *The Argument of "Ulysses."* Middletown, CT: Wesleyan UP, 1987.

Theoharis, Theoharis Constantine. *Joyce's "Ulysses": An Anatomy of the Soul.* Chapel Hill: U of North Carolina P, 1988.

Thomas, Brook. *James Joyce's "Ulysses": A Book of Many Happy Returns.* Baton Rouge: Louisiana State UP, 1982.

Thornton, Weldon. *Allusions in "Ulysses": An Annotated List.* Chapel Hill: U of North Carolina P, 1968.

Tindall, William York. *A Reader's Guide to James Joyce*. New York: Farrar, 1959.

Tucker, Lindsey. *Stephen and Bloom at Life's Feast: Alimentary Symbolism and the Creative Process in James Joyce's "Ulysses."* Columbus: Ohio State UP, 1984.

Tymoczko, Maria. *The Irish "Ulysses."* Berkeley: U of California P, 1994.

Tysdahl, Bjorn J. *Joyce and Ibsen: A Study in Literary Influence*. New York: Humanitas, 1968.

Van Caspel, Paul. *Bloomers on the Liffey: Eisegetical Readings of Joyce's "Ulysses."* Baltimore: Johns Hopkins UP, 1986.

West, Alick. "James Joyce: *Ulysses.*" *Crisis and Criticism, and Selected Literary Essays*. London: Lawrence, 1975.

Wilson, Edmund. *Axel's Castle*. 1931. New York: Scribner's, 1969.

Woolf, Virginia. *A Writer's Diary*. Ed. Leonard Woolf. New York: Harcourt, 1982.

Deconstruction
and
Ulysses

WHAT IS DECONSTRUCTION?

Deconstruction has a reputation for being the most complex and forbidding of contemporary critical approaches to literature, but in fact almost all of us have, at one time, either deconstructed a text or badly wanted to deconstruct one. Sometimes when we hear a lecturer effectively marshal evidence to show that a book means primarily one thing, we long to interrupt and ask what he or she would make of other, conveniently overlooked passages that seem to contradict the lecturer's thesis. Sometimes, after reading a provocative critical article that *almost* convinces us that a familiar work means the opposite of what we assumed it meant, we may wish to make an equally convincing case for our former reading of the text. We may not think that the poem or novel in question better supports our interpretation, but we may recognize that the text can be used to support *both* readings. And sometimes we simply want to make that point: texts can be used to support seemingly irreconcilable positions.

To reach this conclusion is to feel the deconstructive itch. J. Hillis Miller, the preeminent American deconstructor, puts it this way: "Deconstruction is not a dismantling of the structure of a text, but a demonstration that it has already dismantled itself. Its apparently solid ground is no rock but thin air" ("Stevens' Rock" 341). To deconstruct a text isn't to show that all the high old themes aren't there to be found in it. Rather, it is to show that a text—not unlike DNA with its double helix—can have intertwined, opposite "discourses"—strands of narrative, threads of meaning.

Ultimately, of course, deconstruction refers to a larger and more complex enterprise than the practice of demonstrating that a text can have contradictory meanings. The term refers to a way of reading texts practiced by critics who have been influenced by the writings of the French philosopher Jacques Derrida. It is important to gain some understanding of Derrida's project and of the historical backgrounds of his work before reading the deconstruction that follows, let alone attempting to deconstruct a text.

Derrida, a philosopher of language who coined the term *deconstruction*, argues that we tend to think and express our thoughts in terms of opposites. Something is black but not white, masculine and therefore not feminine, a cause rather than an effect, and so forth. These mutually exclusive pairs or dichotomies are too numerous to list but would include beginning/end, conscious/unconscious, presence/absence, and speech/writing. If we think hard about these dichotomies, Derrida suggests, we will realize that they are not simply oppositions; they are also hierarchies in miniature. In other words, they contain one term that our culture views as being superior and one term viewed as negative or inferior. Sometimes the superior term seems only subtly superior (*speech, cause*), but at other times we know immediately which term is culturally preferable (*presence, beginning*, and *consciousness* are easy choices). But the hierarchy always exists.

Of particular interest to Derrida, perhaps because it involves the language in which all the other dichotomies are expressed, is the hierarchical opposition "speech/writing." Derrida argues that the "privileging" of speech, that is, the tendency to regard speech in positive terms and writing in negative terms, cannot be disentangled from the privileging of presence. (Postcards are written by absent friends; we read Plato because he cannot speak from beyond the grave.) Furthermore, according to Derrida, the tendency to privilege both speech and presence is part of the Western tradition of *logocentrism*, the belief that in some ideal beginning were creative *spoken* words, such as "Let there be light," spoken by an ideal, *present* God.[1] According to logocentric

---

[1]Derrida sometimes uses the word *phallogocentrism* to indicate that there is "a certain indissociability" between logocentrism and the "phallocentrism" (Derrida, *Acts* 57) of a culture whose God created light, the world, and man before creating woman—

tradition, these words can now be represented only in unoriginal speech or writing (such as the written phrase in quotation marks above). Derrida doesn't seek to reverse the hierarchized opposition between speech and writing, or presence and absence, or early and late, for to do so would be to fall into a trap of perpetuating the same forms of thought and expression that he seeks to deconstruct. Rather, his goal is to erase the boundary between oppositions such as speech and writing, and to do so in such a way as to throw the order and values implied by the opposition into question.

Returning to the theories of Ferdinand de Saussure, who invented the modern science of linguistics, Derrida reminds us that the association of speech with present, obvious, and ideal meaning—and writing with absent, merely pictured, and therefore less reliable meaning—is suspect, to say the least. As Saussure demonstrated, words are *not* the things they name and, indeed, they are only arbitrarily associated with those things. A word, like any sign, is what Derrida has called a "deferred presence"; that is to say, "the signified concept is never present in itself," and "every concept is necessarily . . . inscribed in a chain or system, within which it refers to another and to other concepts" ("Différance" 138, 140). Neither spoken nor written words have present, positive, identifiable attributes themselves. They have meaning only by virtue of their difference from other words (*red, read, reed*) and, at the same time, their contextual relationship to those words. Take *read* as an example. To know whether it is the present or past tense of the verb—whether it rhymes with *red* or *reed*—we need to see it in relation to some other words (for example, *yesterday*).

Because the meanings of words lie in the differences between them and in the differences between them and the things they name, Derrida suggests that all language is constituted by *différance,* a word he has coined that puns on two French words meaning "to differ" and "to defer": words are the deferred presences of the things they "mean," and their meaning is grounded in difference. Derrida, by the way, changes the *e* in the French word *différence* to an *a* in his neologism *différance;* the change, which can be seen in writing but cannot be heard in spoken French, is itself a playful, witty challenge to the notion that writing is inferior or "fallen" speech.

In *Dissemination* (1972) and *De la grammatologie* [*Of Grammatology*] (1967), Derrida begins to redefine writing by deconstructing

from Adam's rib. "Phallocentrism" is another name for patriarchy. The role that deconstruction has played in feminist analysis will be discussed later.

some old definitions. In *Dissemination,* he traces logocentrism back to Plato, who in the *Phaedrus* has Socrates condemn writing and who, in all the great dialogues, powerfully postulates that metaphysical longing for origins and ideals that permeates Western thought. "What Derrida does in his reading of Plato," Barbara Johnson points out in her translator's introduction to *Dissemination,* "is to unfold dimensions of Plato's *text* that work against the grain of (Plato's own) Platonism" (xxiv). Remember: that is what deconstruction does, according to Miller; it shows a text dismantling itself.

In *Of Grammatology,* Derrida turns to the *Confessions* of Jean-Jacques Rousseau and exposes a grain running against the grain. Rousseau—who has often been seen as another great Western idealist and believer in innocent, noble origins—on one hand condemned writing as mere representation, a corruption of the more natural, childlike, direct, and therefore undevious speech. On the other hand, Rousseau acknowledged his own tendency to lose self-presence and blurt out exactly the wrong thing in public. He confesses that, by writing at a distance from his audience, he often expressed himself better: "If I were present, one would never know what I was worth," Rousseau admitted (Derrida, *Of Grammatology* 142). Thus, Derrida shows that one strand of Rousseau's discourse made writing seem a secondary, even treacherous supplement, while another made it seem necessary to communication.

Have Derrida's deconstructions of *Confessions* and the *Phaedrus* explained these texts, interpreted them, opened them up and shown us what they mean? Not in any traditional sense. Derrida would say that anyone attempting to find a single, homogeneous or universal meaning in a text is simply imprisoned by the structure of thought that would oppose two readings and declare one to be right and not wrong, correct rather than incorrect. In fact, any work of literature that we interpret defies the laws of Western logic, the laws of opposition and noncontradiction. From deconstruction's point of view, texts don't say "A and not B." They say "A and not-A." "Instead of a simple 'either/or' structure," Johnson explains, "deconstruction attempts to elaborate a discourse that says *neither* 'either/or' *nor* 'both/and' nor even 'neither/nor,' while at the same time not totally abandoning these logics either. The word deconstruction is meant to undermine the either/or logic of the opposition 'construction/ destruction.' Deconstruction is both, it is neither, and it reveals the way in which both construction and destruction are themselves not what they appear to be" (Johnson, *World* 12–13).

Although its ultimate aim may be to criticize Western idealism and logic, deconstruction began as a response to structuralism and to formalism, another structure-oriented theory of reading. Using Saussure's theory as Derrida was to do later, European structuralists attempted to create a *semiology*, or science of signs, that would give humankind at once a scientific and a holistic way of studying the world and its human inhabitants. Roland Barthes, a structuralist who later shifted toward poststructuralism, hoped to recover literary language from the isolation in which it had been studied and to show that the laws that govern it govern all signs, from road signs to articles of clothing. Claude Lévi-Strauss, a structural anthropologist who studied everything from village structure to the structure of myths, found in myths what he called *mythemes*, or building blocks, such as basic plot elements. Recognizing that the same mythemes occur in similar myths from different cultures, he suggested that all myths may be elements of one great myth being written by the collective human mind.

Derrida did not believe that structuralists had the concepts that would someday explain the laws governing human signification and thus provide the key to understanding the form and meaning of everything from an African village to Greek myth to Rousseau's *Confessions*. In his view, the scientific search by structural anthropologists for what unifies humankind amounts to a new version of the old search for the lost ideal, whether that ideal be Plato's bright realm of the Idea or the Paradise of Genesis or Rousseau's unspoiled Nature. As for the structuralist belief that texts have "centers" of meaning, in Derrida's view that derives from the logocentric belief that there is a reading of the text that accords with "the book as seen by God." Jonathan Culler, who thus translates a difficult phrase from Derrida's *L'Écriture et la différence* [*Writing and Difference*] (1967) in his book *Structuralist Poetics* (1975), goes on to explain what Derrida objects to in structuralist literary criticism:

> [When] one speaks of the structure of a literary work, one does so from a certain vantage point: one starts with notions of the meaning or effects of a poem and tries to identify the structures responsible for those effects. Possible configurations or patterns that make no contribution are rejected as irrelevant. That is to say, an intuitive understanding of the poem functions as the "centre" . . . : it is both a starting point and a limiting principle. (244)

Deconstruction calls into question assumptions made about literature by formalist, as well as by structuralist, critics. Formalism, or the

New Criticism as it was once commonly called, assumes a work of literature to be a freestanding, self-contained object, its meanings found in the complex network of relations that constitute its parts (images, sounds, rhythms, allusions, and so on). To be sure, deconstruction is somewhat like formalism in several ways. Both formalism and deconstruction are text-oriented approaches whose practitioners pay a great deal of attention to rhetorical *tropes* (forms of figurative language including allegory, symbol, metaphor, and metonymy). And formalists, long before deconstructors, discovered counterpatterns of meaning in the same text. Formalists find ambiguity: deconstructors find undecidability. On close inspection, however, the formalist understanding of rhetorical tropes or figures is quite different from that of deconstruction, and undecidability turns out to be different from the ambiguity formalists find in texts.

Formalists, who associated literary with figurative language, made qualitative distinctions between types of figures of speech; for instance, they valued symbols and metaphors over metonyms. (A metonym is a term standing for something with which it is commonly associated or contiguous; we use metonymy when we say we had "the cold plate" for lunch.) From the formalist perspective, metaphors and symbols are less arbitrary figures than metonyms and thus rank more highly in the hierarchy of tropes: a metaphor ("I'm feeling blue") supposedly involves a special, intrinsic, nonarbitrary relationship between its two terms (the feeling of melancholy and the color blue); a symbol ("the river of life") allegedly involves a unique fusion of image and idea.

From the perspective of deconstruction, however, these distinctions are suspect. In "The Rhetoric of Temporality," Paul de Man deconstructs the distinction between symbol and allegory; elsewhere, he, Derrida, and Miller have similarly questioned the metaphor/metonymy distinction, arguing that all figuration is a process of linguistic substitution. In the case of a metaphor (or symbol), they claim, we have forgotten what juxtaposition or contiguity gave rise to the association that now seems mysteriously special. Derrida, in "White Mythology," and de Man, in "Metaphor (*Second Discourse*)," have also challenged the priority of literal over figurative language, and Miller has gone so far as to deny the validity of the literal/figurative distinction, arguing that all words are figures because all language involves *catachresis,* "the violent, forced, or abusive importation of a term from another realm to name something which has no proper name" (Miller, *Ariadne* 21).

The difference between the formalist concept of literary ambiguity and the deconstructive concept of undecidability is as significant as the gap between formalist and deconstructive understandings of figurative language. Undecidability, as de Man came to define it, is a complex notion easily misunderstood. There is a tendency to assume that it refers to readers who, when forced to decide between two or more equally plausible and conflicting readings, throw up their hands and decide that the choice can't be made. But undecidability in fact debunks this whole notion of reading as a decision-making process carried out on texts by readers. To say we are forced to choose or decide, or that we are unable to do so, is to locate the problem of undecidability falsely within ourselves, rather than recognizing that it is an intrinsic feature of the text.

Undecidability is thus different from ambiguity, as understood by formalists. Formalists believed that a complete understanding of a literary work is possible, an understanding in which ambiguities will be resolved objectively by the reader, even if only in the sense that they will be shown to have definite, meaningful functions. Deconstructors do not share that belief. They do not accept the formalist view that a work of literary art is demonstrably unified from beginning to end, in one certain way, or that it is organized around a single center that ultimately can be identified and defined. Neither do they accept the concept of irony as simply saying one thing and meaning another thing that will be understood with certainty by the reader. As a result, deconstructors tend to see texts as more radically heterogeneous than do formalists. The formalist critic ultimately makes sense of ambiguity; undecidability, by contrast, is never reduced, let alone mastered by deconstructive reading, although the incompatible possibilities between which it is impossible to decide can be identified with certainty.

For critics practicing deconstruction, a literary text is neither a sphere with a center nor an unbroken line with a definite beginning and end. In fact, many assumptions about the nature of texts have been put in question by deconstruction, which in Derrida's words "dislocates the borders, the framing of texts, everything which should preserve their immanence and make possible an internal reading or merely reading in the classical sense of the term" ("Some Statements" 86). A text consists of words inscribed in and inextricable from the myriad discourses that inform it; from the point of view of deconstruction, the boundaries between any given text and that larger text we call language are always shifting.

It was that larger text that Derrida was referring to when he made his famous statement "*there is nothing outside the text*" (*Grammatology* 158). To understand what Derrida meant by that statement, consider the following: we know the world through language, and the acts and practices that constitute that "real world" (the Oklahoma City bombing, the decision to marry) are inseparable from the discourses out of which they arise and as open to interpretation as any work of literature. Derrida is not alone in deconstructing the world/text opposition. De Man viewed language as something that has great power in individual, social, and political life. Geoffrey Hartman, who was closely associated with deconstruction during the 1970s, wrote that "nothing can lift us out of language" (xii).

Once we understand deconstruction's view of the literary text—as words that are part of and that resonate with an immense linguistic structure in which we live and move and have our being—we are in a better position to understand why deconstructors reach points in their readings at which they reveal, but cannot decide between, incompatible interpretive possibilities. A text is not a unique, hermetically sealed space. Perpetually open to being seen in the light of new contexts, any given text has the potential to be different each time it is read. Furthermore, as Miller has shown in *Ariadne's Thread: Story Lines* (1992), the various "terms" and "famil[ies] of terms" we use in performing our readings invariably affect the results. Whether we choose to focus on a novel's characters or its realism, for instance, leads us to different views of the same text. "No one thread," Miller asserts, "can be followed to a central point where it provides a means of overseeing, controlling, and understanding the whole" (21).

Complicating matters still further is the fact that the individual words making up narratives—the words out of which we make our mental picture of a character or place—usually have several (and often have conflicting) meanings due to the complex histories of their usage. (If your professor tells the class that you have written a "fulsome report" and you look up the word *fulsome* in a contemporary dictionary, you will learn that it can mean either "elaborate" or "offensive"; if, for some reason, you don't know what *offensive* means, you will find out that it can equally well describe your favorite quarterback and a racist joke.) "Each word," as Miller puts it, "inheres in a labyrinth of branching interverbal relationships"; often there are "forks in the etymological line leading to bifurcated or trifurcated roots." Deconstructors often turn to etymology, not to help them decide whether a statement means this or that, but rather as a way of revealing the coincidence of several meanings in the same text. "The effect of etymological retracing," Miller writes, "is not to ground the work solidly but to render it unstable, equivocal, wavering, groundless" (*Ariadne* 19).

Deconstruction is not really interpretation, the act of choosing between or among possible meanings. Derrida has glossed de Man's statement that "there is no need to deconstruct Rousseau" by saying that "this was another way of saying: there is always already deconstruction, at work *in* works, especially *literary* works. It cannot be applied, after the fact and from outside, as a technical instrument. Texts deconstruct *themselves* by themselves" (Derrida, *Memoires* 123). If deconstruction is not interpretation, then what is it? Deconstruction may be defined as reading, as long as reading is defined as de Man defined it—as a process involving moments of what he called *aporia* or terminal uncertainty, and as an act performed with full knowledge of the fact that all texts are ultimately unreadable (if reading means reducing a text to a single, homogeneous meaning). Miller explains unreadability by saying that although there are moments of great lucidity in reading, each "lucidity will in principle contain its own blind spot requiring a further elucidation and exposure of error, and so on, ad infinitum. . . . One should not underestimate, however, the productive illumination produced as one moves through these various stages of reading" (*Ethics* 42, 44).

Miller's point is important because, in a sense, it deconstructs or erases the boundary between the readings of deconstructors and the interpretations of more traditional critics. It suggests that all kinds of critics have had their moments of lucidity; it also suggests that critics practicing deconstruction know that their *own* insights—even their insights into what is or isn't contradictory, undecidable, or unreadable in a text—are hardly the last word. As Art Berman writes, "In *Blindness and Insight* de Man demonstrates that the apparently well-reasoned arguments of literary critics contain contradiction at their core; yet there is no alternative path to insight. . . . The readers of criticism recognize the blindness of their predecessors, reorganize it, and thereby gain both the insight of the critics and a knowledge of the contradiction that brings forth insight. Each reader, of course, has his own blindness; and the criticism of criticism is not a matter of rectifying someone else's mistakes" (Berman 239–40).

When de Man spoke of the resistance to theory he referred generally to the antitheoretical bias in literary studies. But he might as well have been speaking specifically of the resistance to deconstruction, as expressed not only in academic books and journals but also in popular magazines such as *Newsweek*. Attacks on deconstruction became more common and more personal some four years after de Man's death in

1983. That was the year that a Belgian scholar working on a doctoral thesis discovered ninety-two articles that de Man had written during World War II for the Brussels newspaper *Le Soir*, a widely read French-language daily that had fallen under Nazi control during the German occupation of Belgium. Ultimately, one hundred and seventy articles by de Man were found in *Le Soir;* another ten were discovered in *Het Vlaamsche Land*, a collaborationist newspaper published in Flemish. These writings, which date from 1941 (when de Man was twenty-one years old), ceased to appear before 1943, by which time it had become clear to most Belgians that Jews were being shipped to death camps such as Auschwitz. De Man's wartime journalism consists mainly, but not entirely, of inoffensive literary pieces. In one article de Man takes Germany's triumph in World War II as a given, places the German people at the center of Western civilization, and foresees a mystical era involving suffering but also faith, exaltation, and rapture. In another article, entitled *"Les Juifs dans la littérature actuelle"* ["Jews in Present-day Literature"], de Man scoffs at the notion that Jewish writers have significantly influenced the literature of his day and, worse, considers the merits of creating a separate Jewish colony that would be isolated from Europe.

No one who had known de Man since his immigration to the United States in 1948 had found him to be illiberal or anti-Semitic. Furthermore, de Man had spent his career in the United States demystifying or, as he would have said, "debunking" the kind of ideological assumptions (about the relationship between aesthetics and national cultures) that lie behind his most offensive Belgian newspaper writings. The critic who in *The Resistance to Theory* (1986) argued that literature must not become "a substitute for theology, ethics, etc." (de Man 24) had either changed radically since writing of the magical integrity and wholeness of the German nation and its culture or had not deeply believed what he had written as a young journalist.

These points have been made in various ways by de Man's former friends and colleagues. Geoffrey Hartman has said that de Man's later work, the work we associate with deconstruction, "looks like a belated, but still powerful, act of conscience" (26–31). Derrida, who like Hartman is a Jew, has read carefully de Man's wartime discourse, showing it to be "split, disjointed, engaged in incessant conflicts" (Hamacher, Hertz, and Keenan 135). "On the one hand," Derrida finds "*unpardonable*" de Man's suggestion that a separate Jewish colony be set up; "on the other hand," he notes that of the four writers de Man praises in the same article (André Gide, Franz Kafka, D. H. Lawrence, and Ernest Hemingway), not one was German, one (Kafka) *was* Jewish, and all four "represent everything that Nazism . . . would have liked to extirpate from history and the great tradition" (Hamacher, Hertz, and Keenan 145).

While friends asserted that some of de Man's statements were unpardonable, deconstruction's severest critics tried to use a young man's sometimes deplorable statements as evidence that a whole critical movement was somehow morally as well as intellectually flawed. As Andrej Warminski summed it up, "the 'discovery' of the 1941–42 writings is being used to perpetuate the old myths about so-called 'deconstruction'" (Hamacher, Hertz, and Keenan 389). Knowing what some of those myths are—and why, in fact, they *are* myths—aids our understanding in an indirect, contrapuntal way that is in keeping with the spirit of deconstruction.

In his book *The Ethics of Reading* (1987), Miller refutes two notions commonly repeated by deconstruction's detractors. One is the idea that deconstructors believe a text means nothing in the sense that it means whatever the playful reader *wants* it to mean. The other is the idea that deconstruction is "immoral" insofar as it refuses to view literature in the way it has traditionally been viewed, namely, "as the foundation and embodiment, the means of preserving and transmitting, the basic humanistic values of our culture" (9). Responding to the first notion, Miller points out that neither Derrida nor de Man "has ever asserted the freedom of the reader to make the text mean anything he or she wants it to mean. Each has in fact asserted the reverse" (10). As for the second notion—that deconstructors are guilty of shirking an ethical responsibility because their purpose is not to (re)discover and (re)assert the transcendent and timeless values contained in great books—Miller argues that "this line of thought" rests "on a basic misunderstanding of the way the ethical moment enters into the act of reading" (9). That "ethical moment," Miller goes on to argue, "is not a matter of response to a thematic content asserting this or that idea about morality. It is a much more fundamental 'I must' responding to the language of literature in itself. . . . Deconstruction is nothing more or less than good reading as such" (9–10). Reading itself, in other words, is an act that leads to further ethical acts, decisions, and behaviors in a real world involving relations to other people and to society at large. For these, the reader must take responsibility, as for any other ethical act.

A third commonly voiced objection to deconstruction is to its playfulness, to the evident pleasure its practitioners take in teasing out

all the contradictory interpretive possibilities generated by the words
in a text, their complex etymologies and contexts, and their potential
to be read figuratively or even ironically. Certainly, playfulness and
pleasure are aspects of deconstruction. In his book *The Post Card*
(1987), Derrida specifically associates deconstruction with pleasure; in
an interview published in a collection of his essays entitled *Acts of Literature* (1992), he speculates that "it is perhaps this *jouissance* which
most irritates the all-out adversaries of deconstruction" (56). But such
adversaries misread deconstruction's "jouissance," its pleasurable playfulness. Whereas they see it as evidence that deconstructors view texts
as tightly enclosed fields on which they can play delightfully useless
little word games, Derrida has said that the "subtle and intense pleasure" of deconstruction arises from the "dismantl[ing]" of repressive
assumptions, representations, and ideas—in short, from the "lifting of
repression" (*Acts* 56–57). As Gregory S. Jay explains in his book
*America the Scrivener: Deconstruction and the Subject of Literary His-
tory* (1990), "Deconstruction has been not only a matter of reversing
binary oppositions but also a matter of disabling the hierarchy of values they enable and of speculating on alternative modes of knowing
and of acting" (xii).

Far from viewing literature as a word-playground, Derrida, in
Derek Attridge's words, "emphasizes . . . literature as an institution,"
one "not given in nature or the brain but brought into being by
processes that are social, legal, and political, and that can be mapped
historically and geographically" (*Acts* 23). By thus characterizing Derrida's emphasis, Attridge counters the commonest of the charges that
have been leveled at deconstructors, namely, that they divorce literary
texts from historical, political, and legal institutions.

In *Memoires for Paul de Man* (1986), Derrida argues that, where
history is concerned, "deconstructive discourses" have pointedly and
effectively questioned "the classical assurances of history, the genealogical narrative, and periodizations of all sorts" (15)—in other
words, the tendency of historians to view the past as the source of
(lost) truth and value, to look for explanations in origins, and to view
as unified epochs (for example, the Victorian period, 1837–1901)
what are in fact complex and heterogeneous times in history. As for
politics, Derrida points out that de Man invariably "says something
about institutional structures and the political stakes of hermeneutic
conflicts," which is to say that de Man's commentaries acknowledge
that conflicting interpretations reflect and are reflected in the politics
of institutions (such as the North American university).

In addition to history and politics, the law has been a subject on which deconstruction has had much to say of late. In an essay on Franz Kafka's story "Before the Law," Derrida has shown that for Kafka the law as such exists but can never be confronted by those who would do so and fulfill its commands. Miller has pointed out that the law "may only be confronted in its delegates or representatives or by its effects on us or others" (*Ethics* 20). What or where, then, is the law itself? The law's presence, Miller suggests, is continually deferred by narrative, that is, writing about or on the law which constantly reinterprets the law in the attempt to reveal what it really is and means. This very act of (re)interpretation, however, serves to "defer" or distance the law even further from the case at hand, since the (re)interpretation takes precedence (and assumes prominence) over the law itself. (As Miller defines it, narrative would include everything from a Victorian novel that promises to reveal moral law to the opinion of a Supreme Court justice regarding the constitutionality of a given action, however different these two documents are in the conventions they follow and the uses to which they are put.) Miller likens the law to a promise, "the validity of [which] does not lie in itself but in its future fulfillment," and to a story "divided against itself" that in the end "leaves its readers . . . still in expectation" (*Ethics* 33).

Because the facts about deconstruction are very different from the myth of its playful irreverence and irrelevance, a number of contemporary thinkers have found it useful to adapt and apply deconstruction in their work. For instance, a deconstructive theology has been developed. Architects have designed and built buildings grounded, as it were, in deconstructive architectural theory. In the area of law, the Critical Legal Studies movement has, in Christopher Norris's words, effectively used "deconstructive thinking" of the kind de Man used in analyzing Rousseau's *Social Contract* "to point up the blind spots, conflicts, and antinomies that plague the discourse of received legal wisdom." Critical legal theorists have debunked "the formalist view of law," that is, the "view which holds law to be a system of neutral precepts and principles," showing instead how the law "gives rise to various disabling contradictions," such as "the problematic distinction between 'private' and 'public' domains." They have turned deconstruction into "a sophisticated means of making the point that all legal discourse is performative in character, i.e., designed to secure assent through its rhetorical power to convince or persuade" (Norris, *Deconstruction and the Interests* 17). Courtroom persuasion, Gerald

Lopez has argued in a 1989 article in the *Michigan Law Review*, consists of storytelling as much as argument (Clayton 13).

In the field of literary studies, the influence of deconstruction may be seen in the work of critics ostensibly taking some other, more political approach. Barbara Johnson has put deconstruction to work for the feminist cause. She and Shoshana Felman have argued that chief among those binary oppositions "based on repression of differences with entities" is the opposition man/woman (Johnson, *Critical* x). In a reading of the "undecidability" of "femininity" in Balzac's story "The Girl with the Golden Eyes," Felman puts it this way: "the rhetorical hierarchization of the . . . opposition between the sexes is . . . such that woman's *difference* is suppressed, being totally subsumed by the reference of the feminine to masculine identity" ("Rereading" 25).

Elsewhere, Johnson, Felman, and Gayatri Spivak have combined Derrida's theories with the psychoanalytic theory of Jacques Lacan to analyze the way in which gender and sexuality are ultimately textual, grounded in language and rhetoric. In an essay on Edmund Wilson's reading of Henry James's story *The Turn of the Screw*, Felman has treated sexuality as a form of rhetoric that can be deconstructed, shown to contain contradictions and ambiguities that more traditional readings of sexuality have masked. Gay and lesbian critics have seen the positive implications of this kind of analysis, hence Eve Kosofsky Sedgwick's admission in the early pages of her book *Epistemology of the Closet* (1990): "One main strand of argument in this book is deconstructive, in a fairly specific sense. The analytic move it makes is to demonstrate that categories presented in a culture as symmetrical binary oppositions . . . actually subsist in a more unsettled and dynamic tacit relation" (9–10).

In telling "The Story of Deconstruction" in his book on contemporary American literature and theory, Jay Clayton assesses the current status of this unique approach. Although he notes how frequently deconstructive critics have been cited for their lack of political engagement, he concludes that deconstruction, "a movement accused of formalism and arid intellectualism, participates in the political turn of contemporary culture" (34). He suggests that what began as theory in the late 1960s and 1970s has, over time, developed into a method employed by critics taking a wide range of approaches to literature—ethnic, feminist, new historicist, Marxist—in addition to critics outside of literary studies per se who are involved in such areas as Critical Legal Studies and Critical Race Theory, which seeks to "sustain a complementary relationship between the deconstructive energies of

Critical Legal Studies and the constructive energies of civil rights activism" (58).

Clayton cites the work of Edward Said as a case in point. Through 1975, the year that his *Beginnings: Intention and Method* was published, Said was employing a form of deconstructive criticism that, in Clayton's words, emphasized the "power" of texts "to initiate projects in the real world" (45–46). Said became identified with cultural and postcolonial criticism, however, beginning in 1978 with the publication of his book *Orientalism*, in which he deconstructs the East/West, Orient/Occident opposition. Said argues that Eastern and Middle Eastern peoples have for centuries been stereotyped by the Western discourses of "orientalism," a textuality that in no way reflects the diversity and differences that exist among the peoples it claims to represent. According to Said, that stereotyping not only facilitated the colonization of vast areas of the globe by the so-called West but also still governs, to a great extent, relations with the Arab and the so-called Eastern world. The expansion of Said's field of vision to include not just literary texts but international relations is powerfully indicative of the expanding role that deconstruction currently plays in developing contemporary understandings of politics and culture, as well as in active attempts to intervene in these fields.

Jacques Derrida, the theorist most closely associated with deconstruction, begins the essay that follows, entitled "Ulysses Gramophone" with *"Oui,"* a French word that might seem to "quote" or "translate" the last word of Joyce's *Ulysses*. But *"oui,"* Derrida suggests in this article written in French and translated by Tina Kendall, may itself be untranslatable. Indeed, Derrida goes on to suggest that *all* words, indeed all languages, defy translation: "according to a distinction I have hazarded elsewhere concerning history and the name of Babel," Derrida writes, "what remains *untranslatable* is at bottom the only thing *to translate*, the only thing *translatable*. What must be translated (*l'à-traduire*) of that which is translatable (*traductible*) can only be the untranslatable (*intraduisible*)."

Having undercut the possibility of writing in French about a novel written in English, and having done so via a characteristically paradoxical statement that seems to equate opposite terms, Derrida subsequently suggests that the slippery associations involved in translation also pertain to "all the genealogical chances that set afloat the notion of legitimate consanguinity in *Ulysses* and no doubt elsewhere." By this he presumably means that when we identify ourselves via our biological lineage or "family tree," or through names determinable due to patriarchal naming practices that conceal more associations than they reveal, we define ourselves via connections at least as questionable and open to contradiction as those between words and their supposed, closest relatives in another language. In *Ulysses*, the encounter between Leopold Bloom and Stephen Dedalus raises questions about whether it is biology and a shared name that makes a relationship paternal or filial, or whether it can be some other connection—involving sympathy, understanding, or shared qualities, for instance.

Derrida then proceeds, via a long digression on lakes, dice, Tokio (in the news in *Ulysses* because of the Russo-Japanese war), and Tokyo (where Derrida says he began writing his essay and shopped for postcards) by applying arguments he made in his book *La Carte Postale* (*The Post Card*) to Joyce's views on published texts. Joyce, Derrida recalls, "speaks of the equivalence of a postcard and a publication," suggesting that both constitute an "open text," an "exhibited surface, . . . an open letter." *Ulysses*, Derrida points out, contains a "trace," or "relay," of this view of the postcard as an "open text"; we can, for instance, follow a "narrative path" that leads from Mr. Reggy Wylie's postcard to Gerty MacDowell to Leopold Bloom's unaddressed postcard to Flynn to the letter Bloom is looking for when he remembers the unaddressed postcard.

For Derrida, that path also leads to the idea of a postcard addressed to a fictitious recipient and bearing no message (*correspondence*), an idea suggested in *Ulysses* by the passage in which a sailor shows Bloom a postcard bearing "a group of savage women in striped loincloths" on one side and only an address on the other. Derrida views *Ulysses* itself as an unaddressed postcard, an open text. Any reader—for it has no addressee—can follow any of an infinite number of paths, or "correspondences," through the novel, much as Homer's Odysseus moved from adventure to adventure. The reader of *Ulysses*, like Odysseus, is an "autobiographic-encyclopedic navigator," which is to say that his or her understanding stems from patterns of association grounded in personal autobiographical (including literary) experience.

Every reader of Joyce's novel is, in a sense, like Derrida, who began his essay on *Ulysses* while in Tokyo looking for postcards, who therefore could hardly help noticing the word Tokio in Joyce's novel, and who subsequently began tracking the correspondences suggested by this noncorrespondence. Every reader of *Ulysses* is also like the reader of Derrida's essay, which is itself "a postcard cast to sea" with no particular addressee or address; that is, the individual members of this essay's audience will follow different traces or tracks through its intentionally meandering argument, full of cross-references and occasions for interpretive "translation," "transfers," and "crossovers" (to use a few of Derrida's recurring terms).

Although it runs against the grain of deconstruction to call any reading "typical of deconstruction" or "typically Derridean," several features of Derrida's essay on Joyce can be traced back to his earlier work. He repeats (albeit with the inevitable *différance*) critical moves made in earlier readings when he indulges in creative wordplay, utilizes false etymologies that nonetheless lead down intellectually stimulating paths, and embeds Joyce's fiction in an autobiographical narrative. By contextualizing *Ulysses* in a story of his own travels from Ithaca (New York) to Oxford (Ohio) to Tokyo, Derrida gives his reading of the novel the metafictional status of a story about—in the double sense of "based on" and "around"—Joyce's story.

In this essay, originally given as an address in French to an audience of Joyce scholars gathered in Frankfurt, Germany, Derrida makes other moves consistent with the strategies of deconstruction. By showing the labyrinthine quality of writing—not just in Joyce's *Ulysses* but in the general text of literature and language in which it participates—he "undermines" the concept of linguistic (and scholarly) "competence" on which learned societies rest. (In Derrida's view, linguistic competence is illusory due to the collapsible nature of the signifier/signified distinction and the fact that each person has his or her own personal, idiosyncratic, associational flows that make any utterance or text untranslatable.) Via a complex discussion of telephones, of the "telephonic 'yes'" or *oui* with which we typically reassure interlocutors that what they have thought and said has been reproduced and "heard" (that is, listened to and understood) at our end of the line, and of what he calls "telephonic spacing" in the text of *Ulysses*, Derrida shows how a scene in the novel involving a professor, a telephone, and Bloom's voice "crosses all the lines in our network, the paradoxes of competence and institution, represented here in the shape of the professor." Subsequently returning to the suspect subjects of genealogy and familial legitimacy raised earlier, Derrida playfully admits to having felt intimidated by the invitation to speak about *Ulysses* in front of Joyce experts—with what, he suggests, will surely be deemed "incompetence"—but also flattered by the opportunity "to be part of this mighty family," to achieve the "legitimation so generously offered."

At several points in "Ulysses Gramophone," Derrida deconstructs the speech/writing opposition and the privilege granted speech over writing in Western metaphysics. He does so in a discussion of his essay's rejected title, which involved a play on *oui* ("yes") and *ouï* ("hear" in the composite word meaning "hearsay"). (The distinction between *oui* and *ouï* is easier to see than to hear, a fact that contradicts the valuative speech-over-writing hierarchy.) Later, Derrida interrogates the privilege granted speech over writing when he says that "The final 'Yes,' the last word, the eschatology of the book, gives itself up only to *reading*, since it distinguishes itself from the others by an inaudible capital letter; what also remains equally inaudible, although visible, is the lateral incorporation of *yes* in *eyes*. Languages of eyes, of ayes." Through the subsequent analysis of a scene involving a typewriter, telephone, and the repeated word "Yes," Derrida refers to a "gramophony" inscribed in *Ulysses*, a speech/writing that "responds, of course, to the dream of a reproduction which *preserves* as its truth the living *yes*, archived into the very quick of the voice" but that "gives way to the possibility of parody, of a *yes* technique that persecutes the most spontaneous, the most giving desire of the *yes*."

Ross C Murfin

DECONSTRUCTION:
A SELECTED BIBLIOGRAPHY

Writings on Deconstruction

Arac, Jonathan, Wlad Godzich, and Wallace Martin, eds. *The Yale Critics: Deconstruction in America*. Minneapolis: U of Minnesota P, 1983. See especially the essays by Bové, Godzich, Pease, and Corngold.

Berman, Art. *From the New Criticism to Deconstruction: The Reception of Structuralism and Post-Structuralism*. Urbana: U of Illinois P, 1988.

Butler, Christopher. *Interpretation, Deconstruction, and Ideology: An Introduction to Some Current Issues in Literary Theory*. Oxford: Oxford UP, 1984.

Clayton, Jay. *The Pleasure of Babel: Contemporary American Literature and Theory*. New York: Oxford UP, 1993.

Culler, Jonathan. *On Deconstruction: Theory and Criticism After Structuralism*. Ithaca: Cornell UP, 1982.

———. *Structuralist Poetics: Structuralism, Linguistics, and the Study of Literature*. Ithaca: Cornell UP, 1975. See especially ch. 10.

Esch, Deborah. "Deconstruction." *Redrawing the Boundaries: The Transformation of English and American Literary Studies.* Ed. Stephen Greenblatt and Giles Gunn. New York: MLA, 1992. 374–91.

Feminist Studies 14 (1988). Special issue on deconstruction and feminism.

Hamacher, Werner, Neil Hertz, and Thomas Keenan. *Responses: On Paul de Man's Wartime Journalism.* Lincoln: U of Nebraska P, 1989.

Hartman, Geoffrey. "Blindness and Insight." *The New Republic,* 7 Mar. 1988.

Jay, Gregory S. *America the Scrivener: Deconstruction and the Subject of Literary History.* Ithaca: Cornell UP, 1990.

Leitch, Vincent B. *American Literary Criticism from the Thirties to the Eighties.* New York: Columbia UP, 1988. See especially ch. 10, "Deconstructive Criticism."

———. *Cultural Criticism, Literary Theory, Poststructuralism.* New York: Columbia UP, 1992.

Loesberg, Jonathan. *Aestheticism and Deconstruction: Pater, Derrida, and de Man.* Princeton: Princeton UP, 1991.

Melville, Stephen W. *Philosophy Beside Itself: On Deconstruction and Modernism.* Theory and History of Lit. 27. Minneapolis: U of Minnesota P, 1986.

Norris, Christopher. *Deconstruction and the Interests of Theory.* Oklahoma Project for Discourse and Theory 4. Norman: U of Oklahoma P, 1989.

———. *Deconstruction: Theory and Practice.* London: Methuen, 1982. Rev. ed. London: Routledge, 1991.

———. *Paul de Man, Deconstruction and the Critique of Aesthetic Ideology.* New York: Routledge, 1988.

Weber, Samuel. *Institution and Interpretation.* Minneapolis: U of Minnesota P, 1987.

Works by de Man, Derrida, and Miller

de Man, Paul. *Allegories of Reading.* New Haven: Yale UP, 1979. See especially ch. 1, "Semiology and Rhetoric," and ch. 7, "Metaphor *(Second Discourse)."*

———. *Blindness and Insight.* New York: Oxford UP, 1971. Minneapolis: U of Minnesota P, 1983. The 1983 edition contains important essays not included in the original edition. See especially "Rhetoric of Temporality."

————. "Phenomenality and Materiality in Kant." *Hermeneutics: Questions and Prospects.* Ed. Gary Shapiro and Alan Sica. Amherst: U of Massachusetts P, 1984. 121–44.

————. *The Resistance to Theory.* Minneapolis: U of Minnesota P, 1986.

————. *Romanticism and Contemporary Culture.* Ed. E. S. Burt, Kevin Newmarkj, and Andrzej Warminski. Baltimore: Johns Hopkins UP, 1993.

————. *Wartime Journalism, 1939–1943.* Lincoln: U of Nebraska P, 1989.

Derrida, Jacques. *Acts of Literature.* Ed. Derek Attridge. New York: Routledge, 1992.

————. "Différance." *Speech and Phenomena.* Trans. David B. Alison. Evanston: Northwestern UP, 1973.

————. *Dissemination.* 1972. Trans. Barbara Johnson. Chicago: U of Chicago P, 1981. See especially the concise, incisive "Translator's Introduction," which provides a useful point of entry into this work and others by Derrida.

————. "Force of Law: The 'Mystical Foundation of Authority.'" Trans. Mary Quaintance. *Deconstruction and the Possibility of Justice.* Ed. Drucilla Cornell, Michel Rosenfeld, and David Gray Carlson. New York: Routledge, 1992. 3–67.

————. *Given Time. 1, Counterfeit Money.* Trans. Peggy Kamuf. Chicago: U of Chicago P, 1992.

————. *Margins of Philosophy.* Trans. Alan Bass. Chicago: U of Chicago P, 1982. Contains the essay "White Mythology: Metaphor in the Text of Philosophy."

————. *Memoires for Paul de Man.* Wellek Library Lectures. Trans. Cecile Lindsay, Jonathan Culler, and Eduardo Cadava. New York: Columbia UP, 1986.

————. *Of Grammatology.* Trans. Gayatri C. Spivak. Baltimore: Johns Hopkins UP, 1976. Trans. of *De la grammatologie.* 1967.

————. "Passions." *Derrida: A Critical Reader.* Ed. David Wood. Cambridge: Basil Blackwell, 1992.

————. *The Post Card: From Socrates to Freud and Beyond.* Trans. with intro. Alan Bass. Chicago: U of Chicago P, 1987.

————. "Some Statements and Truisms about Neo-logisms, Newisms, Postisms, and Other Small Seisisms." *The States of "Theory."* New York: Columbia UP, 1990. 63–94.

————. *Specters of Marx.* Trans. Peggy Kamuf. New York: Routledge, 1994.

————. *Writing and Difference.* 1967. Trans. Alan Bass. Chicago: U of Chicago P, 1978.

Miller, J. Hillis. *Ariadne's Thread: Story Lines.* New Haven: Yale UP, 1992.

————. *The Ethics of Reading: Kant, de Man, Eliot, Trollope, James, and Benjamin.* New York: Columbia UP, 1987.

————. *Fiction and Repetition: Seven English Novels.* Cambridge: Harvard UP, 1982.

————. *Hawthorne and History: Defacing It.* Cambridge: Basil Blackwell, 1991. Contains a bibliography of Miller's work from 1955 to 1990.

————. *Illustrations.* Cambridge: Harvard UP, 1992.

————. "Stevens' Rock and Criticism as Cure." *Georgia Review* 30 (1976): 3–31, 330–48.

————. *Typographies.* Stanford: Stanford UP, 1994.

————. *Versions of Pygmalion.* Cambridge: Harvard UP, 1990.

Essays on Deconstruction and Poststructuralism

Barthes, Roland. *S/Z.* Trans. Richard Miller. New York: Hill, 1974. In this influential work, Barthes turns from a structuralist to a poststructuralist approach.

Benstock, Shari. *Textualizing the Feminine: On the Limits of Genre.* Norman: U of Oklahoma P, 1991.

Bloom, Harold, et al., eds. *Deconstruction and Criticism.* New York: Seabury, 1979. Includes essays by Bloom, de Man, Derrida, Miller, and Hartman.

Chase, Cynthia. *Decomposing Figures.* Baltimore: Johns Hopkins UP, 1986.

Cohen, Tom. *Anti-Mimesis: From Plato to Hitchcock.* Cambridge: Cambridge UP, 1994.

Elam, Diane. *Feminism and Deconstruction: Ms. en Abyme.* New York: Routledge, 1994.

Felman, Shoshana. "Rereading Femininity." Special Issue on "Feminist Readings: French Texts/American Contexts," *Yale French Studies* 62 (1981): 19–44.

————. "Turning the Screw of Interpretation." *Literature and Psychoanalysis: The Question of Reading: Otherwise.* Special issue, *Yale French Studies* 55–56 (1978): 3–508. Baltimore: Johns Hopkins UP, 1982.

Harari, Josué, ed. *Textual Strategies: Perspectives in Post-Structuralist Criticism.* Ithaca: Cornell UP, 1979.

Johnson, Barbara. *The Critical Difference: Essays in the Contemporary Rhetoric of Reading.* Baltimore: Johns Hopkins UP, 1980.

———. *A World of Difference.* Baltimore: Johns Hopkins UP, 1987.

Krupnick, Mark, ed. *Displacement: Derrida and After.* Bloomington: Indiana UP, 1987.

Meese, Elizabeth, and Alice Parker, eds. *The Difference Within: Feminism and Critical Theory.* Philadelphia: John Benjamins, 1989.

Sedgwick, Eve Kosofsky. *Epistemology of the Closet.* Berkeley: U of California P, 1990.

Ulmer, Gregory L. *Applied Grammatology.* Baltimore: Johns Hopkins UP, 1985.

———. *Teletheory: Grammatology in the Age of Video.* New York: Routledge, 1989.

Poststructuralist Approaches to Joyce

Attridge, Derek. "Criticism's Wake." *James Joyce: The Augmented Ninth.* Ed. Bernard Benstock. Syracuse: Syracuse UP, 1988.

Attridge, Derek, and Daniel Ferrer, eds. *Post-structuralist Joyce: Essays from the French.* Cambridge: Cambridge UP, 1984.

Boheemen-Saaf, Christine van. "Deconstruction after Joyce." *New Alliances in Joyce Studies.* Ed. Bonnie Kime Scott. Newark: U of Delaware P, 1988. 29–36.

Cixous, Hélène. *The Exile of James Joyce.* Trans. Sally A. J. Purcell. New York: David Lewis, 1972.

Eco, Umberto. *The Aesthetics of Chaosmos: The Middle Ages of James Joyce.* Trans. Ellen Esrock. Tulsa: U of Tulsa, 1982.

Kristeva, Julia. *Desire in Language.* Ed. Leon S. Roudiez. Trans. Thomas Gora, Alice Jardine, and Leon S. Roudiez. New York: Columbia UP, 1980.

Lernout, Geert. *The French Joyce.* Ann Arbor: U of Michigan P, 1990.

MacCabe, Colin. *James Joyce and the Revolution of the Word.* London: Macmillan, 1978.

Norris, Margot. *The Decentered Universe of "Finnegans Wake."* Baltimore: Johns Hopkins UP, 1976.

Roughley, Alan. *James Joyce and Critical Theory: An Introduction.* London: Harvester, 1991.

A DECONSTRUCTIVE PERSPECTIVE

JACQUES DERRIDA

Ulysses Gramophone
Hear say yes in Joyce[1]

Oui Oui, you are receiving me, these are French words.[2]
To be sure, and I do not even need to reinforce my message with another phrase, all you need is to have heard the first word, *oui*, to know, that is if you understand enough French, that, thanks to the authorization graciously bestowed on me by the organizers of this James Joyce Symposium, I shall address you, more or less, in the language presumed to be mine (*ma langue supposée*), though the last expression can be almost seen as an anglicism.

But can *oui* be quoted or translated? This is one of the questions I intend (*j'entends*) to pose during this talk. How can the sentences that I have just thrown out at you be translated? The one I began with, just as Molly begins and ends what is too lightly referred to as her monologue, that is, the repetition of a *oui*, is not content just to *mention*, it *uses* in its own way these two *ouis*, the ones that I now quote. In my opening, you could not decide and you are still incapable of deciding if I was saying *oui* or quoting, or shall we say more generally, if I was mentioning the word *oui* twice, as a reminder, and I quote, that these are indeed French words.

In the first case, I affirm, acquiesce, subscribe to, approve, reply, or make a promise; at any rate, I agree to something and I sign: to take up again the old *speech act theory* distinction, which is useful up to a certain point, between *use* and *mention*, the usage of *oui* is always at least implied when signing takes place.

In the second case, I would rather have quoted or mentioned the *oui, oui*. Now if the act of quoting or mentioning also undoubtedly presupposes some signature, some confirmation of the act of mentioning,

---

[1]This text was translated by Tina Kendall, with emendations by Shari Benstock. All *Ulysses* quotations are taken from the 1968 London Penguin edition. Footnotes marked with the initials JD are from the original French text; additional explanatory notes for the English text are by Shari Benstock and are marked with the initials SB. The footnotes have been renumbered by Margot Norris for this excerpted version of the essay.

[2]The French verb *entendre* includes in its range of meanings "to hear" and "to understand," both of which are implied in the translation "receiving." In its reflexive form (*s'entendre*), a form also used in this essay, it means to hear each other, to understand each other, to get along with each other. (SB)

this remains implicit and the implicit *oui* is not to be confused with the quoted or mentioned *oui*.

So you still do not know what I wanted to *say* or *do* when I began with this sentence, "*Oui, oui,* you are receiving me, these are French words." In fact you are not receiving me loud and clear at all.

I repeat the question: how will the sentences that I have just thrown out at you be translated? In so far as they mention or quote *oui*, they repeat the French word, and translation is, in principle, absurd or illegitimate: yes, yes, these are not French words. When at the end of *Discours de la Méthode*, Descartes explains why he had decided to write in the language of his country, the Latin translation of *Discours* simply omits this paragraph. What is the sense of writing a sentence in Latin, the gist of which is: the following reasons illustrate why I am now writing in French? It is true that the Latin translation was the only one violently to erase this affirmation of the French language. For it was not just one translation among many; it alleged, according to the laws of the philosophical society of the time, to bring *Discours de la Méthode* back to what should have been the true original in its true language. But we'll leave that for another lecture.[3] I simply wanted to mark that the affirmation of a language through itself is untranslatable. An act which in one language *remarks* the language itself, and which in this way affirms doubly, once by speaking it and once by saying that it has thus been spoken, opens up the space for a *re-marking*, which, at the same time and in the same double way, defies and calls for translation. According to a distinction I have hazarded elsewhere concerning history and the name of Babel, what remains *untranslatable* is at bottom the only thing *to translate*, the only thing *translatable*. What must be translated (*l'à-traduire*) of that which is translatable (*traductible*) can only be the untranslatable (*intraduisible*).

You have already realized that I have been preparing the ground to speak to you about *oui*, or at the very least, about some of the modalities of *oui*, and I should like to specify straightaway, as a kind of rough outline, that this is in some of the sequences in *Ulysses*.[4]

---

[3]To be published. (JD)

[4]The French verb *s'apprêter* (translated here as "preparing the ground," or, more literally, "preparing myself") is one of some two dozen verb forms used throughout the essay that, in their reflexivity, call attention to self-actions, where grammatically the subject and object of the verb are the same. Thus these verbs echo, underwrite, and call out two of Derrida's major concerns here: (1) the always already implicated affirmative of any statement (which, simultaneously internal and external to her, is articulated in Molly's double "yes"); and (2) the putting into question of the independent status of "subject" and "object," of "sender" and "receiver" in speech act theory. Primary among

To put an end, without further ado, to circulation or to an inter-minable circumnavigation, in order to avoid the aporia with a view to a better beginning, I threw myself in the water, as we say in French, and I decided to open myself, together with you, to a chance encounter.[5] With Joyce, luck is always taken in hand by the law, its sense and its agenda, using overdetermination of figures and ruses.[6] And yet the chance nature (*l'aléa*) of meetings, the randomness of coincidences lends itself to being affirmed, accepted, yes, even approved in all their occurrences. In all their occurrences, that is to say, in all the genealogi-cal chances that set afloat the notion of legitimate consanguinity in

---

these verbs are *se rappeler* ("to remember," "to recall," "to recollect"—more literally, to call again to oneself), *se lire* ("to read," "be read"—or "to read itself"), and *se donner* ("to give oneself up," "to devote oneself to," "to abandon oneself to"). When possible, the translation has been kept close to the implied self-action of the verb (as a reminder that the verb is calling to itself). The essay also explores the reciprocal nature of certain interchanges, sometimes exploiting simultaneously the reflexive and reciprocal elements in a single term. When it has not been possible to retain the reflexivity, the French verb has been placed in parentheses following the translation.

Derrida also uses a group of verbs whose prefixes suggest repetition, doubling, an action folding back on itself, notably: *retrouver* ("to re-find"), *rappeler* ("to re-call"), *répondre* ("to re-spond," "to answer"), *revenir* ("to come back," "to come again"), *reparler* ("to speak again"), *raconter* ("to re-count," "to tell"). Again, it has not always been possible to retain the sense of this repeating and doubling through the translation. And the double sense of certain French words (*fils*, meaning both "son" and "threads") is sometimes lost in the English as are the resonating doubles of the French text, silently attesting to Derrida's argument that what remains "untranslatable" in that which is "translatable" is the only thing to "translate."

Also often lost in the English translation are repetitions of the same word through a variety of contexts, for example: *marquer, la marque; propre; appeler; interpeller; passage; traverser; mémoire; mémoriser, parasiter; correspondance.* (SB)

[5]The "chance encounter" here carries greater risk in French: *l'aléatoire d'une rencontre.* The Latin, *alea*, translates into French as *un coup de dé* (the title of a Mallarmé text about which Derrida has written elsewhere; *un coup de dés* in English is translated by making the singular *dé* plural: a roll of the dice. Derrida plays on *un coup de dé* at every chance in this text (especially with other strokes of luck, taps and telephone calls, *un coup de téléphone*, or more forceful blows, *à coups de coudes*, elbowing one's way through). Often it has not been possible to retain seemingly random occurrences. A certain dependence upon luck, chance, and an uncertain outcome has become a game of "chance" in both languages (musically speaking, the "aleatory" are sound sequences played at random or by chance). *Aléa* translates into English as hazardous or risky, carrying with it the risks of "chance." (SB)

[6]In French, this sentence is: *Avec Joyce, la chance est toujours ressaisie par la loi, le sens et le programme, selon la surdétermination des figures et des ruses.* The verb *ressaisir* means literally "to seize again" (carrying with it the juridical meaning of *saisir*—"a seizure") and to "take control." The English translation, "to take in hand," carries with it both "to seize authoritatively" and to supervise, instruct, control, direct. *Le sens* has multiple meanings (which echo here): "sense" (including in the "figural," which appears as "figures"), "meaning," "signification," "understanding," "direction," and "way." (SB)

Ulysses and no doubt elsewhere. This is all too clear in the encounter between Bloom and Stephen to which I shall return shortly.

To throw oneself in the water, I was saying. I was, to be specific, thinking of the water of a lake. But, knowing Joyce's word, you may have thought that I was referring to the bottle in the sea. But lakes were not so foreign to him, as I shall presently demonstrate.

The throw of the dice (*l'aléa*) to which I said *oui*, deciding in the same way to subject *you* to it too, I give the proper name—Tokyo.

Tokyo: does this city lie on the western circle that leads back to Dublin or to Ithaca?

An aimless wandering, a random trek (*la randonnée d'une "randomness"*) led me one day to the passage (Eumaeus, The Shelter, 1 A.M.) in the course of which Bloom names "the coincidence of meeting, discussion, dance, row, old salt, of the here today and gone tomorrow type, night loafers, the whole galaxy of events, all went to make up a miniature cameo of the world we live in" (*U*, 567). The "galaxy of events" was translated into French by "*gerbe des événements*," which omits the milk and therefore the milky tea that runs through (*irrigue*) *Ulysses*, turning it into a milky way or "galaxy." Allow me one more slight detour, a parenthesis: we were wondering what happens to the *yes* when it is repeated in a *mention* or in a quotation. But what happens when it becomes a trademark, a kind of non-transferable commercial license? And since we are spinning in the milk here, what happens when *yes* becomes, yes, a brand, or a brandname, of yoghurt? I shall come back to Ohio, this place marked in *Ulysses*. Now in Ohio there exists a type of Dannon yoghurt which is simply called *YES*. Underneath the *YES* legible on the lid, we find the slogan: "Bet You Can't Say No to Yes."

"Coincidence of meeting" declares the passage I was in the middle of quoting. A little later the name Tokyo crops up: suddenly, like a telegram or a newspaper heading, *The Telegraph*, which is to be found under Bloom's elbow, "as luck would have it"—as it says at the beginning of the paragraph.

The name Tokyo is associated with a battle. "Great battle Tokio." It is not Troy, but Tokyo, in 1904; the battle with internal Russia. Now, I was in Tokyo just over a month ago, and that is where I began writing this lecture—or rather, I began to dictate the main ideas into a pocket cassette recorder.

I decided to date it like this—and dating is signing—on the morning of 11 May when I was looking for postcards in a sort of news agency in the *basement* of the Okura Hotel. I was looking for postcards that would show Japanese lakes, or let's call them inland seas (*mers intérieures*). It had crossed my mind to follow the edges of lakes in *Ulysses*, to venture out on a grand lakeside tour between the lake of life which is the Mediterranean Sea and the *Lacus Mortis* referred to in the hospital scene, to be exact, and dominated by the symbol of the mother: "they came trooping to the sunken sea, *Lacus Mortis*. . . . Onward to the dead sea they tramp to drink" (*U*, 411). This is, in fact, what I had initially thought of for this lecture on *Ulysses*, to address (*adresser*), as you say in English, the postcard scene, rather the inverse of what I did in *La carte postale*, where I tried to restage the babelization of the postal system in *Finnegans Wake*. You will no doubt know better than I that the whole pack of postcards perhaps hints at the hypothesis that the geography of Ulysses' trips around the Mediterranean lake could have the structure of a postcard or a cartography of postal dispatches. This will gradually be illustrated, but for the moment I should like to take up a remark made by J. J. in which he speaks of the equivalence of a postcard and a publication. Any public piece of writing, any open text, is also offered like the exhibited surface, in no way private, of an open letter, and therefore of a postcard with its address incorporated in the message and hereafter open to doubt, and with its coded and at the same time stereotyped language, trivialized by the very code and number. Conversely, any postcard is a public document, deprived of all privacy and, moreover, in this way laying itself open to the law (*tombe sous le coup de la loi*). This is indeed what J. J. says: "—And moreover, says J. J. [they are not just any initials], a postcard is publication. It was held to be sufficient evidence of malice in the testcase Sadgrove *v*. Hole. In my opinion an action might lie" (*U*, 320). Translated: there would be cause for a certain action to be pursued before the law, to sue, but also that the action itself might lie.

The trace, the relay, of the postcard that we are following can be found in Mr. Reggy Wylie's postcard, "his silly postcard" that Gerty could tear "into a dozen pieces" (*U*, 360). Among others, there is also the "postcard to Flynn" that Bloom remembers, furthermore, having forgotten to address, which underlines the nature of anonymous publicity: a postcard has no proper addressee, apart from the person who acknowledges having received it with some inimitable signature. *Ulysses*, an immense postcard. "Mrs Marion. Did I forget to write the address on that letter like the postcard I sent to Flynn?" (*U*, 367). I refer to these postcards along a discursive path, or more precisely, along a narrative path, which I cannot always trace (*reconstituer*).

There is the ineluctable problem of method to which I shall return in a moment. The postcard without an address does not let itself be forgotten; it recalls itself to Bloom's memory just when he is looking for a misplaced letter: "Where did I put the letter? Yes, all right" (*U*, 365). We can assume that the reassuring "yes" accompanies and confirms the return of memory: the letter has been relocated (*le lieu de la lettre est retrouvé*). A little further, after Reggy's "silly postcard," there is the "silly letter": "Damned glad I didn't do it in the bath this morning over her silly I will punish you letter" (*U*, 366). Let us leave enough time for the bath fragrance to reach us. You could pursue the intensification of derision up to Molly's sarcastic remarks about the man Breen: "now [he's] going about in his slippers to look for £1000 for a postcard up up O Sweetheart May" (*U*, 665).

So I was in the middle of buying postcards in Tokyo, in an underground passage in the Hotel Okura. Now the sequence which, in telegraphic style, mentions the "Great Battle Tokio," after having recalled the "coincidence of meeting," the illegitimate genealogy and erratic seed that links Stephen to Bloom, "the galaxy of events," and so on, is a passage from another postcard. Not this time a postcard without an address but a messageless postcard (*une carte postale sans correspondance*). So one could say a postcard without a text, which could be reduced to the mere association of a picture and an address. Now it so happens that here the address is fictitious too. The addressee of this messageless card is a sort of fictitious reader. Before returning to this question, let us complete the "Tokyo" circle sequence, which I must quote. It follows closely from the extraordinary exchange between Bloom and Stephen on the subject of *belonging*, *l'appartenance*: "You suspect, Stephen retorted with a sort of half laugh, that I may be important because I belong to the *faubourg Saint Patrice* called Ireland for short" (*U*, 565).

"I would go a step farther, Mr Bloom insinuated" (the French translation, which renders "a step farther" as *un peu plus loin*, and which met the approval of J. J., who co-signed it, lacks among other things the association "stepfather," which superimposes at the bottom of all these genealogical fantasies, with their genetic crossovers and chance disseminations, a dream of legitimation through adoption, and the return of the son or, through marriage, with the daughter. But we can never tell who belongs to whom, what to whom, what to what, who to what. There is no subject of belonging, no more than there is an owner (*propriétaire*) of the postcard: it remains without any assigned addressee).

—But I suspect, Stephen interrupted, that Ireland must be important because it belongs to me.

—What belongs? queried Bloom, bending, fancying he was perhaps under some misapprehension. Excuse me. Unfortunately I didn't catch the latter portion. What was it you? . . .

Stephen speeds things up: "We can't change the country. Let us change the subject" (U, 565–66).

But going to Tokyo is not enough to change the country, let alone the language.

A little later, then; the return of the messageless postcard made out to a fictitious addressee. Bloom thinks of the aleatory encounters, the galaxy of events, and he dreams of writing, as I am doing here, of what happens to him, his story, "my experiences," as he puts it, and he wants to keep some kind of chronicle of this, a diary within a diary (*journal*) or a personal newspaper (*journal*), by making free associations without constraint. So here it is, we are drawing close to the postcard in the vicinity of Tokyo: "The coincidence of meeting . . . the whole galaxy of events . . . To improve the shining hour he wondered whether he might meet with anything approaching the same *luck* [my italics] as Mr Philip Beaufoy if taken down in writing. Supposing he were to pen something out of the common groove (as he fully intended doing) at the rate of one guinea per column, *My Experiences*, let us say, *in a Cabman's Shelter*" (U, 567).

My Experiences is both my "phenomenology of the mind" in the Hegelian sense of a "science of the experience of the consciousness" and the great circular return, the autobiographic-encyclopedic circumnavigation of Ulysses: there has often been talk of the Odyssey of the phenomenology of the mind. Here the phenomenology of mind would have the form of a diary of the conscious and the unconscious in the chance form of letters, telegrams, of newspapers called *The Telegraph*, for example, long-distance writing, and also of postcards for which sometimes the only text, taken out of some sailor's pocket, merely exhibits a fantasy in the form of an address.

Bloom has just spoken of "My Experiences":

The pink edition, extra sporting, of the *Telegraph*, tell a graphic lie, lay, as luck would have it, beside his elbow and as he was just puzzling again, far from satisfied, over a country belonging to him and the preceding rebus the vessel came from Bridgwater and the postcard was addressed to A. Boudin, find the captain's age, his *eyes* [my italics of the words *eyes*, to which we shall return] went

aimlessly over the respective captions which came under his special
province, the allembracing give us this day our daily press. First he
got a bit of a start but it turned out to be only something about
somebody named H. du Boyes, agent for typewriters or something like that. Great battle Tokio. Lovemaking in Irish £200
damages. (*U*, 567)

I am not going to analyze here the statigraphy of the "Tokio
battlefield": experts can do that ad infinitum; the limitations of a lecture permit me only to recount to you, like a postcard cast to sea, *my
experiences in Tokyo*, and then to pose the question in passing of *yes*, of
chance, and of Joycean experience as expertise: but what is an expert,
Ph.D. scholar in things Joycean? What of the Joycean institution and
what should I think of the hospitality with which it honors me today
in Frankfurt?

Bloom juxtaposes the allusion to the postcard to something that
already offers a pure associative juxtaposition, the contiguity of
which is apparently insignificant and yet this insignificance is underlined: it is the question of the captain's age, which we should guess
rather than calculate, after the presentation of a series of facts, the
figures of a *rebus*, with no evident connection to the question in
hand. Nevertheless, always understood (*sous-entendu*) in the joke is
the fact that the captain is the captain of a ship. Now the postcard is
in fact the very same one the sailor spoke about, a sea-traveler, a captain who, like Ulysses, returns one day from a long circular voyage
around the Mediterranean lake. A few pages earlier, same place, same
time: "—Why, the sailor answered, upon reflection upon it, I've
circumnavigated a bit since I first joined on. I was in the Red Sea.
I was in China and North America and South America. I seen ice-
bergs plenty, growlers. I was in Stockholm and the Black Sea, the
Dardanelles, under Captain Dalton, the best bloody man that ever
scuttled a ship. I seen Russia . . . I seen maneaters in Peru"
(*U*, 545–46).

He has been everywhere except Japan, I said to myself. And here
he is taking a messageless postcard out of his pocket. As for the address, it is fictitious, as fictitious as *Ulysses*, and it is the only thing that
this Ulysses has in his pocket:

> He fumbled out a picture postcard from his inside pocket,
> which seemed to be in its way a species of repository, and pushed
> it along the table. The printed matter on it stated: *Choza de In-
> dios. Beni, Bolivia.*

All focused their attention on the scene exhibited, at a group of savage women in striped loincloths. . . .
His postcard proved a centre of attraction for Messrs the greenhorns for several minutes, if not more.

• • •

Mr Bloom, without evincing surprise, unostentatiously turned over the card to peruse the partially obliterated address and postmark. It ran as follows: *Tarjeta Postal. Señor A. Boudin, Galeria Becche, Santiago, Chile.* There was no message evidently, as he took particular notice. Though not an implicit believer in the lurid story narrated . . . having detected a discrepancy between his name (assuming he was the person he represented himself to be and not sailing under false colours after having boxed the compass on the strict q.t. somewhere) and the fictitious addressee of the missive which made him nourish some suspicions of our friend's *bona fides*, nevertheless. . . . (*U*, 546–47)

. . . Up until now I have been speaking to you about letters in *Ulysses*, and postcards, about typewriters and telegraphs, but the telephone is missing, and I must relate to you a telephone experience. For a long time, I have thought—and this is still true today—that I would never be ready to give a talk on Joyce to an audience of Joyce experts. But when it comes to Joyce, what is an expert? that's my question. Still just as intimidated and behind schedule, I felt highly embarrassed when, in March, my friend Jean-Michel Rabaté telephoned me to ask for a title. I didn't have one. I only knew that I wanted to discuss *yes* in *Ulysses*. I had even tried casually counting them; more than 222 *yes*es in the so-called original version (and we know better than ever what precautions we must take when we use this expression). I came up with this no doubt approximate figure after an initial counting up, which took into consideration only the *yes*es in their explicit form.[7] I mean the word *yes*, since there are other examples of *yes* without the word *yes*, and indeed, the number of *yes*es is not the same in translation, which is a major problem; the French version adds quite a few. More than a quarter of these *yes*es are to be found in what is so ingenuously termed Molly's monologue: wherever there is a *yes*, whatever break may have taken place in the monologue, the other is hooked up somewhere on the telephone.

[7]Later, in the week following this lecture, a student and friend whom I met in Toronto drew my attention to another counting up of *yes*es. This calculation arrived at a far higher figure, having no doubt included all the *ayes* which I noted only in passing, and which are pronounced like the word *I*, signifying the word *I* (*je*). This counting poses a problem, to which I will return later. There is another estimation, that of Noel

When Jean-Michel Rabaté phoned me, I had, then, already decided to interrogate, if we can put it like that, the *yes*es of *Ulysses* as well as the institution of Joycean experts, as well as to question what happens when the word *yes* is written, quoted, repeated, archived, *recorded*, gramophoned, or is the subject of translation or transfer. But I still had no title, only a statistic and a few notes on a single sheet. I asked Rabaté to wait a second, went up to my room, cast a glance at the page of notes and a title crossed my mind with a kind of irresistible brevity, the authority of a telegraphic order: *hear say yes (oui dire) in Joyce*. So, you are receiving me, saying *yes* in Joyce but also saying it so that the yes *(le oui)* which can be noticed, the *saying yes (le dire oui)*, sallies forth like a quotation or a rumor going about, circumnavigating, as it were, the ear's labyrinth, which is what we know only by hear-say *(oui-dire)*. The play on "hear say yes," *l'oui-dire* and *l'ouï-dire*, can only be fully effective in French, which exploits the obscure, babelian homonomy of *oui* with just a dotted "i," and *ouï* with a diaresis. This untranslatable homonomy can be heard (by *oui dire*, that is) rather than read *with the eyes*, with the last word, *eyes*, noticed in passing, saying *yes* in the passage, giving itself to reading the grapheme *yes* rather than hearing it. *Yes* can only be a mark in *Ulysses*, a mark at once written and spoken, vocalized as a grapheme and written as a phoneme, *yes*, in a word, gramophoned.

So *hear say yes (l'oui-dire)* seemed to me to be a good title, sufficiently untranslatable and potentially capable of captioning what I wanted to say about the *yes*es in Joyce. Rabaté said "yes" to me on the telephone, that this title was fine. . . . All of you are experts and you belong to one of the most remarkable institutions. It bears the name

---

Riley Fitch in *Sylvia Beach and the Lost Generation: A History of Literary Paris in the Twenties and Thirties* (New York: Norton; London: Penguin, 1983), 109–10. If I quote the whole of the paragraph, it is because it seems to go beyond the mere arithmeticality of the *yes*:

> One consultation with Joyce concerned Benoist-Méchin's translation of the final words of *Ulysses*: "and his heart was going like mad and yes I said Yes I will." The young man wanted the novel to conclude with a final "yes" following the "I will." Earlier Joyce had considered using "yes" (which appears 354 times in the novel) as his final word, but had written "I will" in the draft that Benoist-Méchin was translating. There followed a day of discussion in which they dragged in all the world's great philosophers. Benoist-Méchin, who argued that in French the "*oui*" is stronger and smoother, was more persuasive in the philosophical discussion. "I will" sounds authoritative and Luciferian. "Yes," he argued, is optimistic, an affirmation to the world beyond oneself. Joyce, who may have changed his mind earlier in the discussion, conceded hours later, "yes," the young man was right, the book would end with "the most positive word in the language." (JD)

of a man who did everything, and admitted it, to make this institution indispensable, to keep it busy for centuries, as though on some new Tower of Babel to *make a name* for himself again. The institution can be seen as a powerful reading machine, a signature and countersignature machine in the service of his name, of his "patent." But as with God and the Tower of Babel, it is an institution for which he did everything he could to make it impossible and improbable in its very principle, to de-construct it in advance, even going as far as to undermine the very concept of competence, upon which one day an institutional legitimacy might be founded, whether we are dealing with a competence of knowledge or know-how. Before returning to this question, that is, of what you and I are doing here, as an exemplification of competence and incompetence, I shall hang on to the telephone for a little longer, before breaking off a more or less telepathic communication with Jean-Michel Rabaté. Up until now we have amassed letters, postcards, telegrams, typewriters, et cetera. We should remember that if *Finnegans Wake* is the sublime babelization of a *penman* and *postman*, the motif of postal difference, of remote control and telecommunication, is already powerfully at work in *Ulysses*. And, as always, this is *remarked en abyme*. For example, in "THE WEARER OF THE CROWN": "Under the porch of the general post office shoeblacks called and polished. Parked in North Prince's street, His Majesty's vermillion mailcars, bearing on their sides the royal initials, E. R., received loudly flung sacks of letters, postcards, lettercards, parcels, insured and paid, for local, provincial, British and overseas delivery" (*U*, 118). This *remote control* technology, as we say of television remote control, is not an element outside of this context; it affects the inside of meaning in the most elementary sense, even so far as the statement or the inscription of practically the shortest word, the gramophony of *yes*. This is why the wandering circumnavigation of a postcard, letter, or a telegram only shifts destinations in the perpetual buzzing of a telephone obsession, or again, a telegramophonic obsession, if you take into account a gramophone or answering service.

If I am not mistaken, the first phone call sounds with Bloom's words: "Better phone him up first" in a sequence entitled "AND IT WAS THE FEAST OF THE PASSOVER" (*U*, 124). A little before, he had somewhat mechanically, like a record, repeated this prayer, the most serious of all prayers for a Jew, the one that should never be allowed to become mechanical, to be gramophoned: *Shema Israel Adonai Elohanu*. If, more or less legitimately (for everything and nothing is legitimate when we lift out segments as examples of narrative metonymy) we subtract this element from the most obvious narrative frame in the book, then we can speak of the telephonic *Shema Israel* between God, who is infinitely removed (*a long-distance call, a collect call from or to the collector of prepuces*) and Israel. *Shema Israel* means, as you know, call to Israel, listen Israel, hello Israel, to the address of the name of Israel, *a person-to-person call*.[8] The "Better phone him up first" scene takes place in the offices of *The Telegraph (Le Télégramme)* newspaper (and not *The Tetragram*) and Bloom has just paused to watch a kind of typewriter, a composing machine, a typographic womb (*matrice*): "He stayed in his walk to watch a typesetter neatly distributing type." And as he first of all reads it backwards ("Reads it backwards first"), composing the name of Patrick Dignam, the name of the father, Patrick, from right to left, he remembers his own father reading the hagadah in the same direction. In the same paragraph, around the name of Patrick, you can follow the whole series of fathers, the twelve sons of Jacob, et cetera, and the word "practice" crops up twice to scan this patristic and *perfectly* paternal litany ("Quickly he does it. Must require some practice that." And twelve lines lower, "How quickly he does that job. Practice makes perfect.") This comes almost immediately after we read, "Better phone him up first": "*plutôt un coup de téléphone pour commencer*," the French translation says. Let's say that it's better to begin with a phone call. In the beginning, there must have been some phone calls.

In the beginning, there was the telephone. Before the act or the word, the telephone. In the beginning was the telephone. We can hear the telephone constantly ringing, this *coup de téléphone* plays on apparently random figures, but about which there is so much to say; we hear it resonate unceasingly. And it incorporates within itself this *yes* toward which we slowly, moving in circles around it, return. There are several

---

[8]Elsewhere, in the brothel, it is the circumcised who say the "Shema Israel," and there is also the *Lactus Morte*, the dead sea: "THE CIRCUMCISED: (*In a dark guttural chant as they cast dead fruit upon him, no flowers) Shema Israel Adonai Elohena Adonai Echad*" (*U*, 496).
And while we are speaking of Ulysses, the dead sea, gramophones, and soon the laugh, there is *Remembrance of Things Past*: "He stopped laughing; I should have liked to recognize my friend, but, like Ulysses in the Odyssey when he rushes forward to embrace his dead mother, like the spiritualist who tries in vain to elicit from a ghost an answer which will reveal its identity, like the visitor at an exhibition of electricity who cannot believe that the voice which the gramophone restores unaltered to life is not a voice spontaneously emitted by a human being, I was obliged to give up the attempt." A little higher up: "The familiar voice seemed to be emitted by a gramophone more perfect than any I had ever heard." *The Past Recaptured*, trans. Andreas Mayor. New York: Vintage Books, 1971, pp. 188–89. (JD)

modalities or tonalities of the telephonic *yes*, but one of them, without saying anything else, returns to mark, simply, that we are *here*, present, listening, on the other end of the line, ready to answer but not for the moment responding to anything other than the preparation to answer (hello, yes; I'm listening, I can hear that you are there, ready to speak just when I am ready to speak to you). In the beginning was the telephone, yes, in the beginning a telephone call. A few pages after "*Shema Israel*" and the first telephone call, just after the unforgettable Ohio scene entitled "MEMORABLE BATTLES RECALLED" (you can hear that a voice can trip quickly from Ohio to the Battle of Tokyo), a certain telephonic *yes* resounds with a "Bingbang" which recalls the origin of the universe. A competent professor has just passed by "—A perfect cretic! the professor said. Long, short and long," after the cry "In Ohio!" "My Ohio!" Then, at the beginning of "O, HARP EOLIAN" (*U*, 129), there is the sound of teeth chattering as dental floss is applied (and if I were to tell you that this year, before going to Tokyo, I went to Oxford, Ohio, and that I even bought some dental floss— that is to say, an eolian harp—in a drugstore in Ithaca, you would not believe me. You would be wrong; it is true and can be verified). When "the resonant unwashed teeth" vibrate to the dental floss, we hear "—Bingbang, bingbang." Bloom then asks to ring: "I just want to phone about an ad." Then "the telephone whirred inside." This time the eolian harp is not dental floss but the telephone, the cables of which are elsewhere "the navel cords," which harp back to Eden. "—Twenty eight . . . No, twenty . . . Double four . . . Yes." We cannot tell if this *Yes* is part of a monologue, approving the Other within (yes that's the right number) or if he is already in communication with the other end of the line. We cannot know. The context is cut, end of sequence.

But at the end of the following sequence ("SPOT THE WINNER"), a telephonic "yes" rings again in the same offices of *The Telegraph*: "Yes . . . *Evening Telegraph* here, Mr Bloom phoned from the inner office. Is the boss . . . ? Yes, *Telegraph* . . . To where? . . . Aha! Which auction rooms? . . . Aha! I see . . . Right. I'll catch him" (*U*, 130).

It is repeatedly said that the phone call is *internal*. "Mr Bloom . . . made for the *inner* door" when he wants to ring; then "the telephone whirred *inside*," and finally, "Mr Bloom phoned from the *inner* office." So, a telephonic interiority: for before any appliance bearing the name "telephone" in modern times, the telephonic *tekhnè* is at work within the voice, multiplying the writing of voices without any instruments, as Mallarmé would say, a mental telephony, which, inscribing remoteness, distance, difference, and spacing in sound (*phoné*), institutes, forbids, *and at the same time* interferes with the so-called monologue. At the same time, in the same way (*du même coup*), from the first phone call (*dès le premier coup de téléphone*) and from the simplest vocalization, from the monosyllabized quasi-interjection of the word *oui*, "yes," "ay." More conclusively, we have the instance of these *yes*, *yeses* which *speech act* theorists use as an illustration of the performative and which Molly repeats at the end of the so-called monologue, the "*Yes, Yes, I do*," her consent in the marriage ceremony. When I speak of mental telephony, or even of masturbation, I am implicitly quoting "THE SINS OF THE PAST"; "(*In a medley of voices*) He went through a form of clandestine marriage with at least one woman in the shadow of the Black Church. Unspeakable messages he telephoned mentally to Miss Dunne at an address in d'Olier Street while he presented himself indecently to the instrument in the callbox" (*U*, 491–92).

Telephonic spacing is particularly superimposed in the scene entitled "A DISTANT VOICE." The scene crosses all the lines in our network, the paradoxes of competence and institution, represented here in the shape of the professor, and, in every sense of the word, the *repetition* of the word *yes* between *eyes and ears, entre les yeux and les oreilles*. All these telephonic lines can be drawn from one paragraph:

A DISTANT VOICE

—I'll answer it, the professor said going . . .

—Hello? *Evening Telegraph* here . . . Hello? . . .

Who's there? . . . Yes . . . Yes . . . Yes . . .

    The professor came to the inner door. [*inner* again]

—Bloom is at the telephone, he said. (*U*, 137–38)

Bloom-is-at-the-telephone. In this way, the professor defines a particular situation at a certain moment in the novel, no doubt, but as is always the case in the stereophony of a text that gives several outlines to each statement, always allowing metonymic extracts to be taken— and I am not the only reader of Joyce to indulge in this pursuit, at once legitimate and abusive, authorized and improper—the professor is also naming the permanent essence of Bloom. This can be read in this particular paradigm: *he is at the telephone*, he is always there, he belongs to the telephone, he is riveted yet destined there. His being is a being-at-the-telephone. He is hooked up to a multiplicity of voices and answering machines. His being-there is a being at the telephone, in the way that Heidegger speaks of a being for the death of *Dasein*. And I am not playing with words when I say that: Heideggerian *Dasein* is also a being-called, it always is, as we are informed in *Sein und Zeit*, and as my friend Sam Weber reminded me, a *Dasein* that can only comply with itself using the Call (*der Ruf*) as a starting point, a call which has come from afar, which does not necessarily use words, and which, in a certain way, is not saying anything. To such an analysis, we could apply down to the last detail the whole of chapter 57 of *Sein und Zeit* on the subject of *der Ruf*, drawing, for example, on phrases like the following: *Der Angerufene ist eben dieses Dasein; aufgerufen zu seinem eigensten Seinkönnen (Sich-vorweg . . .) Und aufgerufen ist das Dasein durch den Anruf aus dem Verfallen in das Man . . .* The called one is precisely this *Dasein*; summoned, called forth, called up toward this possibility of being the most proper (before himself). And in this way the *Dasein* is hailed by this call, called out to, called out of the collapse of the "one," of anonymity. Unfortunately, we do not have the time to enter further into this analysis over and above the jargon of *Eigentlichkeit*, which is particularly remembered in this university [Frankfurt].

—Bloom is at the telephone, he said.

—Tell him to go to hell, the editor said promptly. X is Burke's public house, see? (*U*, 138)

Bloom is at the telephone, hooked up to a powerful network to which I shall return in an instant. He belongs in his essence to a polytelephonic structure. But he is at the telephone in the sense that he is also being *waited for* on the telephone. When the professor says, "Bloom is at the telephone," and I shall shortly say, "Joyce is at the telephone," he is saying: he is waiting for someone to respond to him, waiting for an answer, which the editor—who must decide the future of his text, its safekeeping and its truth—does not want to give, and who at this point sends him to hell, a *Verfallen* then into the hell of censured books. Bloom is waiting for an answer, for someone to say, "hello, yes," that is, for someone to say, "Yes, yes," beginning with the telephonic *yes* indicating that there is indeed another voice, or an answering machine, on the other end of the line. When, at the end of the book, Molly says, "yes, yes," she is answering a request, but a request that she requests. She is at the telephone, even when she is in bed, asking, and waiting to be asked, on the telephone (since she is alone) to say, "yes, yes." And the fact that she asks "with my eyes" does not prevent this demand being made by telephone; on the contrary: "well as well him as another and then I asked him with my eyes to ask again yes and then he asked me would I yes to say yes my mountain flower and first I put my arms around him yes and drew him down to me so he could feel my breasts all perfume yes and his heart was going like mad and yes I said yes I will Yes" (*U*, 704).

The final "Yes," the last word, the eschatology of the book, gives itself up only to *reading*, since it distinguishes itself from the others by an inaudible capital letter; what also remains equally inaudible, although visible, is the literal incorporation of *yes* in *eyes*. Languages of eyes, of ayes.

We still do not know what *yes* means and how this small word, if it is one, operates in language and in what we calmly refer to as speech acts. We do not know whether this word shares anything at all with any other word in any language, even with the word *no*, which is most certainly not symmetrical to it. We do not know if a grammatical, semantic, linguistic, rhetorical, or philosophical concept exists capable of this event marked *yes*. Let us leave that aside for the moment. Let us, and this is not merely fiction, act *as if* this would not prevent us, on the contrary, from hearing what the word *yes* governs. We will move on to the difficult questions later, if we have time.

Yes on the telephone can be crossed in one and the same occurrence, by a variety of intonations whose differentiating qualities are potentialized on stereophonic long waves. They may appear only to go as far as interjection, as far as the mechanical quasi signal that indicates either the mere presence of interlocutory *Dasein* at the other end of the line (Hello, yes?) or the passive docility of a secretary or a subordinate who, like some archiving machine, is ready to record orders (*yes sir*) or who is satisfied with purely informative answers (*yes, sir; no, sir*). This is just one example among many. I have deliberately chosen the section where a typewriter and the trade name H.E.L.Y.'s lead us to the last piece of furniture in the hall, or, as a techno-telecommunication type of introduction, to a certain gramophone, and at the same time connects us to the network of the prophet Elijah. So here we are, though of course I have sectioned and selected, filtering away the noise on the line:

> Miss Dunne hid the Capel street library copy of *The Woman in White* far back in her drawer and rolled a sheet of gaudy notepaper into her typewriter.

Too much mystery business in it. Is he in love with that one, Marion? Change it and get another by Mary Cecil Haye. The disk shot down the groove, wobbled a while, ceased and ogled them: six.
Miss Dunne clicked at the keyboard:
— 16 June 1904. [almost eighty years.]
Five tallwhitehatted sandwichmen between Monypeny's corner and the slab where Wolfe Tone's statue was not, eeled themselves turning H.E.L.Y.'S and plodded back as they had come. . . .
The telephone rang rudely by her ear.
—Hello. Yes, sir. No, sir. Yes, sir. I'll ring them up after five. Only those two, sir, for Belfast and Liverpool. All right, sir. Then I can go after six if you're not back. A quarter after. Yes, sir. Twenty-seven and six. I'll tell him. Yes: one, seven, six.
She scribbled three figures on an envelope.
—Mr Boylan! Hello! That gentleman from *Sport* was in looking for you. Mr Lenehan, yes. He said he'll be in the Ormond at four. No, sir. Yes, sir. I'll ring them up after five. (*U*, 228–29)

It is not by accident that the repetition of *yes* can be seen to assume mechanical, servile forms, often bending the woman to her master, even if any answer to the other as a singular other must, it seems, escape it. In order for the *yes* of affirmation, assent, consent, alliance, of engagement, signature, or gift to have the value it has, it must carry the repetition within itself. It must *a priori* and immediately confirm its promise and promise its confirmation. This essential repetition lets itself be haunted by an intrinsic threat, by an internal telephone which interferes (*parasiter*) with it like a mimetic, mechanical double, like its incessant parody. We shall return to this fatality. But we can already hear a gramophony which records writing in the liveliest voice. *A priori* it reproduces it, in the absence of all intentional presence of the affirmer. Such gramophony responds, of course, to the dream of a reproduction which *preserves* as its truth the living *yes*, archived into the very quick of the voice. But in this way it gives way to the possibility of parody, of a *yes* technique that persecutes the most spontaneous, the most giving desire of the *yes*. To meet (*répondre à*) its destination, this *yes* must reaffirm itself immediately. Such is the condition of a signed commitment. *Yes* can only express *itself* by promising itself its own memory. (*Le oui ne peut se dire que s'il se promet la mémoire de soi.*) The affirmation of the word *yes* is the affirmation of memory. *Yes* must preserve itself, reiterate itself, must archive its voice in order to give itself once again to be heard (*la redonner à entendre*).

This is what I call the gramophone effect. *Yes* gramophones itself and, *a priori*, telegramophones itself.

The desire for memory and the mourning implicit in the word *yes* set in motion an anamnesic machine. And its hypermnesic overacceleration. The machine reproduces the quick (*le vif*), it doubles it with its automaton. The example I have chosen offers the privilege of a double contiguity: from the word *yes* to the word *voice* and to the word *gramophone* in a sequence expressing the desire for memory, desire as memory of desire and memory for desire. It takes place in Hades, in the cemetery, at about 11 o'clock in the morning, the time reserved for the *heart* (that is, as Heidegger would put it again, the place reserved for memory that is retained and for truth), here in the sense of the Sacred Heart:

> The Sacred Heart that is: showing it. Heart on his sleeve. . . .
> How many! All these here once walked round Dublin. Faithful departed.
> As you are now so once were we.
> Besides how could you remember everybody? Eyes, walk, voice. Well, the voice, yes: gramophone. Have a gramophone in every grave or keep it in the house. After dinner on a Sunday. Put on poor old greatgrandfather Kraahraark! Hellohellohello amawfullyglad kraark awfullygladaseeragain hellohello amarawf kopthsth. Remind you of the voice like the photograph reminds you of the face. Otherwise you couldn't remember the face after fifteen years, say. For instance some fellow that died when I was in Wisdom Hely's. (*U*, 115–16)[9]

What right do we have to select or interrupt a quotation from *Ulysses*? This is always legitimate and illegitimate, to be made legitimate like an illegitimate child. I could follow the sons of Hely (Bloom's old boss), threading them through all sorts of genealogies. Rightly or wrongly, I judge it more economical here to rely on the association with the name of the prophet Elijah, to whom a good many passages are devoted, or rather whose coming at regular intervals can be foretold. I pronounce *Elie* in the French way, but in the English name for Elijah, Molly's *Ja* can be heard echoing if Molly gives voice to the flesh (*la chair*, hang on to this word) which always says *yes* (*stets bejaht*, Joyce reminds us, reversing Goethe's words). I shall not investigate further the part of the text where it is said, "voice out of heaven,

[9]I am told that James Joyce's grandson is here, now, in this room. This quotation is naturally dedicated to him. (JD)

calling: *Elijah! Elijah!* and he answered with a main cry: *Abba! Abba!* And they beheld Him even Him, ben Bloom Elijah, amid clouds of angels" (*U*, 343).

No, without transition, I give myself up to repetition, to that which is called "the second coming of Elijah" in the brothel. The Gramophone, the character and the voice, if I can put it like this, of the gramophone just shouted:

Jerusalem!
Open your gates and sing
Hosanna . . . (*U*, 472)

In the second coming of Elijah after "the end of the world," Elijah's voice acts as a kind of telephone exchange or marshalling yard. All communication, transport, transfer, and translation networks go through him. Polytelephony goes through Elijah's programophony. But do not forget, whatever you do, that Molly reminds us that ben Bloom Elijah lost his job at Hely's. Bloom had thought at that time of prostituting Molly, of making her pose naked for a very rich man.

Elijah is just a voice, a skein of voices. It says, "*C'est moi qui opère tous les téléphones de ce réseau-là*" in the French translation approved by Joyce for "Say, I am operating all this trunk line. Boys, do it now. God's time is 12.25. Tell mother you'll be there. Rush your order and you play a slick ace. Join on right here! Book through to eternity junction, the nonstop run" (*U*, 473). I want to insist (in French) on the fact that seats must be *booked* (*louer*), reserved near Elijah, Elijah must be *praised (louer)* and the *booking* (*location*) of this *praise* (*louange*) is none other than the book which stands in lieu of *eternity junction*, like a transferential and teleprogramophonic exchange.[10] "Just one word more," continues Elijah, who also evokes the second coming of Christ and asks us if we are ready, "Florry Christ, Stephen Christ, Zoe Christ, Bloom Christ," et cetera. "Are you all in this vibration? I say you are"—which is translated into French by "*Moi je dis que oui,*" a problematic though not illicit translation about which we must speak again. And the voice of the one who says "yes," Elijah, saying to those who are in the *vibration* (a key word in my view) that they can call him any time, straightaway, instantaneously, without using any technique or postal system, but going by the sun, by solar

---

[10]The French plays upon both meanings of *louer* ("to book" or "to rent" and "to praise"), of *location* (a "hiring" or "renting"), and of *louange* ("praise" or "commendation") as well as *livre* ("book"). (SB)

cables and rays, by the voice of the sun—we could say photophone or heliophone. He says "by sunphone": "Got me? That's it. You call me up by sunphone any old time. Bumboosers, save your stamps" (*U*, 473). So do not write me any letters, save your stamps, you can collect them, like Molly's father.

We have arrived at this point because I was telling you about my travel experiences, my round trip, and about a few phone calls. If I am telling stories, it is to put off speaking about serious things and because I am too intimidated. Nothing intimidates me more than a community of experts in Joycean matters. Why? I wanted first of all to speak to you about this, to speak to you about authority and intimidation. . . .

I did not feel worthy of the honor that had been bestowed on me, far from it, but I must have been nourishing some obscure desire to be part of this mighty family which tends to sum up all others, including their hidden narratives of bastardy, legitimation, and illegitimacy. If I have accepted, it is mainly for having suspected some perverse challenge in a legitimation so generously offered. You know better than I the concern regarding familial legitimation; it is this which makes *Ulysses*, as well as *Finnegans Wake*, vibrate. I was thinking, in the plane, of the challenge and the trap, because experts, I said to myself, with the lucidity and experience that a long acquaintance with Joyce confers on them, ought to know better than most to what extent, beneath the simulacrum of a few signs of complicity, of references or quotations in each of my books, Joyce remains a stranger to me, as if I did not know him. Incompetence, as they know, is the profound truth of my relationship to this work which I know deep down only indirectly, through hearsay, through rumors, through what people say (*des* *"on-dit"*), second-hand exegeses, always partial readings. For these experts, I said to myself, the time has come for the deception to burst out (*éclater*), and how best could this be demonstrated or denounced if not at the opening of a large symposium?

So, in order to defend myself against this hypothesis, which was almost a certainty, I asked myself: but in the end what does competence come down to in the case of Joyce? And what can a Joycean institution, a Joycean family, a Joycean international organization be? I do not know how far we can speak of the modernity of Joyce, but if this exists, beyond the apparatus for postal and programophonic technologies, it is linked to the declared project of keeping generations of university scholars at work for centuries of babelian edification, which must itself have been drawn up using a technological model and the division of university labor that could not be that of former centuries. The scheme of bending vast communities of readers and writers to this law, to detain them by means of an interminable transferential chain of translation and tradition, can equally well be attributed to Plato and Shakespeare, to Dante and Vico, without mentioning Hegel and other finite divinities. But none of these could calculate, as well as Joyce did, his feat (*son coup*), by modifying it to certain types of world research institutions prepared to use not only means of transport, of communication, of organizational programming allowing an accelerated capitalization, a crazy accumulation of interest in terms of knowledge blocked in Joyce's name, while he even lets you all sign in his name, as Molly would say ("I could often have written out a fine cheque for myself and write his name on it" [*U, 702*]), but also the modes of archivization and consultation of data unheard of (*inouïes*) for all the grandfathers whom I have just named, omitting Homer. The intimidation holds to this: Joyce experts are the representatives as well as the effects of the most powerful project for programming the totality of research in onto-logico-encyclopedic fields for centuries, all the while commemorating his own, proper signature. A Joyce scholar has rightly at his/her disposal, has the right to dispose of, the totality of competence in the encyclopedic field of the *universitas*. He has at his command the computer of all memory, he plays with the entire archive of culture—at least of what is said to be Western culture, and of what in this returns to itself according to the Ulyssean circle of encyclopedia; and this is why one can always at least dream of writing *on* Joyce and not *in* Joyce from the fantasy of some Far Eastern capital, without, in my case, having too many illusions about it. The effects of this preprogramming, you know better than I, are admirable and terrifying, and sometimes of intolerable violence. One of them has the following form: nothing can be invented *on the subject* of Joyce. Everything we can say about *Ulysses*, for example, has already been anticipated, including as we have seen, the scene about academic competence and the ingenuity of metadiscourse. We are caught in the net. All the gestures sketched in to allow an initiatory movement are already announced in an overpotentialized text that will remind you, at a given moment, that you are captive in a language, writing, knowledge, and *even narration* network. This is one of the things I wanted to demonstrate before, in recounting all these stories, moreover true ones, about the postcard in Tokyo, the trip to Ohio, or the phone call from Rabaté. We have verified that all this had its narrative paradigm and was *already* recounted in *Ulysses*. Everything that happened to me, including the narrative that I would attempt to make of it, was already foretold and forenarrated, this unusualness being dated, prescribed in a sequence of knowledge and narration: within *Ulysses*, to say nothing of *Finnegans Wake*, by a hypermnesis machine capable of storing in an immense epic work, with the Western memory and virtually all the languages in the world *including traces of the future*. Yes, everything has already happened to us with *Ulysses* and has been signed in advance by Joyce. . . .

Reader-Response Criticism
and
Ulysses

WHAT IS READER-RESPONSE CRITICISM?

Students are routinely asked in English courses for their reactions to the texts they are reading. Sometimes there are so many different reactions that we may wonder whether everyone has read the same text. And some students respond so idiosyncratically to what they read that we say their responses are "totally off the wall." This variety of response interests reader-response critics, who raise theoretical questions about whether our responses to a work are the same as its meanings, whether a work can have as many meanings as we have responses to it, and whether some responses are more valid than others. They ask what determines what is and what isn't "off the wall." What, in other words, is the wall, and what standards help us define it?

In addition to posing provocative questions, reader-response criticism provides us with models that aid our understanding of texts and the reading process. Adena Rosmarin has suggested that a literary text may be likened to an incomplete work of sculpture: to see it fully, we must complete it imaginatively, taking care to do so in a way that responsibly takes into account what exists. Other reader-response critics have suggested other models, for reader-response criticism is not a monolithic school of thought but, rather, an umbrella term covering a variety of approaches to literature.

Nonetheless, as Steven Mailloux has shown, reader-response critics *do* share not only questions but also goals and strategies. Two of the basic goals are to show that a work gives readers something to do and to describe what the reader does by way of response. To achieve those goals, the critic may make any of a number of what Mailloux calls "moves." For instance, a reader-response critic might typically (1) cite direct references to reading in the text being analyzed, in order to justify the focus on reading and show that the world of the text is continuous with the one in which the reader reads; (2) show how other non-reading situations in the text nonetheless mirror the situation the reader is in ("Fish shows how in *Paradise Lost* Michael's teaching of Adam in Book XI resembles Milton's teaching of the reader throughout the poem"); and (3) show, therefore, that the reader's response is, or is analogous to, the story's action or conflict. For instance, Stephen Booth calls *Hamlet* the tragic story of "an audience that cannot make up its mind" (Mailloux, "Learning" 103).

Although reader-response criticism is often said to have emerged in the United States in the 1970s, it is in one respect as old as the foundations of Western culture. The ancient Greeks and Romans tended to view literature as rhetoric, a means of making an audience react in a certain way. Although their focus was more on rhetorical strategies and devices than on the reader's (or listener's) response to those methods, the ancients by no means left the audience out of the literary equation. Aristotle thought, for instance, that the greatness of tragedy lay in its "cathartic" power to cleanse or purify the emotions of audience members. Plato, by contrast, worried about the effects of artistic productions, so much so that he advocated evicting poets from the Republic on the grounds that their words "feed and water" the passions!

In our own century, long before 1970, there were critics whose concerns and attitudes anticipated those of reader-response critics. One of these, I. A. Richards, is usually associated with formalism, a supposedly objective, text-centered approach to literature that reader-response critics of the 1970s roundly attacked. And yet in 1929 Richards managed to sound surprisingly *like* a 1970s-vintage reader-response critic, writing in *Practical Criticism* that "the personal situation of the reader inevitably (and within limits rightly) affects his reading, and many more are drawn to poetry in quest of some reflection of their latest emotional crisis than would admit it" (575). Rather than deploring this fact, as many of his formalist contemporaries would have done, Richards argued that the reader's feelings and experiences provide a kind of reality check, a way of testing the authenticity of emotions and events represented in literary works.

Approximately a decade after Richards wrote *Practical Criticism,* an American named Louise M. Rosenblatt published *Literature as Exploration* (1938). In that seminal book, now in its fourth edition (1983), Rosenblatt began developing a theory of reading that blurs the boundary between reader and text, subject and object. In a 1969 article entitled "Towards a Transactional Theory of Reading," she sums up her position by writing that "a poem is what the reader lives through under the guidance of the text and experiences as relevant to the text" (127). Rosenblatt knew her definition would be difficult for many to accept: "The idea that a *poem* presupposes a *reader* actively involved with a *text,*" she wrote, "is particularly shocking to those seeking to emphasize the objectivity of their interpretations" ("Transactional" 127).

Rosenblatt implicitly and generally refers to formalists (also called the "New Critics") when she speaks of supposedly objective interpreters shocked by the notion that a "poem" is something cooperatively produced by a "reader" and a "text." Formalists spoke of "the poem itself," the "concrete work of art," the "real poem." They had no interest in what a work of literature makes a reader "live through." In fact, in *The Verbal Icon* (1954), William K. Wimsatt and Monroe C. Beardsley defined as fallacious the very notion that a reader's response is relevant to the meaning of a literary work:

> The Affective Fallacy is a confusion between the poem and its *results* (what it *is* and what it *does*). . . . It begins by trying to derive the standards of criticism from the psychological effects of a poem and ends in impressionism and relativism. The outcome . . . is that the poem itself, as an object of specifically critical judgment, tends to disappear. (21)

Reader-response critics have taken issue with their formalist predecessors. Particularly influential has been Stanley Fish, whose early work is seen by some as marking the true beginning of contemporary reader-response criticism. In "Literature in the Reader: Affective Stylistics" (1970), Fish took on the formalist hegemony, the New Critical establishment, by arguing that any school of criticism that would see a work of literature as an object, claiming to describe what it *is* and never what it *does,* is guilty of misconstruing the very essence of literature and reading. Literature exists when it is read, Fish suggests, and its force is an affective force. Furthermore, reading is a temporal process. Formalists assume it is a spatial one as they step back and survey the literary work as if it were an object spread out before them. They may find elegant patterns in the texts they examine and reexamine, but they fail to take into account that the work is quite different to a reader who is turning the pages and being moved, or affected, by lines that appear and disappear as the reader reads.

In a discussion of the effect that a sentence penned by the seventeenth-century physician Thomas Browne has on a reader reading, Fish pauses to say this about his analysis and also, by extension, about his critical strategy: "Whatever is persuasive and illuminating about [it] is the result of my substituting for one question—what does this sentence mean?—another, more operational question—what does this sentence do?" He then quotes a line from John Milton's *Paradise Lost*, a line that refers to Satan and the other fallen angels: "Nor did they not perceive their evil plight." Whereas more traditional critics might say that the "meaning" of the line is "They did perceive their evil plight," Fish relates the uncertain movement of the reader's mind *to* that half-satisfying interpretation. Furthermore, he declares that "the reader's inability to tell whether or not 'they' do perceive and his involuntary question . . . are part of the line's *meaning,* even though they take place in the mind, not on the page" (*Text* 26).

The stress on what pages *do* to minds (and what minds do in response) pervades the writings of most, if not all, reader-response critics. Stephen Booth, whose book *An Essay on Shakespeare's Sonnets* (1969) greatly influenced Fish, sets out to describe the "reading experience that results" from a "multiplicity of organizations" in a sonnet by Shakespeare (*Essay* ix). Sometimes these organizations don't make complete sense, Booth points out, and sometimes they even seem curiously contradictory. But that is precisely what interests reader-response critics, who, unlike formalists, are at least as interested in fragmentary, inconclusive, and even unfinished texts as in polished, unified works. For it is the reader's struggle to *make sense* of a challenging work that reader-response critics seek to describe.

The German critic Wolfgang Iser has described that sense-making struggle in his books *The Implied Reader* (1972) and *The Act of Reading: A Theory of Aesthetic Response* (1976). Iser argues that texts are full of "gaps" (or "blanks," as he sometimes calls them). These gaps powerfully affect the reader, who is forced to explain them, to connect what they separate, to create in his or her mind aspects of a poem or novel or play that aren't *in* the text but that the text incites. As Iser puts it in *The Implied Reader*, the "unwritten aspects" of a story "draw the reader into the action" and "lead him to shade in the many outlines suggested by the given situations, so that these take on a reality of their own." These "outlines" that "the reader's imagination animates" in turn "influence" the way in which "the written part of the text" is subsequently read (276).

In *Self-Consuming Artifacts: The Experience of Seventeenth-Century Literature* (1972), Fish reveals his preference for literature that makes readers work at making meaning. He contrasts two kinds of literary presentation. By the phrase "rhetorical presentation," he describes literature that reflects and reinforces opinions that readers already hold; by "dialectical presentation," he refers to works that prod and provoke. A dialectical text, rather than presenting an opinion as if it were truth, challenges readers to discover truths on their own. Such a text may not even have the kind of symmetry that formalist critics seek. Instead of offering a "single, sustained argument," a dialectical text, or self-consuming artifact, may be "so arranged that to enter into the spirit and assumptions of any one of [its] . . . units is implicitly to reject the spirit and assumptions of the unit immediately preceding" (*Artifacts* 9). Whereas a critic of another school might try to force an explanation as to why the units are fundamentally coherent, the reader-response critic proceeds by describing how the reader deals with the sudden twists and turns that characterize the dialectical text, returning to earlier passages and seeing them in an entirely new light.

"The value of such a procedure," Fish has written, "is predicated on the idea of meaning as *an event*," not as something "located (presumed to be embedded) *in* the utterance" or "verbal object as a thing in itself" (*Text* 28). By redefining meaning as an event rather than as something inherent in the text, the reader-response critic once again locates meaning in time: the reader's time. A text exists and signifies while it is being read, and what it signifies or means will depend, to no small extent, on *when* it is read. (*Paradise Lost* had some meanings for a seventeenth-century Puritan that it would not have for a twentieth-century atheist.)

With the redefinition of literature as something that exists meaningfully only in the mind of the reader, with the redefinition of the literary work as a catalyst of mental events, comes a concurrent redefinition of the reader. No longer is the reader the passive recipient of those ideas that an author has planted in a text. "The reader is *active*," Rosenblatt insists ("Transactional" 123). Fish begins "Literature in the Reader" with a similar observation: "If at this moment someone were to ask, 'what are you doing,' you might reply, 'I am reading,' and thereby acknowledge that reading is . . . something *you do*" (*Text* 22). Iser, in focusing critical interest on the gaps in texts, on what is not expressed, similarly redefines the reader as an active maker.

Amid all this talk of "the reader," it is tempting and natural to ask, "Just who *is* the reader?" (Or, to place the emphasis differently, "Just who is *the* reader?") Are reader-response critics simply sharing their own idiosyncratic responses when they describe what a line from *Paradise Lost* does in and to the reader's mind? "What about my responses?" you may want to ask. "What if they're different? Would reader-response critics be willing to say that my responses are equally valid?"

Fish defines "the reader" in this way: "*the* reader is the *informed* reader." The informed reader (whom Fish sometimes calls "the *intended* reader") is someone who is "sufficiently experienced as a reader to have internalized the properties of literary discourses, including everything from the most local of devices (figures of speech, etc.) to whole genres." And, of course, the informed reader is in full possession of the "semantic knowledge" (knowledge of idioms, for instance) assumed by the text (*Artifacts* 406).

Other reader-response critics define "*the* reader" differently. Wayne C. Booth, in *A Rhetoric of Irony* (1974), uses the phrase "the implied reader" to mean the reader "created by the work." (Only "by agreeing to play the role of this created audience," Susan Suleiman explains, "can an actual reader correctly understand and appreciate the work" [8].) Gerard Genette and Gerald Prince prefer to speak of "the narratee, . . . the necessary counterpart of a given narrator, that is, the person or figure who receives a narrative" (Suleiman 13). Like Booth, Iser employs the term "the implied reader," but he also uses "the educated reader" when he refers to what Fish called the "informed reader."

Jonathan Culler, who in 1981 criticized Fish for his sketchy definition of the informed reader, set out in *Structuralist Poetics* (1975) to describe the educated or "competent" reader's education by elaborating those reading conventions that make possible the understanding of poems and novels. In retrospect, however, Culler's definitions seem sketchy as well. By "competent reader," Culler meant competent reader of "literature." By "literature," he meant what schools and colleges mean when they speak of literature as being part of the curriculum. Culler, like his contemporaries, was not concerned with the fact that curricular content is politically and economically motivated. And "he did not," in Mailloux's words, "emphasize how the literary competence he described was embedded within larger formations and traversed by political ideologies extending beyond the academy" ("Turns" 49). It remained for a later generation of reader-oriented critics to do those things.

The fact that Fish, following Rosenblatt's lead, defined reader-response criticism in terms of its difference from and opposition to the New Criticism or formalism should not obscure the fact that the formalism of the 1950s and early 1960s had a great deal in common with the reader-response criticism of the late 1960s and early 1970s. This has become increasingly obvious with the rise of subsequent critical approaches whose practitioners have proved less interested in the close reading of texts than in the way literature represents, reproduces, and/or resists prevailing ideologies concerning gender, class, and race. In a retrospective essay entitled "The Turns of Reader-Response Criticism" (1990), Mailloux has suggested that, from the perspective of hindsight, the "close reading" of formalists and "Fish's early 'affective stylistics'" seem surprisingly similar. Indeed, Mailloux argues, the early "reader talk of . . . Iser and Fish enabled the continuation of the formalist practice of close reading. Through a vocabulary focused on a text's manipulation of readers, Fish was especially effective in extending and diversifying the formalist practices that continued business as usual within literary criticism" (48).

Since the mid-1970s, however, reader-response criticism (once commonly referred to as the "School of Fish") has diversified and taken on a variety of new forms, some of which truly *are* incommensurate with formalism, with its considerable respect for the integrity and power of the text. For instance, "subjectivists" like David Bleich, Norman Holland, and Robert Crosman have assumed what Mailloux calls the "absolute priority of individual selves as creators of texts" (*Conventions* 31). In other words, these critics do not see the reader's response as one "guided" by the text but rather as one motivated by deep-seated, personal, psychological needs. What they find in texts is, in Holland's phrase, their own "identity theme." Holland has argued that as readers we use "the literary work to symbolize and finally to replicate ourselves. We work out through the text our own characteristic patterns of desire" ("UNITY" 816). Subjective critics, as you may already have guessed, often find themselves confronted with the following question: If all interpretation is a function of private, psychological identity, then why have so many readers

interpreted, say, Shakespeare's *Hamlet* in the same way? Different subjective critics have answered the question differently. Holland simply
has said that common identity themes exist, such as that involving an
oedipal fantasy.

Meanwhile, Fish, who in the late 1970s moved away from reader-
response criticism as he had initially helped define it, came up with
a different answer to the question of why different readers tend to read
the same works the same way. His answer, rather than involving
common individual identity themes, involved common *cultural* identity. In "Interpreting the *Variorum*" (1976), he argues that the "stability of interpretation among readers" is a function of shared "interpretive strategies." These strategies, which "exist prior to the act of
reading and therefore determine the shape of what is read," are held in
common by "interpretive communities" such as the one constituted
by American college students reading a novel as a class assignment
(*Text* 167, 171). In developing the model of interpretive communities, Fish truly has made the break with formalist or New Critical
predecessors, becoming in the process something of a social, structuralist, reader-response critic. Recently, he has been engaged in studying reading communities and their interpretive conventions in order to
understand the conditions that give rise to a work's intelligibility.

Fish's shift in focus is in many ways typical of changes that have
taken place within the field of reader-response criticism—a field that,
because of those changes, is increasingly being referred to as "reader-
oriented" criticism. Less and less common are critical analyses examining the transactional interface between the text and its individual
reader. Increasingly, reader-oriented critics are investigating reading
communities, as the reader-oriented cultural critic Janice A. Radway
has done in her study of female readers of romance paperbacks (*Reading the Romance*, 1984). They are also studying the changing reception of literary works across time; see, for example, Mailloux in his
"pragmatic readings" of American literature in *Interpretive Conventions* (1982) and *Rhetorical Power* (1989).

An important catalyst of this gradual change was the work of
Hans Robert Jauss, a colleague of Iser's whose historically oriented
reception theory (unlike Iser's theory of the implied reader) was not
available in English book form until the early 1980s. Rather than
focusing on the implied, informed, or intended reader, Jauss examined
actual past readers. In *Toward an Aesthetic of Reception* (1982), he
argued that the reception of a work or author tends to depend upon
the reading public's "horizons of expectations." He noted that, in the

morally conservative climate of mid-nineteenth-century France, *Madame Bovary* was literally put on trial, its author Flaubert accused of glorifying adultery in passages representing the protagonist's fevered delirium via free indirect discourse, a mode of narration in which a third-person narrator tells us in an unfiltered way what a character is thinking and feeling.

As readers have become more sophisticated and tolerant, the popularity and reputation of *Madame Bovary* have soared. Sometimes, of course, changes in a reading public's horizons of expectations cause a work to be *less* well received over time. As American reception theorists influenced by Jauss have shown, Mark Twain's *Adventures of Huckleberry Finn* has elicited an increasingly ambivalent reaction from a reading public increasingly sensitive to demeaning racial stereotypes and racist language. The rise of feminism has prompted a downward revaluation of everything from Andrew Marvell's "To His Coy Mistress" to D. H. Lawrence's *Women in Love*.

Some reader-oriented feminists, such as Judith Fetterley, Patrocinio Schweickart, and Monique Wittig, have challenged the reader to become what Fetterley calls "the resisting reader." Arguing that literature written by men tends, in Schweickart's terms, to "immasculate" women, they have advocated strategies of reading that involve substituting masculine for feminine pronouns and male for female characters in order to expose the sexism inscribed in patriarchal texts. Other feminists, such as Nancy K. Miller in *Subject to Change* (1988), have suggested that there may be essential differences between the way women and men read and write.

That suggestion, however, has prompted considerable disagreement. A number of gender critics whose work is oriented toward readers and reading have admitted that there is such a thing as "reading like a woman" (or man), but they have also tended to agree with Peggy Kamuf that such forms of reading, like gender itself, are cultural rather than natural constructs. Gay and lesbian critics, arguing that sexualities have been similarly constructed within and by social discourse, have argued that there is a homosexual way of reading; Wayne Koestenbaum has defined "the (male twentieth-century first world) gay reader" as one who "reads resistantly for inscriptions of his condition, for texts that will confirm a social and private identity founded on a desire for other men. . . . Reading becomes a hunt for histories that deliberately foreknow or unwittingly trace a desire felt not by author but by reader, who is most acute when searching for signs of himself" (in Boone and Cadden, 176–77).

Given this kind of renewed interest in the reader and reading, some students of contemporary critical practice have been tempted to conclude that reader-oriented theory has been taken over by feminist, gender, gay, and lesbian theory. Others, like Elizabeth Freund, have suggested that it is deconstruction with which the reader-oriented approach has mixed and merged. Certainly, all of these approaches have informed and been informed by reader-response or reader-oriented theory. The case can be made, however, that there is in fact still a distinct reader-oriented approach to literature, one whose points of tangency are neither with deconstruction nor with feminist, gender, and so-called queer theory but, rather, with the new historicism and cultural criticism.

This relatively distinct form of reader theory is practiced by a number of critics, but is perhaps best exemplified by the work of scholars like Mailloux and Peter J. Rabinowitz. In *Before Reading: Narrative Conventions and the Politics of Interpretation* (1987), Rabinowitz sets forth four conventions or rules of reading, which he calls the rules of "notice," "signification," "configuration," and "coherence"—rules telling us which parts of a narrative are important, which details have a reliable secondary or special meaning, which fit into which familiar patterns, and how stories fit together as a whole. He then proceeds to analyze the misreadings and misjudgments of critics and to show that politics governs the way in which those rules are applied and broken. ("The strategies employed by critics when they read [Raymond Chandler's] *The Big Sleep*," Rabinowitz writes, "can teach us something about the structure of misogyny, not the misogyny of the novel itself, but the misogyny of the world outside it" [195].) In subsequent critical essays, Rabinowitz proceeds similarly, showing how a society's ideological assumptions about gender, race, and class determine the way in which artistic works are perceived and evaluated.

Mailloux, who calls his approach "rhetorical reception theory" or "rhetorical hermeneutics," takes a similar tack, insofar as he describes the political contexts of (mis)interpretation. In a recent essay on "Misreading as a Historical Act" (1993), he shows that a mid-nineteenth-century review of Frederick Douglass's *Narrative* by proto-feminist Margaret Fuller seems to be a misreading until we situate it "within the cultural conversation of the 'Bible politics' of 1845" (Machor 9). Woven through Mailloux's essay on Douglass and Fuller are philosophical pauses in which we are reminded, in various subtle ways, that all reading (including Mailloux's and our own) is culturally situated and likely to seem like *mis*reading someday. One such reflective pause, however, accomplishes more; in it, Mailloux reads the map of where reader-oriented criticism is today, affords a rationale for its being there, and plots its likely future direction. "However we have arrived at our present juncture," Mailloux writes,

> the current talk about historical acts of reading provides a welcome opportunity for more explicit consideration of how reading is historically contingent, politically situated, institutionally embedded, and materially conditioned; of how reading any text, literary or nonliterary, relates to a larger cultural politics that goes well beyond some hypothetical private interaction between an autonomous reader and an independent text; and of how our particular views of reading relate to the liberatory potential of literacy and the transformative power of education. (5)

In the essay that follows, "Patterns of Communication in Joyce's *Ulysses*," influential reader-response theorist Wolfgang Iser points out that, despite the novel's Homeric title and Dublin setting, "No Homeric figures actually appear in *Ulysses*, and yet the novel cannot be described as a realistic depiction of ordinary life in Dublin." Although *Ulysses* contains a wealth of detail concerning Dublin and people's lives there, the novel is hardly a realistic work of fiction; indeed, rather than creating "the illusion of reality," these details "become a sort of end in themselves, such as one finds in the art-form of the collage." Readers, realizing that these details "illustrate nothing," feel compelled to make something of the classical parallel implied by the novel's title; hence, they "try to create—through recourse to the *Odyssey*—some sort of frame of reference that will bring this chaos of detail under control and will endow everyday life with a pattern, with meaning, and with significance." But Homer's *Odyssey*, Iser argues, no more suffices to contain and explain all we experience in *Ulysses* than do the address books and newspaper cuttings from which Joyce drew the novel's details of everyday Dublin life.

Iser maintains that

> by giving his novel this structure—whether consciously or unconsciously—Joyce was complying with a basic disposition of the reader, described by Northrop Frye as follows: "Whenever we read anything, we find our attention moving in two directions at once. One direction is outward or centrifugal, in which we keep going outside our reading, from the individual words to the things they mean, or, in practice, to our memory of the conventional association between them. The other direction is inward or centripetal, in

which we try to develop from the words a sense of the larger verbal pattern they make."

In the case of *Ulysses*, we read in terms of possible "outward" Homeric parallels while, at the same time, looking for "internal" patterns like those we have observed in our personal lives and experiences. "Both approaches are, in themselves, rather flabby, and the task of stiffening them up, and indeed bringing them together, is what the novel sets its reader."

Iser develops his argument regarding the reader's dual-track task by discussing the way in which Joyce chose to present the material in *Ulysses:* through eighteen chapters, each written from its own distinct perspective. (One of these, "The Oxen of the Sun" chapter, shows the inadequacy of various linguistic styles associated with different historical periods.) Joyce thereby shows "the one-sidedness" of "characterizations" and "presentations"—that is, the degree to which they are idiosyncratic interpretations bound to leave us with a "surplus of nonintegrated, unstructured material." To "moderate, if not actually neutralize, the interpretive nature of style," Iser goes on to argue, "Joyce called upon virtually every stylistic mode that the novel had evolved during its comparatively short history. These he enriched with the whole armory of allusions and with the recall of archetypes." As a result, style cannot be accused of controlling or limiting the novel's possible interpretations.

In a novel in which such things as allusion and style do not establish meaning by limiting interpretive possibility, Iser proposes, "readers themselves [must] reduce the amount of observable material to manageable proportions." This hardly means that all readers will reduce the material in the same way, or even that individual readers will reduce it the same way every time they read the novel. "Each reading," Iser maintains, "gives us a new chance to integrate the details in a different way," but also leaves us with surplus details unaccounted for by that reading—details calling out for yet other readings. *Ulysses*, in Iser's view, "offers only a potential presentation, the working out of which has to be done actively by the reader. Thus it is possible to discover many different 'pictures' of the everyday world, but they will never converge into a defined picture—and it is this very fact that compels the reader to continue his/her search."

In his several discussions of actual passages from the novel, Iser shows how readers of *Ulysses* become "involved personally" in the making of meaning. In reading a scene in which Stephen tries to teach a history lesson, Iser argues that readers must choose between or synthesize "interior monologue, direct speech, and literary quotation" and then ultimately bridge the gap between that sort of passage and later ones, such as the passage in which Mr. Deasy makes "unequivocal utterances." The text, Iser maintains,

> says nothing about any relationship between these two passages, but the reader will soon find a relatively straightforward way to bridge this gap. Viewed against the background of infinite possibilities, Mr. Deasy's self-confidence appears absurdly narrowminded, and so the reader will most likely come to two conclusions: first, that Mr. Deasy is a pompous ass; second, and far more important, that any claim to knowledge is an automatic reduction of the infinite and discounts above all the changeability of phenomena.

Such an interpretation, however, is the reader's and the reader's alone, for, as Iser emphasizes, "there is no such statement in the text itself."

Even as Iser reads *Ulysses* anew, he advances and extends arguments he has made about the act of reading in *The Act of Reading* and *The Implied Reader*. He remains interested in textual gaps, especially as manifested in "the unconnected allusions and the abrupt alternation of stylistic devices" in *Ulysses*. But these gaps, he insists, account for

> the stimulating quality of the text. On the one hand, the density of allusions and the continual segmentation of style involve an incessant changing of perspectives, which seem to go out of control whenever the reader tries to pin them down; on the other hand, the gaps resulting from cuts and abbreviations tempt the reader to fill them in. He/she will try to group things, because this is the only way in which he/she can recognize situations or understand characters in the novel.

Iser ultimately argues, however, that Joyce's gap-filled structure and style inspire readers to do more than try to recognize situations or understand characters. Rather, Joyce "makes us aware that the degree of indeterminacy is irreducible, thus indicating that all the semiconsistent conceptions we have of everyday phenomena can only become conceptions because they ignore the inexplicability of reality."

Ross C Murfin

READER-RESPONSE CRITICISM:
A SELECTED BIBLIOGRAPHY

Some Introductions to
Reader-Response Criticism

Beach, Richard. *A Teacher's Introduction to Reader-Response Theories.* Urbana: NCTE, 1993.

Fish, Stanley E. "Literature in the Reader: Affective Stylistics." *New Literary History* 2 (1970): 123–61. Rpt. in Fish, *Text* 21–67, and in Primeau 154–79.

Freund, Elizabeth. *The Return of the Reader: Reader-Response Criticism.* London: Methuen, 1987.

Holub, Robert C. *Reception Theory: A Critical Introduction.* New York: Methuen, 1984.

Leitch, Vincent B. *American Literary Criticism from the Thirties to the Eighties.* New York: Columbia UP, 1988.

Mailloux, Steven. "Learning to Read: Interpretation and Reader-Response Criticism." *Studies in the Literary Imagination* 12 (1979): 93–108.

———. "Reader-Response Criticism?" *Genre* 10 (1977): 413–31.

———. "The Turns of Reader-Response Criticism." *Conversations: Contemporary Critical Theory and the Teaching of Literature.* Ed. Charles Moran and Elizabeth F. Penfield. Urbana: NCTE, 1990. 38–54.

Rabinowitz, Peter J. "Whirl Without End: Audience-Oriented Criticism." *Contemporary Literary Theory.* Ed. G. Douglas Atkins and Laura Morrow. Amherst: U of Massachusetts P, 1989. 81–100.

Rosenblatt, Louise M. "Towards a Transactional Theory of Reading." *Journal of Reading Behavior* 1 (1969): 31–47. Rpt. in Primeau 121–46.

Suleiman, Susan R. "Introduction: Varieties of Audience-Oriented Criticism." Suleiman and Crosman 3–45.

Tompkins, Jane P. "An Introduction to Reader-Response Criticism." Tompkins ix–xxiv.

Reader-Response Criticism in
Anthologies and Collections

Flynn, Elizabeth A., and Patrocinio P. Schweickart, eds. *Gender and Reading: Essays on Readers, Texts, and Contexts.* Baltimore: Johns Hopkins UP, 1986.

Garvin, Harry R., ed. *Theories of Reading, Looking, and Listening.* Lewisburg: Bucknell UP, 1981. Essays by Cain and Rosenblatt.

Machor, James L., ed. *Readers in History: Nineteenth-Century American Literature and the Contexts of Response.* Baltimore: Johns Hopkins UP, 1993. Contains Mailloux essay "Misreading as a Historical Act: Cultural Rhetoric, Bible Politics, and Fuller's 1845 Review of Douglass's *Narrative.*"

Primeau, Ronald, ed. *Influx: Essays on Literary Influence.* Port Washington: Kennikat, 1977. Essays by Fish, Holland, and Rosenblatt.

Suleiman, Susan R., and Inge Crosman, eds. *The Reader in the Text: Essays on Audience and Interpretation.* Princeton: Princeton UP, 1980. See especially the essays by Culler, Iser, and Todorov.

Tompkins, Jane P., ed. *Reader-Response Criticism: From Formalism to Post-Structuralism.* Baltimore: Johns Hopkins UP, 1980. See especially the essays by Bleich, Fish, Holland, Prince, and Tompkins.

Reader-Response Criticism: Some Major Works

Bleich, David. *Subjective Criticism.* Baltimore: Johns Hopkins UP, 1978.

Booth, Stephen. *An Essay on Shakespeare's Sonnets.* New Haven: Yale UP, 1969.

Booth, Wayne C. *A Rhetoric of Irony.* Chicago: U of Chicago P, 1974.

Eco, Umberto. *The Role of the Reader: Explorations in the Semiotics of Texts.* Bloomington: Indiana UP, 1979.

Fish, Stanley Eugene. *Doing What Comes Naturally: Change, Rhetoric, and the Practice of Theory in Literary and Legal Studies.* Durham: Duke UP, 1989.

———. *Is There a Text in This Class? The Authority of Interpretive Communities.* Cambridge: Harvard UP, 1980. This volume contains most of Fish's most influential essays, including "Literature in the Reader: Affective Stylistics," "What It's Like to Read *L'Allegro* and *Il Penseroso*," "Interpreting the *Variorum*," "How to Recognize a Poem When You See One," "Is There a Text in This Class?" and "What Makes an Interpretation Acceptable?"

———. *Self-Consuming Artifact: The Experience of Seventeenth-Century Literature.* Berkeley: U of California P, 1972.

———. *Surprised by Sin: The Reader in "Paradise Lost."* 2nd ed. Berkeley: U of California P, 1971.

Holland, Norman N. *5 Readers Reading.* New Haven: Yale UP, 1975.

————. "UNITY IDENTITY TEXT SELF." *PMLA* 90 (1975): 813–22.

Iser, Wolfgang. *The Act of Reading: A Theory of Aesthetic Response.* Baltimore: Johns Hopkins UP, 1978.

————. *The Implied Reader: Patterns of Communication in Prose Fiction from Bunyan to Beckett.* Baltimore: Johns Hopkins UP, 1974.

Jauss, Hans Robert. *Toward an Aesthetic of Reception.* Trans. Timothy Bahti. Intro. Paul de Man. Brighton, Eng.: Harvester, 1982.

Mailloux, Steven. *Interpretive Conventions: The Reader in the Study of American Fiction.* Ithaca: Cornell UP, 1982.

————. *Rhetorical Power.* Ithaca: Cornell UP, 1989.

Messent, Peter. *New Readings of the American Novel: Narrative Theory and Its Application.* New York: Macmillan, 1991.

Prince, Gerald. *Narratology.* New York: Mouton, 1982.

Rabinowitz, Peter J. *Before Reading: Narrative Conventions and the Politics of Interpretation.* Ithaca: Cornell UP, 1987.

Radway, Janice A. *Reading the Romance: Women, Patriarchy, and Popular Literature.* Chapel Hill: U of North Carolina P, 1984.

Rosenblatt, Louise M. *Literature as Exploration.* 4th ed. New York: MLA, 1983.

————. *The Reader, the Text, the Poem: The Transactional Theory of the Literary Work.* Carbondale: Southern Illinois UP, 1978.

Slatoff, Walter J. *With Respect to Readers: Dimensions of Literary Response.* Ithaca: Cornell UP, 1970.

Steig, Michael. *Stories of Reading: Subjectivity and Literary Understanding.* Baltimore: Johns Hopkins UP, 1989.

Exemplary Short Readings of Major Texts

Anderson, Howard. "*Tristram Shandy* and the Reader's Imagination." *PMLA* 86 (1971): 966–73.

Berger, Carole. "The Rake and the Reader in Jane Austen's Novels." *Studies in English Literature, 1500–1900* 15 (1975): 531–44.

Booth, Stephen. "On the Value of *Hamlet.*" *Reinterpretations of English Drama: Selected Papers from the English Institute.* Ed. Norman Rabkin. New York: Columbia UP, 1969. 137–76.

Easson, Robert R. "William Blake and His Reader in *Jerusalem.*" *Blake's Sublime Allegory.* Ed. Stuart Curran and Joseph A. Wittreich. Madison: U of Wisconsin P, 1973. 309–28.

Kirk, Carey H. "*Moby-Dick:* The Challenge of Response." *Papers on Language and Literature* 13 (1977): 383–90.

Leverenz, David. "Mrs. Hawthorne's Headache: Reading *The Scarlet Letter*." *Nathaniel Hawthorne, "The Scarlet Letter."* Ed. Ross C Murfin. Case Studies in Contemporary Criticism. Boston: Bedford–St. Martin's, 1991. 263–74.

Lowe-Evans, Mary. "Reading with a 'Nicer Eye': Responding to *Frankenstein*." *Mary Shelley, "Frankenstein."* Ed. Johanna M. Smith. Case Studies in Contemporary Criticism. Boston: Bedford–St. Martin's, 1992. 215–29.

Rabinowitz, Peter J. "'A Symbol of Something': Interpretive Vertigo in 'The Dead.'" *James Joyce, "The Dead."* Ed. Daniel R. Schwarz. Case Studies in Contemporary Criticism. Boston: Bedford–St. Martin's, 1994. 137–49.

Treichler, Paula. "The Construction of Ambiguity in *The Awakening*." *Kate Chopin, "The Awakening."* Ed. Nancy A. Walker. Case Studies in Contemporary Criticism. Boston: Bedford–St. Martin's, 1993. 308–28.

Other Works Referred to in "What Is Reader-Response Criticism?"

Booth, Wayne C. *A Rhetoric of Irony*. Chicago: U of Chicago P, 1974.

Culler, Jonathan. *Structural Poetics: Structuralism, Linguistics, and the Study of Literature*. Ithaca: Cornell UP, 1975.

Koestenbaum, Wayne. "Wilde's Hard Labor and the Birth of Gay Reading." *Engendering Men: The Question of Male Feminist Criticism*. Ed. Joseph A. Boone and Michael Cadden. New York: Routledge, 1990.

Richards, I. A. *Practical Criticism*. New York: Harcourt, 1929. Rpt. in *Criticism: The Major Texts*. Ed. Walter Jackson Bate. Rev. ed. New York: Harcourt, 1970. 575.

Wimsatt, William K., and Monroe C. Beardsley. *The Verbal Icon*. Lexington: U of Kentucky P, 1954. See especially the discussion of "The Affective Fallacy," with which reader-response critics have so sharply disagreed.

Reader-Response Approaches to Joyce

Iser, Wolfgang. "Doing Things in Style: An Interpretation of 'The Oxen of the Sun' in James Joyce's *Ulysses*." *The Implied Reader: Patterns of Communication in Prose Fiction from Bunyan to Beckett*. Baltimore: Johns Hopkins UP, 1974.

James Joyce Quarterly 16 (Fall 1978/Winter 1979). "Structuralist/Reader-Response" issue.

Lawrence, Karen. *The Odyssey of Style in "Ulysses."* Princeton: Princeton UP, 1981.

Riquelme, John Paul. *Teller and Tale in Joyce's Fiction: Oscillating Perspectives.* Baltimore: Johns Hopkins UP, 1983.

Senn, Fritz. *Joyce's Dislocutions: Essays on Reading as Translation.* Ed. John Paul Riquelme. Baltimore: Johns Hopkins UP, 1984.

Thomas, Brook. *James Joyce's "Ulysses": A Book of Many Happy Returns.* Baton Rouge: Louisiana State UP, 1982.

A READER-RESPONSE PERSPECTIVE

WOLFGANG ISER

Patterns of Communication in Joyce's *Ulysses*

No Homeric figures actually appear in *Ulysses*, and yet the novel cannot be described as a realistic depiction of ordinary life in Dublin, despite the vast number of verifiable details that run right through it. We have since learned that a great deal of this material was drawn from Dublin address books, topographical descriptions, and the daily press of that time, so that an astonishing wealth of names, addresses, local events, and even newspaper cuttings can actually be identified (Adams), though in the text they frequently form a montage that is stripped of its context. Sometimes the details vanish away into the impenetrable private sphere of Joyce himself, and sometimes they seem to lead the reader into a veritable labyrinth when he/she attempts to collate them. In searching for and visualizing connections, he/she often loses the organizing principle of the connections thought to have been discovered. And frequently it seems as though the many details are simply there for their own sake and, through sheer weight of numbers, more or less deliberately blur the outline of events in the narrative.

The effect of all this is somewhat paradoxical, for it runs completely contrary to the expectations that the realistic novel had established in its readers. There, too, one was confronted with a wealth of details which the reader could see reflected in his/her own world of experience. Their appearance in the novel served mainly to authenticate the view of life offered (Jauss 161 f., 241 f.). But in *Ulysses* they are, to a great extent, deprived of this function. When details no longer serve to reinforce probability or to stabilize the illusion of reality, they must become a sort of end in themselves, such as one finds in the art-form of the collage. The unstructured material of *Ulysses* is taken directly *from* life itself, but since it no longer testifies to the author's preconception of reality, it cannot be taken *for* life itself. Thus the details illustrate nothing; they simply present themselves, and since they bear witness to nothing beyond themselves, they revoke the normal assumption that a novel represents a given reality. It is not surprising, then, that one is constantly returning to the title in order to try to create—through recourse to the *Odyssey*—some sort of frame of reference that will bring this chaos of detail under control and will endow everyday life with a pattern, with meaning, and with significance.

We now have a double frustration of our expectations: not only do the Homeric figures fail to appear in *Ulysses* but also the many details are deprived of their usual function. As a result, our attention is drawn to the evocative nature of the novel. We realize that all these details constitute a surplus that projects far beyond any organizational schema that the novel may offer us. And so each reading gives us a new chance to integrate the details in a different way—with the result, however, that each form of integration brings about a sort of kaleidoscopic reshuffling of the material excluded.

By giving his novel this structure—whether consciously or unconsciously—Joyce was complying with a basic disposition of the reader, described by Northrop Frye as follows: "Whenever we read anything, we find our attention moving in two directions at once. One direction is outward or centrifugal, in which we keep going outside our reading, from the individual words to the things they mean, or, in practice, to our memory of the conventional association between them. The other direction is inward or centripetal, in which we try to develop from the words a sense of the larger verbal pattern they make" (Frye, *Anatomy* 73). These two tendencies seem to take the reader of *Ulysses* in completely different directions, which are divergent rather than convergent. As he/she reads, he/she finds that everyday life in Dublin is, so to speak, continually breaking its banks, and the resultant flood of detail induces the reader to try and build his/her own dams of meaning—though these in turn are inevitably broken down. Even the signal contained in the title seems to dispel rather than fulfill one's hopes of controlling the material, for the central frame of reference that one would so like to deduce from the *Odyssey* is never formulated anywhere in the text. According to whether one reads the novel from the Dublin viewpoint or from that of the *Odyssey*, one will get quite different 'images.' In the first case, the apparent lack of connection between the many details creates the impression of a thoroughly chaotic world; in the second, one wonders what the return of Ulysses in modern trappings is supposed to signify. Both approaches are, in themselves, relatively flabby, and the task of stiffening them up, and indeed bringing them together, is what the novel sets its reader.

The Homeric allusions in *Ulysses* open up an horizon which is certainly not identical with that of the modern "World-Weekday" (Broch 187), for between the present and the archetypes of the Homeric epic lies the whole of history, which could only be passed over if *Ulysses* were concerned with nothing but the return of archetypes. One should not forget, when considering the Homeric parallel, that Joyce permeated his novel with just as many Shakespearean allusions as Homeric. And even if one tries to equate Shakespeare's presence in *Ulysses* with the return of archetypes, nevertheless there is no denying the fact that Joyce was obviously more interested in the various manifestations of such archetypes than in merely establishing their return. This certainly indicates that for him the archetype was, at most, a vehicle, but not a subject. The history of its manifestations takes precedence over its mythical nature. But what is this history, and in what form is it reflected in the novel?

Our answer to this question can, perhaps, best proceed from the experiments in style. These in themselves are an innovation, insofar as the eighteen chapters of the novel present the narrative through eighteen differently structured perspectives. Normally, when reading a novel, we are asked only once to adopt the author's chosen standpoint in order to fulfill his intentions—but here the same demand is made of us no less than seventeen extra times, for each chapter is written in a different style. Style, according to John Middleton Murry, "is a quality of language which communicates . . . a system of emotions or thoughts, peculiar to the author" (Murry 65). We can talk of style when systematic viewpoints bring about a frame of reference that is to direct the reader's observations by selecting which facts are or are not to be presented.

This function of style is both its strength and its weakness, for inevitably it must restrict the field of observation. The meaning that it is to express can only take its shape through the process of selecting particular aspects of phenomena to be presented, and so phenomena are reproduced mainly for the sake of what they will communicate to the reader. As style imposes a specific meaning and edits reality to coincide with this meaning, it reveals itself to be a "mythical analogue" (Lugowski 12), which—as Clemens Lugowski has shown—not only implies a particular conception of reality but is also the agent that actually forms it. Although this "'mythical artifice' . . . is the result of a deeply unconscious and indirect act of interpretation" (Lugowski 206), for this very reason it will freeze the historical conditions under which such acts of interpretation came into being.

In *Ulysses* Joyce shows up these limitations by thematizing the capacity of style itself. In constantly changing the perspective through the eighteen chapters, he draws attention to the normative pressure caused by the modes of observation inherent in any one style, thus revealing the extreme one-sidedness of each individual "act of interpretation." While the change of styles shows up these limitations, the process is underlined in the individual chapters by the surplus of non-integrated, unstructured material. This, too, makes one aware of the limitations of the style in question, so that it often seems more real than the view of reality being presented at the time.

Thus we have changes of style and nonintegrated material to show up the limitations of each style, and in addition to these two factors, there is even a kind of authorial commentary (Goldberg 288) which has these very limitations as its subject. This is the case in "The Oxen of the Sun," which Joyce critics have always approached with a kind of embarrassment (Iser 179–95). T. S. Eliot had the impression that this chapter showed the "futility of all the English styles" (Ellmann 490), and this must certainly have been at least one of the effects that Joyce was aiming at.

In this display of individual and period styles, we are made aware of the various assumptions that condition the different presentations of the theme. By parodying the styles, Joyce makes sure that we do not overlook the 'interpretive' nature of the forms of presentation. Leopold Bloom finds himself transformed into a variety of figures, in accordance with the particular style used: the medieval "traveller Leopold" changes into the Arthurian knight "Sir Leopold," who in turn leaps into a new context as "childe Leopold" (pp. 369–70). The reader cannot help being aware of the one-sidedness of all these characterizations, as he/she has already become familiar in the preceding chapters with the many-sidedness of Bloom's character. This same one-sidedness is equally evident in the central theme of the chapter. This does not deal with love, but only with the way in which Malory, Bunyan, Addison and the other writers conceived of love. The basically comic effect arises out of the impression one has that the views, expressed in such a variety of styles, exclude rather than supplement one another. With each author the main theme takes on a different shape, but as each style automatically and unquestioningly assumes that it has captured the reality of the phenomenon, the latent naiveté comes to the surface. The question arises as to which of these individual views comes closest to the truth, but even then we realize that the individual authors, precisely through their selection of a particular means of presentation, have in fact edited the subject to form a single meaning and a single evaluation. The very fact that these meanings and evaluations seem to assume a normative validity makes us aware of the extent to which they depend on the historical situation from which they have sprung. If "The Oxen of the Sun" is taken, then, as the author's own 'commentary' on his work, one can scarcely expect him to organize his novel as yet another "act of interpretation." It is the *presentation* of everyday life that concerns him, and not the evaluation.

However, such a presentation also requires a form, and inevitably any form that Joyce chose would automatically foreshorten the phenomenon to be presented. And so one might assume that the chapters of the novel were organized, each as a sort of rebuttal to the others, with their respective *principium stilisationis*. The consequences of this principle of construction are very far-reaching. Joyce could parody the different styles in order to show the limitations of their capacity, but if he applied this technique to the whole novel, it would mean that in trying to present the events, etc., of June 16, 1904, he would have to parody himself continually. There are certainly traces of this in the text, but a constant self-parody would ultimately distract the reader from coming to grips with the events of June 16, 1904. And would this not in turn—like all parodies—lead primarily to a negative evaluation, as limited in its own way as the evaluations of the authors parodied? Such a form would itself constitute an "act of interpretation."

Is it possible for anything to be presented, and yet at the same time for the "act of interpretation" to be suspended without the object of presentation becoming incomprehensible? *Ulysses* is the answer to this question. In order to moderate, if not actually neutralize, the interpretive nature of style, Joyce called upon virtually every stylistic mode that the novel had evolved during its comparatively short history. These he enriched with the whole armory of allusions and with the recall of archetypes. The multiplicity of these schemata, together with the complexity of their interrelationships, results in a form of presentation that in fact presents each incipient meaning simultaneously with its own diffusion. Thus the novel does not paint a picture of the "World-Weekday"—which means, ultimately, that it does not 'present' anything in the conventional sense—but, through the great variety of its perspectives, it offers possibilities for conceiving or imagining the "World-Weekday." These possibilities must be fulfilled by the readers themselves, if they want to make contact with the reality of the novel. One must therefore differentiate between 'presentation' (that is, by the author) and 'imagination' (on the part of the reader). Of course, even if the 'interpretive acts' of the novel are obvious, the readers still have to imagine things for themselves. But they will only conduct these 'interpretive acts' if the system of presentation leaves out the coordinating elements between observable phenomena and situations. In *Ulysses* this is brought about mainly through the overprecision of the system, which presents more conceivable material than the reader is capable of processing as he/she reads. And so it is not the style of the novel but the overtaxed readers themselves that reduce the amount of observable material to manageable proportions. In doing so, they can scarcely avoid equating this reduced amount with the meaning. If one considers reactions to *Ulysses* over the last forty years—insofar as these can be gauged by the different interpretations offered—one can see how historically conditioned such meanings are. At the same time, it cannot be denied that the many possible permutations of meaning in *Ulysses* act as a constant inducement to the reader to formulate a meaning—and in doing so, he/she is forced to enter into the action of the novel.

The individual chapters of *Ulysses* act, to a greater or lesser degree, as signposts that point the way through the "World-Weekday," rather than guidebooks that impose on the reader a specific interpretation of the regions they represent. If we want to get a proper understanding of the function of the patterns of presentation, the allusions, and also the archetypes, it might be as well first to examine one or two concrete examples.

The novel begins with the parody of a church ritual. Mulligan, the medical student, holds his shaving-bowl aloft at the top of the Martello tower, and intones: *Introibo ad altare Dei* (1). If this little curtain-raiser is a sign of what is to come, then we appear to be due for one long parody. At first this impression seems to be confirmed by the subsequent conversation between Mulligan and Stephen, for as he talks the former jumps around abruptly from one stylistic level to another, everyday slang alternating with scholarly allusions to Greece, Irish mythology, and even Zarathustra (5, 9, 20). Indeed individual allusions are sometimes broken up and even corrupted. Are we now to have a series of parodied stylistic levels? If so, there would be a danger of the tension soon flagging, for a parody of stylistic levels here might seem trivial after the initial 'exposing' of the mass. Moreover, it is scarcely possible to find a *tertium comparationis* for the various intersecting levels of Mulligan's speech.

It is also impossible to establish a purpose for such a parody, unless one wanted to conclude from the diffusion of stylistic levels that Joyce was advocating a purist use of language—an idea that is hardly worth considering. In fact, one gets the impression that what is stated is nothing but a stimulus to call forth its own reversal. Thus the profane distortions of the ritual of the mass take on a significance other than that of mere parody. Like the subsequent conversation, they point up the limitations of all clearly formulated statements that induce the reader to supply his/her own connections between the segmented stylistic levels. As the text offers no point of convergence for the phenomena it sets before him, the reader tends to load each detail with meaning, and since the meaning cannot be fully realized, there arises a latent tension between the unconnected phenomena. This basic pattern, with a few variations, runs right through the first chapter, which Joyce called "Telemachus" in his 'notesheets' (Litz 39). The most important type of variation is the abrupt switch of narrator. In the middle of a third-person narrative we are suddenly confronted with statements in the first person (7–8), which strike the reader so forcibly that he/she soon becomes more conscious of narrative patterns than of things narrated. And so here, as elsewhere in the novel, one gets the impression that one must constantly differentiate between the linguistic possibilities of style and the possible nature of the phenomena concerned.

The predominant pattern of reversal in this first chapter reduces all that is clear and concrete to a mere position in life, but life itself goes far beyond such positions. The next chapter, originally called "Nestor," reveals the implications of this fact, and naturally another collection of stylistic patterns is necessary to uncover these hidden consequences. Stephen's interior monologue is the dominant pattern in this chapter, but it is broken up by authorial passages, direct speech, and also quotations from Milton's *Lycidas* (22–23), all set against and arising out of the background of the morning lesson. They lead to reflections on history and man's possible place in history:

> For them too history was a tale like any other too often heard, their land a pawnshop.
>   Had Pyrrhus not fallen by a beldam's hand in Argos or Julius Caesar not been knifed to death? They are not to be thought away. Time has branded them and fettered they are lodged in the room of the infinite possibilities they have ousted. But can those have been possible seeing that they never were? Or was that only possible which came to pass? Weave, weaver of the wind . . . It must be a movement then, an actuality of the possible as possible. (22–23)

It is not insignificant that this reflection on the possible is inspired specifically by historical processes in which everything appears to be so irrevocably fixed. Is this determinacy ultimately to be seen as one possibility among many? What about the existences of historical individuals? If, through their deeds and sufferings, they stepped outside the jurisdiction of infinite possibilities, why should they now fall back into it? It seems almost like a sophism when Stephen asks whether Pyrrhus and Caesar even considered the possibility, when they were alive, that one day they would not be there, or that they would end as they did. Although he himself considers such thoughts to be mere speculations, they do not stop him from concluding that real life can only be understood as an actuality of one possibility among many. But if what happened did not happen inevitably, then the real is nothing but a chance track left by the possible. And if reality is nothing but one chance track, then it pales to insignificance beside the vast number of unseen and unfulfilled possibilities; it shrinks to the dimensions of a mere curiosity. The tendency apparent in these reflections of Stephen's runs parallel to that at the beginning of the novel, where whatever was said pointed the way to its own reversal, and whatever possibilities were excluded by each utterance were brought out by another.

The children are bored by the history lesson, and want Stephen to tell them a story: "Tell us a story, sir. — Oh, do, sir. A ghoststory" (22). Stephen himself has just had the impression that, when one thinks

about it, history changes into a ghost story, albeit a different type from
the one the children would like to hear. Bored by the factual, they
are now asking for the fantastic, without realizing how much incom-
prehensibility lies in the factual. The text, of course, does not state
this, but the manner in which the different perspectives are thrust
against one another compels the reader to search for a link between
them. The text offers him/her no guide as to how the different standpoints might be evaluated, and at best he/she can only orient himself/
herself through the next perspective which, like that of the children,
is inserted into Stephen's monologue. There is no "ghoststory"; instead, the children begin to read verses from Milton's *Lycidas*—those
lines where the mourning shepherd is consoled with the assurance that
the dead do not perish. Evidently only poetry eternalizes; but poetry
is fiction.

In this comparatively short section of the text, there are three
different intersecting patterns: interior monologue, direct speech, and
literary quotations—all focused upon a relatively uniform theme
which, however, takes on three different forms as it is presented to
the reader. For Stephen reality is so overshadowed by the possible that
it is deprived of its unique significance. The children are bored by what
has been and want the titillation of the unreal. The literary quotation
shows how clearly that eternalization only exists in the medium of
fiction. The text does not say how these three viewpoints are to be
joined together, but simply offers three different possibilities for relating the real to the unreal. As the individual stylistic patterns intersect
within the text, there is no hierarchic construction. The reflections
of the inner monologue point inevitably to the private nature of the
opinion expressed; the desires of the school children appear as something spontaneous and naive and the quotation as a kind of insurance
without any reality. Although this need not be regarded as the only
possible interpretation of the different patterns of the text, the conditions are certainly there for such an interpretation. Since these patterns
are without a point of convergence, their meaning arises out of their
interaction—a process which is set in motion by the readers themselves and which will therefore involve them personally in the text.

Apart from the patterns we have mentioned, this process is encour-
aged above all by the end of the chapter, which deals with a conversation between Stephen and the headmaster, Mr. Deasy. The headmaster gives Stephen a letter which he wants published in the *Evening
Telegraph*, because it contains his (Deasy's) solution to an important

problem: foot-and-mouth disease. "I have put the matter into a nut-shell, Mr Deasy said. It's about the foot and mouth disease. Just look through it. There can be no two opinions on the matter" (30).

For Mr. Deasy, there can be no two opinions about this or about a number of other political problems in Ireland. But now the segmented text pattern of Stephen's history lesson becomes the background to Mr. Deasy's unequivocal utterances, through which he seeks once and for all to set right existing realities. Again the text says nothing about any relationship between these two passages, but the reader will soon find a relatively straightforward way to bridge this gap. Viewed against the background of infinite possibilities, Mr. Deasy's self-confidence appears absurdly narrow-minded, and so the reader will most likely come to two conclusions: first, that Mr. Deasy is a pompous ass; second, and far more important, that any claim to knowledge is an automatic reduction of the infinite and discounts above all the changeability of phenomena. However, let it be empha-sized once again—this interpretation will be the reader's, for there is no such statement in the text itself.

As regards the original chapter heading—"Nestor"—this offers yet another perspective, insofar as the reader will try to link the wis-dom of Nestor with the pretension of Mr. Deasy. He/she will proba-bly find that not only does Mr. Deasy suffer from the comparison, but so, too, does Nestor. For if, in Mr. Deasy's case, claims to knowledge presuppose unawareness of the changeability of phenomena, then the mythical wisdom of Nestor is open to re-evaluation by the reader.

As it would be beyond the scope of this essay to deal with all the experiments of style in *Ulysses*, we shall confine ourselves to those that evince the most striking variations. One of these is undoubtedly the "Aeolus" chapter. Bloom's visit to the newspaper office provides the framework for a curiously patterned form of narration. Analysis reveals two separate levels of the text, which one might call, for the sake of convenience, the micro- and the macrostructure of the chapter. The microstructural level consists of a large number of allusions which basically can be divided into three different groups: (1) those dealing with the immediate situation, Bloom's effort to place an advertisement at the newspaper office and the events connected with it; (2) those referring to completely different episodes outside the chapter itself, sometimes relating to incidents already described and sometimes anticipating things; (3) those passages which seem to slide into obscurity when one tries to work out exactly where they might be heading. However, as these allusions are not only distinctly separated, but are in fact woven into an intricate pattern, each one of them tends to entice the reader to follow it. Thus the allusions themselves turn into microperspectives which, because of their very density, simply cannot be followed through to the end. They form abbreviated extracts from reality which inevitably compel the reader to a process of selection.

This is also true of the other stylistic pattern to be discerned within the microstructural stratum. Just as with the allusions, there is throughout an abrupt alternation between dialogue, direct and indirect speech, authorial report, first-person narrative, and interior monologue. Although such techniques do impose a certain order on the abundance of allusions, they also invest them with differing importance. An allusion by the author himself certainly has a function for the context different from one that is made in indirect speech by one of the characters. Thus extracts from reality and individual events are not contracted merely into allusions, but, through the different patterns of style, emerge in forms that endow them with a varied range of relevance. At the same time, the unconnected allusions and the abrupt alternation of stylistic devices disclose a large number of gaps.

All this gives rise to the stimulating quality of the text. On the one hand, the density of allusions and the continual segmentation of style involve an incessant changing of perspectives, which seem to go out of control whenever the reader tries to pin them down; on the other hand, the gaps resulting from cuts and abbreviations tempt the reader to fill them in. He/she will try to group things, because this is the only way in which he/she can recognize situations or understand characters in the novel.

The macrostructure of the chapter lends itself to this need for 'grouping,' though in a peculiar way. Heading and 'newspaper column' form the schema that incorporates the allusions and stylistic changes. The heading is an instruction as to what to expect. But the text which follows the caption reveals the composition described above, and so in most cases does not fulfill the expectation raised by the heading. As the newspaper headlines refer to various incidents in the city, the situation of Ireland, and so forth, they would seem to be concerned with everyday events, the reality of which is beyond question. But the column that follows frustrates this expectation, not only by leading commonplace realities off in unforeseeable directions, thus destroying the grouping effect of the headline, but also by fragmenting facts and occurrences in such a way that to comprehend the commonplace becomes a real effort. While the heading appears to gratify our basic need for grouping, this need is predominantly subverted by the text that follows.

In the "Aeolus" chapter, the reader not only learns something about events in Dublin on June 16, 1904, but he also experiences the difficulties inherent in the comprehension of the barest outline of events. It is precisely because the heading suggests a way of grouping from a particular viewpoint that the text itself seems so thoroughly to contradict our familiar notions of perception. The text appears to defy transcription of the circumstances indicated and instead offers the reader nothing but attitudes or possibilities of perception concerning these circumstances.

Sometimes it does, however, occur in this chapter that the expectations aroused by the headings are fulfilled. At such moments, the text seems banal, for when the reader has adjusted himself to the nonfulfillment of his expectations, he will view things differently when they *are* fulfilled. The reason for this is easy to grasp. If the text of the column does not connect up with the heading, the readers must supply the missing links. Their participation in the intention of the text is thus enhanced. If the text does fulfill the expectations aroused by the heading, no removing of gaps is required of the reader and he/she feels the 'letdown' of banality. In this way, the textual pattern in this chapter arouses continual conflicts with the reader's own modes of perception, and as the author has completely withdrawn from this montage of possibilities, the reader is given no guidance as to how to resolve the conflicts. But it is through these very conflicts, and the confrontation with the array of different possibilities, that the reader of such a text is given the impression that something does happen to him/her.

It is perhaps not by chance that in this chapter the Homeric parallel has shrunk to the barest recollection, for the basic schema of composition is determined not by the scattering of news to all winds, but by the manner in which this scattered news is received. Joyce makes his theme out of what did not concern Homer, and this also reveals something of the strategy of literary allusions that Joyce used in *Ulysses*.

Of a quite different sort is the stylistic experiment in the chapter originally called "Ithaca," which is of particular interest since it deals with the theme of homecoming. This archetypal situation is presented

here as an uninterrupted sequence of questions and answers involving
the main characters. To all appearances this interrogation is conducted
by an anonymous narrator, who more or less asks himself what Bloom
and Stephen think, do, feel, intend, communicate, mean, etc., and
then proceeds himself to give answers that are as wide-ranging as they
are detailed. But what exactly is the purpose of this inquiry, and why
should the narrator be asking all the questions, since he appears to
know all the answers anyway?

The effect of the mode of presentation in this chapter is that it
seems constantly to place a barrier between the reader and the events
of Bloom's nocturnal homecoming that are to be narrated; instead
of describing these events, it appears to be continually interrupting
them. In this way, the characters in the novel seem to fade into the
distance — especially since each question is assigned an answer which
is so loaded with precise detail that the reader's comprehension is in
danger of being utterly swamped. This tends to divert the reader's
attention away from the events and onto the curious nature of this
question-and-answer process. For, obviously, the intention of the
chapter must lie in this and not in the details of the nocturnal events.
But if the mode of presentation sets aside rather than describes the
events, and obtrudes on the reader instead of orienting him/her, then
the only justification for this 'going against the grain' must be that it
exposes something which generally would be obscured by the mode
of presentation.

Let us consider an example. When Bloom comes home, he puts
some water on the stove because he wants to have a shave. The
question-and-answer process now concerns the boiling of the water:

> What concomitant phenomenon took place in the vessel of liq-
> uid by the agency of fire?
> The phenomenon of ebullition. Fanned by a constant
> updraught of ventilation between the kitchen and the chimney-
> flue, ignition was communicated from the faggots of precom-
> bustible fuel to polyhedral masses of bituminous coal, containing
> in compressed mineral form the foliated fossilised decidua of
> primeval forests which had in turn derived their vegetative exis-
> tence from the sun, primal source of heat (radiant), transmitted
> through omnipresent luminiferous diathermanous ether. Heat
> (convected), a mode of motion developed by such combustion,
> was constantly and increasingly conveyed from the source of
> calorification to the liquid contained in the vessel, being radiated
> through the uneven unpolished dark surface of the metal iron, in

part reflected, in part absorbed, in part transmitted, gradually rais-
ing the temperature of the water from normal to boiling point, a
rise in temperature expressible as the result of an expenditure of
72 thermal units needed to raise 1 pound of water from 50° to
212° Fahrenheit. (634)

The amount of scientific data—in this chapter a typical feature which
becomes even more complicated elsewhere—shows how difficult it is
to give the required reason for the phenomenon in question.

An impression akin to fantasy is evoked by the chain of cause and
effect which, instead of going straight back to the primal cause, seems
only to bring out more and more dependent factors. The more precise
the description of these factors, the further into the distance recedes
the primal cause and the more aware we become of the unexplainabil-
ity of what is to be explained. As the narrator asks more and more
questions, the answers demonstrate not his knowledge so much as the
unobtainability of the right answers—and this is emphasized by the
very preciseness of what *is* known. Thus the tendency underlying this
question-and-answer process is one that aims at showing the degree of
indeterminability inherent in all phenomena. It is scarcely surprising
then that new questions are constantly thrown up which are meant to
limit the amount of indeterminacy, but instead—thanks to their very
precision—in fact increase it.

The question-and-answer process makes us aware that the degree of indeterminacy is irreducible, thus indicating that all the semiconsistent conceptions we have of everyday phenomena can only become conceptions because they ignore the inexplicability of reality.
They are, in this sense, a fiction.

Now if indeterminacy is only to be removed by means of fiction,
the reader finds the ground cut away from beneath his/her feet whenever he/she realizes this. The "Ithaca" chapter keeps maneuvering
him/her into a position from which he/she can escape only by taking
up a definite attitude. He/she might decide that the chain of ironic
answers forms a parody of scientific pedantry. But, as Northrop Frye
states in another context, the ironic solution is: "the negative pole of
the allegorical one. Irony presents a human conflict which . . . is unsat-
isfactory and incomplete unless we see in it a significance beyond itself . . . What that significance is, irony does not say: it leaves that question up to the reader or audience" (Frye, "Road" 14). This is the sort of
irony we find in the "Ithaca" chapter, which uses its ironic elements to
give the reader responsibility for finding his/her own solution. This, of

course, involves interpreting, and in order to ensure that interpretation be kept in its proper perspective, certain warning signals are built into the text. To the question: "What qualifying considerations allayed his [that is, Bloom's] perturbations?" comes the answer: "The difficulties of interpretation since the significance of any event followed its occurrence as variably as the acoustic report followed the electrical discharge and of counterestimating against an actual loss by failure to interpret the total sum of possible losses proceeding originally from a successful interpretation" (637).

The main problem of interpretation, then, lies in the fact that the meaning of any one event is incalculably variable. The image of electrical discharge, which disperses its sound waves in all directions, shows that every event, as soon as it happens, sets up a whole spectrum of meanings. If we try to extract one of these meanings and pass it off as *the* meaning of the event, then automatically we are shutting out all other meanings.

Normally we understand by a successful interpretation one that conveys a specific meaning. But according to the answer given here, an interpretation can only be successful if it takes into account the "possible losses" caused by interpretation — in other words, if it succeeds in returning to the phenomenon interpreted its whole spectrum of possible meanings. And this, as the answer makes clear, is difficult.

Meanings have a heuristic character which, particularly in these scientifically couched answers, bring out the many-sidedness of the phenomena described. In such a description, the phenomena will appear all the richer in meaning if no one meaning dominates. In the "Ithaca" chapter, aspects are not static but seem to be moving, offering an infinitely wider range of perspectives than could be offered if the author were merely to present the readers with their own classified interpretation of the phenomenon. And however confused the readers may feel through this bewildering multiplicity, at least they now have the chance of experiencing for themselves something of the essential character of the phenomena. The heightened indeterminacy enables them to view so many different aspects from so many different standpoints, and from the interaction of these aspects and perspectives they themselves continually and dynamically formulate the meaning. In this way it is possible for the readers to experience the phenomenon more as itself than as the expression of something else.

Joyce called this chapter "Ithaca." But what sort of homecoming is this? For Ulysses it meant the end of his adventurous journey, with all its attendant dangers and sufferings, and also his reckoning with the suitors; but for Bloom the homecoming passes with innumerable trivial acts and a fantastic, if impotent, condemnation of all Molly's lovers. No one is excepted from this universal anathema; it applies ultimately to marriage as an institution and even to Bloom himself. "What then remains after this holocaust? Only himself with his desires—not as husband or householder but as Leopold Bloom, an Einziger with no Eigentum" (Budgen 261). Yet again, then, we have in the Homeric allusion a parallel which, if anything, runs in the opposite direction from the original, showing up the individuality of Bloom against the background of what the reader might expect from the archetypal homecoming.

The implication of a novel written in several different styles is that the view expressed by each style is to be taken only as one possible facet of everyday reality. The accumulation of facts has the effect of making these seem like a mere suggestion to the reader as to how he/she might observe reality. The perspectives provided by the various chapters of the novel abruptly join up, overlap, are segmented, even clash, and through their very density they begin to overtax the reader's vision. The density of the presentational screen, the confusing montage and its interplay of perspectives, the invitation to the reader to look at identical incidents from many conflicting points of view—all this makes it extremely difficult for the reader to find his/her way. The novel refuses to divulge any way of connecting up this interplay of perspectives, and so the reader is forced to provide his/her own liaison. This has the inevitable consequence that reading becomes a process of selection, with the reader's own imagination providing the criteria for the selection. For the text of *Ulysses* only offers the conditions that make it possible to conceive of this everyday world—conditions which each reader will exploit in his/her own way.

What does the achievement of the various modes of presentation consist of? First, one can say that they bring to bear a form of observation which underlies the very structure of perception. For we "have the experience of a world, not understood as a system of relations which wholly determine each event, but as an open totality the synthesis of which is inexhaustible . . . From the moment that experience—that is, the opening on to our *de facto* world—is recognized as the beginning of knowledge, there is no longer any way of distinguishing a level of *a priori* truths and one of factual ones, what the world must necessarily be and what it actually is" (Merleau-Ponty 219, 221). Through their countless offshoots, the different styles of *Ulysses* preclude any meaning directed toward integration, but they also fall into a pattern of observation that contains within itself the possibility of a continual extension. It is the very abundance of perspectives that conveys the abundance of the world under observation.

The effect of this continual change is dynamic, unbounded as it is by any recognizable teleology. From one chapter to the next the 'horizon' of everyday life is altered and constantly shifted from one area to another through the links which the reader tries to establish between the chapter styles. Each chapter prepares the 'horizon' for the next, and it is the process of reading that provides the continual overlapping and interweaving of the views presented by each of the chapters. The reader is stimulated into filling the 'empty spaces' between the chapters in order to group them as a coherent whole. This process, however, has the following results: The conceptions of everyday life which the reader forms undergo constant modifications in the reading process. Each chapter provides a certain amount of expectation concerning the next chapter. However, the gaps of indeterminacy which open up between the chapters tend to diminish the importance of these expectations as a means of orientating the reader. As the process continues, a 'feedback' effect is bound to develop, arising from the new chapter and reacting back upon the preceding, which under this new and somewhat unexpected impression is subjected to modifications in the reader's mind. The more frequently the reader experiences this effect, the more cautious and the more differentiated will be his/her expectations, as they arise through his/her realization of the text. Thus what has just been read modifies what had been read before, so that the readers themselves operate the 'fusion of horizons,' with the result that they produce an experience of reality which is real precisely because it happens, without being subjected to any representational function. Reality, then, is a process of realization necessitating the reader's involvement, because only the reader can bring it about. This is why the chapters are not arranged in any sequence of situations that might be complementary to one another; in fact, the unforeseen difference of style rather seems to make each chapter into a turning-point as opposed to a continuation. And as the whole novel consists of such turning-points the process of reading unfolds itself as a continual modification of all previous conceptions, thus inverting the traditional teleological structure of the novel.

Edmund Wilson has summed up both the reader's impression and the structure of the novel as follows: "I doubt whether any human memory is capable, on a first reading, of meeting the demands of 'Ulysses.' And when we reread it, we start in at any point, as if it were indeed something solid like a city which actually existed in space and which could be entered from any direction" (Wilson 210). The reader is virtually free to choose his/her own direction, but he/she will not be able to work his/her way through every possible perspective, for the number of these is far beyond the capacity of any one reader's naturally selective perception. If the novel sometimes gives the impression of unreality, this is not because it presents unreality, but simply because it swamps us with aspects of reality that overburden our limited powers of absorption. We are forced to make our own selections from the perspectives offered and, consequently, in accordance with our own personal disposition, to formulate ideas that have their roots in *some* of the signs and situations confronting us.

This form of reading is predetermined by the novel itself, with its network of superimposed patterns that evoke constantly changing 'pictures' of everyday life. Each reading is a starting-point for the composition of such 'pictures', and indeed the whole process of reading *Ulysses* is a kind of composition. (The same, it is true, can be said of all reading, but in the case of this novel, the demands made on the reader's creativity are far greater than normal.) No one picture is representative, and one cannot even say that any one pattern is in itself determinate or determinant, for the different sections of the text only go so far as to offer signs that can be grouped together to form a context. The patterns are, as it were, transitory units which are necessary if everyday life is to be experienced, but are in no way binding as to the nature of experience.

Each 'picture' composed out of each pattern represents one possible meaning of the text concerned, but the reader will not be content to accept each 'picture' as an end in itself. He/she will search for a 'complete picture' of everyday life, and this is precisely what the novel withholds from him/her. The patterns offer him/her nothing but the conditions for and variations of the presentability of everyday life. There is no overriding tendency, and the mass of details presents itself to the reader to organize in accordance with his/her own acts of comprehension. This, in turn, demands a heightened degree of participation on the reader's part. The novel thus places itself in the category of "cool media" (McLuhan 22–23), as McLuhan called those texts and other media which, through their indeterminacy, allow and even demand a high degree of participation. Herein lies the main difference between *Ulysses* and the tradition of the novel. Instead of providing an illusory coherence of the reality it presents, this novel offers only a potential presentation, the working out of which has to be done actively by the reader. Thus it is possible to discover many different 'pictures' of the everyday world, but they will never converge into a defined picture—and it is this very fact that compels the reader to continue his/her search. Even though he/she will never find the object of his/her search, on his/her way he/she will meet with a vast array of possible conceptions, through which the reality of everyday life will come alive in a corresponding number of ways. As these conceptions are not joined together, every picture remains representative of no more than one aspect of reality. The reading process unfolds as a "categorical aspection" (Aldrich 21–24), in the sense that the aspects of reality that group together into a 'picture' are continually merging and diverging, so that the readers can experience that reality as they go along, but being thus entangled in it they can never hope to encompass it all.

The readers, however, will still be continually tempted to try to establish some consistency in all the signs, patterns, fragments, etc. But whenever we establish consistency, "illusion takes over" (Gombrich 278). "Illusion is whatever is fixed or definable, and reality is best understood as its negation: whatever reality is, it's not *that*" (Frye, *Anatomy* 169–70). The truth of this statement becomes apparent as one reads *Ulysses*. At first the inconsistency of the stylistic patterns and structures impels the reader to formulate illusions, because only by joining things can he/she comprehend an unfamiliar experience. But even while he/she is in the process of linking things up, he/she is bringing into being all the other possibilities of the text that defy integration; and these in turn proceed to overshadow the consistency he/she had begun to establish, so that in the process of illusion-forming the reader also creates the latent destruction of those very illusions. He/she will begin to distrust the convenient patterns he/she has been building and will eventually himself/herself perceive that they are nothing but the instruments he/she uses to grasp and pare down the mass of detail. Now the very fact that it is he/she who produces and destroys the illusions makes it impossible for him/her to stand aside and view 'reality' from a distance—the only reality for him/her to view is the one he/she is creating. He/she is involved in it, in precisely the same way that he/she gets involved in 'real life' situations. Thus for many Joyce readers, 'interpretation' is a form of refuge-seeking—an effort to reclaim the ground which has been cut from under their feet. Perhaps Bloom's attempts to instruct his wife contain the most succinct summary of Joyce's whole method:

> With what success had he attempted direct instruction? She followed not all, a part of the whole, gave attention with interest, comprehended with surprise, with care repeated, with greater difficulty remembered, forgot with ease, with misgiving reremembered, rerepeated with error. What system had proved more effective? Indirect suggestion implicating selfinterest. (647–48)

WORKS CITED

Adams, Robert Martin. *Surface and Symbol: The Consistency of James Joyce's "Ulysses."* New York: Oxford UP, 1962.

Aldrich, Virgil C. *Philosophy of Art.* Englewood Cliffs: Prentice, 1963.

Broch, H. *Dichten und Erkennen.* Zurich: Rhein-Verlag, 1955.

Budgen, Frank. *James Joyce and the Making of "Ulysses."* Bloomington: Indiana UP, 1960.

Ellmann, Richard. *James Joyce.* Oxford: Oxford UP, 1966.

Frye, Northrop. *Anatomy of Criticism: Four Essays.* New York: Atheneum, 1967.

———. "The Road of Excess." *Myth and Symbol: Critical Approaches and Applications.* Ed. Bernice Slote. Lincoln: U of Nebraska P, 1964.

Goldberg, S. L. *The Classical Temper: A Study of James Joyce's "Ulysses."* London: Chatto, 1961.

Gombrich, E. H. *Art and Illusion: A Study in the Psychology of Pictorial Representation.* London: Phaidon, 1962.

Iser, Wolfgang. *The Implied Reader: Patterns of Communication from Bunyan to Beckett.* Baltimore: Johns Hopkins UP, 1974.

Jauss, Hans Robert. "Nachahmungsprinzip und Wirklichkeitsbegriff in der Theorie des Romans von Diderot bis Stendhal." *Nachahmung und Illusion: Poetik und Hermeneutik I.* Ed. Hans Robert Jauss. Munich: Fink, 1964.

Joyce, James. *Ulysses.* London: Bodley Head, 1937.

Litz, A. Walton. *The Art of James Joyce: Method and Design in "Ulysses" and "Finnegans Wake."* London: Oxford UP, 1961.

Lugowski, Clemens. *Die Form der Individualität im Roman.* Berlin: Dunker, 1932.

McLuhan, Marshall. *Understanding Media: The Extensions of Man.* New York: McGraw, 1966.

Merleau-Ponty, Maurice. *Phenomenology of Perception.* Trans. Colin Smith. New York: Humanitas, 1962.

Murry, John Middleton. *The Problem of Style.* London: Oxford UP, 1960.

Wilson, Edmund. *Axel's Castle: A Study in the Imaginative Literature of 1870–1930.* New York: Scribner's, 1969.

Feminist and Gender Criticism and *Ulysses*

WHAT ARE FEMINIST AND GENDER CRITICISM?

Among the most exciting and influential developments in the field of literary studies, feminist and gender criticism participate in a broad philosophical discourse that extends far beyond literature, far beyond the arts in general. The critical *practices* of those who explore the representation of women and men in works by male or female, lesbian or gay writers inevitably grow out of and contribute to a larger and more generally applicable *theoretical* discussion of how gender and sexuality are constantly shaped by and shaping institutional structures and attitudes, artifacts and behaviors.

Feminist criticism was accorded academic legitimacy in American universities "around 1981," Jane Gallop claims in her book *Around 1981: Academic Feminist Literary Theory* (1992). With Gallop's title and approximation in mind, Naomi Schor has since estimated that "around 1985, feminism began to give way to what has come to be called gender studies" (275). Some would argue that feminist criticism became academically legitimate well before 1981. Others would take issue with the notion that feminist criticism and women's studies have been giving way to gender criticism and gender studies, and with the either/or distinction that such a claim implies. Taken together, however, Gallop and Schor provide us with a useful fact—that of feminist criticism's historical precedence—and a chronological focus on the early to mid-1980s, a period during which the feminist approach was unquestionably influential and during which new interests emerged, not all of which were woman centered.

During the early 1980s, three discrete strains of feminist theory and practice—commonly categorized as French, North American, and British—seemed to be developing. French feminists tended to focus their attention on language. Drawing on the ideas of the psychoanalytic philosopher Jacques Lacan, they argued that language as we commonly think of it—as public discourse—is decidedly phallocentric, privileging what is valued by the patriarchal culture. They also spoke of the possibility of an alternative, feminine language and of *l'écriture féminine:* women's writing. Julia Kristeva, who is generally seen as a pioneer of French feminist thought even though she dislikes the feminist label, suggested that feminine language is associated with the maternal and derived from the pre-oedipal fusion between mother and child. Like Kristeva, Hélène Cixous and Luce Irigaray associated feminine writing with the female body. Both drew an analogy between women's writing and women's sexual pleasure, Irigaray arguing that just as a woman's *"jouissance"* is more diffuse and complex than a man's unitary phallic pleasure ("woman has sex organs just about everywhere"), so "feminine" language is more diffuse and less obviously coherent than its "masculine" counterpart (*This Sex* 101–03).

Kristeva, who helped develop the concept of *l'écriture féminine,* nonetheless urged caution in its use and advocacy. Feminine or feminist writing that resists or refuses participation in "masculine" discourse, she warned, risks political marginalization, relegation to the outskirts (pun intended) of what is considered socially and politically significant. Kristeva's concerns were not unfounded: the concept of *l'écriture féminine* did prove controversial, eliciting different kinds of criticism from different kinds of feminist and gender critics. To some, the concept appears to give writing a biological basis, thereby suggesting that there is an *essential* femininity, and/or that women are *essentially* different from men. To others, it seems to suggest that men can write as women, so long as they abdicate authority, sense, and logic in favor of diffusiveness, playfulness, even nonsense.

While French feminists of the 1970s and early 1980s focused on language and writing from a psychoanalytic perspective, North American critics generally practiced a different sort of criticism. Characterized by close textual reading and historical scholarship, it generally took one of two forms. Critics like Kate Millett, Carolyn Heilbrun, and Judith Fetterley developed what Elaine Showalter called the "feminist critique" of "male constructed literary history" by closely examining canonical works by male writers, exposing the patriarchal ideology implicit in such works and arguing that traditions of systematic masculine dominance are indelibly inscribed in our literary tradition. Fetterley urged women to become "resisting readers"—to notice how biased most of the classic texts by male authors are in their language, subjects, and attitudes and to actively reject that bias as they read, thereby making reading a different, less "immasculating" experience. Meanwhile, another group of North American feminists, including Showalter, Sandra Gilbert, Susan Gubar, and Patricia Meyer Spacks, developed a different feminist critical model—one that Showalter referred to as "gynocriticism." These critics analyzed great books by women from a feminist perspective, discovered neglected or forgotten women writers, and attempted to recover women's culture and history, especially the history of women's communities that nurtured female creativity.

The North American endeavor to recover women's history—for example, by emphasizing that women developed their own strategies to gain power within their sphere—was seen by British feminists like Judith Newton and Deborah Rosenfelt as an endeavor that "mystifies" male oppression, disguising it as something that has created a special world of opportunities for women. More important from the British standpoint, the universalizing and "essentializing" tendencies of French theory and a great deal of North American practice disguised women's oppression by highlighting sexual difference, thereby seeming to suggest that the dominant system may be impervious to change. As for the North American critique of male stereotypes that denigrate women, British feminists maintained that it led to counterstereotypes of female virtue that ignore real differences of race, class, and culture among women.

By now, the French, North American, and British approaches have so thoroughly critiqued, influenced, and assimilated one another that the work of most Western practitioners is no longer easily identifiable along national boundary lines. Instead, it tends to be characterized according to whether the category of *woman* is the major focus in the exploration of gender and gender oppression or, alternatively, whether the interest in sexual difference encompasses an interest in other differences that also define identity. The latter paradigm encompasses the work of feminists of color, Third World (preferably called post-colonial) feminists, and lesbian feminists, many of whom have asked whether the universal category of woman constructed by certain French and North American predecessors is appropriate to describe women in minority groups or non-Western cultures.

These feminists stress that, while all women are female, they are something else as well (such as African American, lesbian, Muslim Pakistani). This "something else" is precisely what makes them—including their problems and their goals—different from other women. As Armit Wilson has pointed out, Asian women living in Great Britain are expected by their families and communities to preserve Asian cultural traditions; thus, the expression of personal identity through clothing involves a much more serious infraction of cultural rules than it does for a Western woman. Gloria Anzaldúa has spoken personally and eloquently about the experience of many women on the margins of Eurocentric North American culture. "I am a border woman," she writes in *Borderlands: La Frontera = The New Mestiza* (1987). "I grew up between two cultures, the Mexican (with a heavy Indian influence) and the Anglo. . . . Living on the borders and in margins, keeping intact one's shifting and multiple identity and integrity is like trying to swim in a new element, an 'alien' element" (i).

Instead of being divisive and isolating, this evolution of feminism into femin*isms* has fostered a more inclusive, global perspective. The era of recovering women's texts, especially texts by white Western women, has been succeeded by a new era in which the goal is to recover entire cultures of women. Two important figures of this new era are Trinh T. Minh-ha and Gayatri Spivak. Spivak, in works such as *In Other Worlds: Essays in Cultural Politics* (1987) and *Outside in the Teaching Machine* (1993), has shown how political independence (generally looked upon by metropolitan Westerners as a simple and beneficial historical and political reversal) has complex implications for "subaltern" or subproletarian women.

The understanding of woman not as a single, deterministic category but rather as the nexus of diverse experiences has led some white, Western, "majority" feminists like Jane Tompkins and Nancy K. Miller to advocate and practice "personal" or "autobiographical" criticism. Once reluctant to reveal themselves in their analyses for fear of being labeled idiosyncratic, impressionistic, and subjective by men, some feminists are now openly skeptical of the claims to reason, logic, and objectivity that male critics have made in the past. With the advent of more personal feminist critical styles has come a powerful new interest in women's autobiographical writings, manifested in essays such as "Authorizing the Autobiographical" by Shari Benstock, which first appeared in her influential collection *The Private Self: Theory and Practice of Women's Autobiographical Writings* (1988).

Traditional autobiography, some feminists have argued, is a gendered, "masculinist" genre; its established conventions call for a lifeplot that turns on action, triumph through conflict, intellectual selfdiscovery, and often public renown. The body, reproduction, children, and intimate interpersonal relationships are generally well in the background and often absent. Arguing that the lived experiences of women and men differ—women's lives, for instance, are often characterized by interruption and deferral—Leigh Gilmore has developed a theory of women's self-representation in her book *Autobiographics: A Feminist Theory of Self-Representation.*

Autobiographics was published in 1994, well after the chronological divide that, according to Schor, separates the heyday of feminist criticism and the rise of gender studies. Does that mean that Gilmore's book is a feminist throwback? Is she practicing gender criticism instead, the use of the word "feminist" in her book's subtitle notwithstanding? Or are both of these questions overly reductive? As implied earlier, many knowledgeable commentators on the contemporary critical scene are skeptical of the feminist/gender distinction, arguing that feminist criticism is by definition gender criticism and pointing out that one critic whose work *everyone* associates with feminism (Julia Kristeva) has problems with the feminist label while another critic whose name is continually linked with the gender approach (Teresa de Lauretis) continues to refer to herself and her work as feminist.

Certainly, feminist and gender criticism are not polar opposites but, rather, exist along a continuum of attitudes toward sex and sexism, sexuality and gender, language and the literary canon. There are, however, a few distinctions to be made between those critics whose writings are inevitably identified as being toward one end of the continuum or the other.

One distinction is based on focus: as the word implies, "feminists" have concentrated their efforts on the study of women and women's issues. Gender criticism, by contrast, has not been woman centered. It has tended to view the male and female sexes—and the masculine and feminine genders—in terms of a complicated continuum, much as we are viewing feminist and gender criticism. Critics like Diane K. Lewis have raised the possibility that black women may be more like white men in terms of familial and economic roles, like black men in terms of their relationships with whites, and like white women in terms of their relationships with men. Lesbian gender critics have asked whether lesbian women are really more like straight women than they are like gay (or for that matter straight) men. That we refer to gay and lesbian studies as gender studies has led some to suggest that gender studies is a misnomer; after all, homosexuality is not a gender. This objection may easily be answered once we realize that one purpose of gender criticism is to criticize gender as we commonly conceive of it, to expose its insufficiency and inadequacy as a category.

Another distinction between feminist and gender criticism is based on the terms "gender" and "sex." As de Lauretis suggests in *Technologies of Gender* (1987), feminists of the 1970s tended to equate gender with sex, gender difference with sexual difference. But that equation doesn't help us explain "the differences among women, . . . the differences *within women.*" After positing that "we need a notion of gender that is not so bound up with sexual difference," de Lauretis provides just such a notion by arguing that "gender is not a property of bodies or something originally existent in human beings"; rather, it is "the product of various social technologies, such as cinema" (2). Gender is, in other words, a construct, an effect of language, culture, and its institutions. It is gender, not sex, that causes a weak old man to open a door for an athletic young woman. And it is gender, not sex, that may cause one young woman to expect old men to behave in this way, another to view this kind of behavior as chauvinistic and insulting, and still another to have mixed feelings (hence de Lauretis's phrase "differences *within women*") about "gentlemanly gallantry."

Still another related distinction between feminist and gender criticism is based on the *essentialist* views of many feminist critics and the *constructionist* views of many gender critics (both those who would call themselves feminists and those who would not). Stated simply and perhaps too reductively, the term "essentialist" refers to the view that women are essentially different from men. "Constructionist," by contrast, refers to the view that most of those differences are characteristics not of the male and female sex (nature) but, rather, of the masculine and feminine genders (nurture). Because of its essentialist tendencies, "radical feminism," according to the influential gender critic Eve Kosofsky Sedgwick, "tends to deny that the meaning of gender or sexuality has ever significantly changed; and more damagingly, it can make future change appear impossible" (*Between Men* 13).

Most obviously essentialist would be those feminists who emphasize the female body, its difference, and the manifold implications of
that difference. The equation made by some avant-garde French feminists between the female body and the *maternal* body has proved
especially troubling to some gender critics, who worry that it may
paradoxically play into the hands of extreme conservatives and funda-
mentalists seeking to reestablish patriarchal family values. In her book
The Reproduction of Mothering (1978), Nancy Chodorow, a sociolo-
gist of gender, admits that what we call "mothering"—not having
or nursing babies but mothering more broadly conceived—is commonly associated not just with the feminine gender but also with the
female sex, often considered nurturing by nature. But she critically interrogates the common assumption that it is in women's nature or biological destiny to "mother" in this broader sense, arguing that the
separation of home and workplace brought about by the development
of capitalism and the ensuing industrial revolution made mothering
appear to be essentially a woman's job in modern Western society.

If sex turns out to be gender where mothering is concerned, what
differences *are* grounded in sex—that is, nature? *Are* there *essential*
differences between men and women—other than those that are
purely anatomical and anatomically determined (for example, a man
can exclusively take on the job of feeding an infant milk, but he may
not do so from his own breast)? A growing number of gender critics
would answer the question in the negative. Sometimes referred to as
"extreme constructionists" and "postfeminists," these critics have
adopted the viewpoint of philosopher Judith Butler, who in her book
Gender Trouble (1990) predicts that "sex, by definition, will be shown
to have been gender all along" (8). As Naomi Schor explains their position, "there is nothing outside or before culture, no nature that is
not always and already enculturated" (278).

Whereas a number of feminists celebrate women's difference, postfeminist gender critics would agree with Chodorow's statement that men
have an "investment in difference that women do not have" (Eisenstein
and Jardine 14). They see difference as a symptom of oppression, not a
cause for celebration, and would abolish it by dismantling gender categories and, ultimately, destroying gender itself. Since gender categories
and distinctions are embedded in and perpetuated through language,
gender critics like Monique Wittig have called for the wholesale transformation of language into a nonsexist, and nonheterosexist, medium.

Language has proved the site of important debates between feminist and gender critics, essentialists and constructionists. Gender critics

have taken issue with those French feminists who have spoken of a feminine language and writing and who have grounded differences in language and writing in the female body.[1] For much the same reason, they have disagreed with those French-influenced Anglo-American critics who, like Toril Moi and Nancy K. Miller, have posited an essential relationship between sexuality and textuality. (In an essentialist sense, such critics have suggested that when women write, they tend to break the rules of plausibility and verisimilitude that men have created to evaluate fiction.) Gender critics like Peggy Kamuf posit a relationship only between *gender* and textuality, between what most men and women *become* after they are born and the way in which they write. They are therefore less interested in the author's sexual "signature"—in whether the author was a woman writing—than in whether the author was (to borrow from Kamuf) "Writing Like a Woman."

Feminists like Miller have suggested that no man could write the "female anger, desire, and selfhood" that Emily Brontë, for instance, inscribed in her poetry and in *Wuthering Heights* (*Subject* 72). In the view of gender critics, it is and has been possible for a man to write like a woman, a woman to write like a man. Shari Benstock, a noted feminist critic whose investigations into psychoanalytic and poststructuralist theory have led her increasingly to adopt the gender approach, poses the following question to herself in *Textualizing the Feminine* (1991): "Isn't it precisely 'the feminine' in Joyce's writings and Derrida's that carries me along?" (45). In an essay entitled "Unsexing Language: Pronomial Protest in Emily Dickinson's 'Lay this Laurel,'" Anna Shannon Elfenbein has argued that "like Walt Whitman, Emily Dickinson crossed the gender barrier in some remarkable poems," such as "We learned to like the Fire / By playing Glaciers—when a Boy—" (Berg 215).

It is also possible, in the view of most gender critics, for women to read as men, men as women. The view that women can, and indeed have been forced to, read as men has been fairly noncontroversial. Everyone agrees that the literary canon is largely "androcentric" and that writings by men have tended to "immasculate" women, forcing

---

[1]Because feminist/gender studies, not unlike sex/gender, should be thought of as existing along a continuum of attitudes and not in terms of simple opposition, attempts to highlight the difference between feminist and gender criticism are inevitably prone to reductive overgeneralization and occasional distortion. Here, for instance, French feminism is made out to be more monolithic than it actually is. Hélène Cixous has said that a few men (such as Jean Genet) have produced "feminine writing," although she suggests that these are exceptional men who have acknowledged their own bisexuality.

them to see the world from a masculine viewpoint. But the question of whether men can read as women has proved to be yet another issue dividing feminist and gender critics. Some feminists suggest that men and women have some essentially different reading strategies and outcomes, while gender critics maintain that such differences arise entirely out of social training and cultural norms. One interesting outcome of recent attention to gender and reading is Elizabeth A. Flynn's argument that women in fact make the best interpreters of imaginative literature. Based on a study of how male and female students read works of fiction, she concludes that women come up with more imaginative, open-ended readings of stories. Quite possibly the imputed hedging and tentativeness of women's speech, often seen by men as disadvantages, are transformed into useful interpretive strategies—receptivity combined with critical assessment of the text—in the act of reading (Flynn and Schweickart 286).

In singling out a catalyst of the gender approach, many historians of criticism have pointed to Michel Foucault. In his *History of Sexuality* (1976, tr. 1978), Foucault distinguished sexuality (that is, sexual behavior or practice) from sex, calling the former a "technology of sex." De Lauretis, who has deliberately developed her theory of gender "along the lines of . . . Foucault's theory of sexuality," explains his use of "technology" this way: "Sexuality, commonly thought to be a natural as well as a private matter, is in fact completely constructed in culture according to the political aims of the society's dominant class" (*Technologies* 2, 12). Foucault suggests that homosexuality as we now think of it was to a great extent an invention of the nineteenth century. In earlier periods there had been "acts of sodomy" and individuals who committed them, but the "sodomite" was, according to Foucault, "a temporary aberration," not the "species" he became with the advent of the modern concept of homosexuality (42–43). By historicizing sexuality, Foucault made it possible for his successors to consider the possibility that all of the categories and assumptions that currently come to mind when we think about sex, sexual difference, gender, and sexuality are social artifacts, the products of cultural discourses.

In explaining her reason for saying that feminism began to give way to gender studies "around 1985," Schor says that she chose that date "in part because it marks the publication of *Between Men*," a seminal book in which Eve Kosofsky Sedgwick "articulates the insights of feminist criticism onto those of gay-male studies, which had up to then pursued often parallel but separate courses (affirming the existence of a homosexual or female imagination, recovering lost traditions, decoding the cryptic discourse of works already in the canon by homosexual or feminist authors)" (276). Today, gay and lesbian criticism is so much a part of gender criticism that some people equate it with the gender approach, while others have begun to prefer the phrase "sexualities criticism" to "gender criticism."

Following Foucault's lead, some gay and lesbian gender critics have argued that the heterosexual/homosexual distinction is as much a cultural construct as is the masculine/feminine dichotomy. Arguing that sexuality is a continuum, not a fixed and static set of binary oppositions, a number of gay and lesbian critics have critiqued heterosexuality as a norm, arguing that it has been an enforced corollary and consequence of what Gayle Rubin has referred to as the "sex/gender system." (Those subscribing to this system assume that persons of the male sex should be masculine, that masculine men are attracted to women, and therefore that it is natural for masculine men to be attracted to women and unnatural for them to be attracted to men.) Lesbian gender critics have also taken issue with their feminist counterparts on the grounds that they proceed from fundamentally heterosexual and even heterosexist assumptions. Particularly offensive to lesbians like the poet-critic Adrienne Rich have been those feminists who, following Doris Lessing, have implied that to make the lesbian choice is to make a statement, to act out feminist hostility against men. Rich has called heterosexuality "a beachhead of male dominance" that, "like motherhood, needs to be recognized and studied as a political institution" ("Compulsory Heterosexuality" 143, 145).

If there is such a thing as reading like a woman and such a thing as reading like a man, how then do lesbians read? Are there gay and lesbian ways of reading? Many would say that there are. Rich, by reading Emily Dickinson's poetry as a lesbian—by not assuming that "heterosexual romance is the key to a woman's life and work"—has introduced us to a poet somewhat different from the one heterosexual critics have made familiar (*Lies* 158). As for gay reading, Wayne Koestenbaum has defined "the (male twentieth-century first world) gay reader" as one who "reads resistantly for inscriptions of his condition, for texts that will confirm a social and private identity founded on a desire for other men. . . . Reading becomes a hunt for histories that deliberately foreknow or unwittingly trace a desire felt not by author but by reader, who is most acute when searching for signs of himself" (Boone and Cadden 176–77).

Lesbian critics have produced a number of compelling reinterpretations, or in-scriptions, of works by authors as diverse as Emily Dickinson, Virginia Woolf, and Toni Morrison. As a result of these provocative readings, significant disagreements have arisen between straight and lesbian critics and among lesbian critics as well. Perhaps the most famous and interesting example of this kind of interpretive controversy involves the claim by Barbara Smith and Adrienne Rich that Morrison's novel *Sula* can be read as a lesbian text—and author Toni Morrison's counterclaim that it cannot.

Gay male critics have produced a body of readings no less revisionist and controversial, focusing on writers as staidly classic as Henry James and Wallace Stevens. In Melville's *Billy Budd* and *Moby-Dick,* Robert K. Martin suggests, a triangle of homosexual desire exists. In the latter novel, the hero must choose between a captain who represents "the imposition of the male on the female" and a "Dark Stranger" (Queequeg) who "offers the possibility of an alternate sexuality, one that is less dependent upon performance and conquest" (5).

Masculinity as a complex construct producing and reproducing a constellation of behaviors and goals, many of them destructive (like performance and conquest) and most of them injurious to women, has become the object of an unprecedented number of gender studies. A 1983 issue of *Feminist Review* contained an essay entitled "Anti-Porn: Soft Issue, Hard World," in which B. Ruby Rich suggested that the "legions of feminist men" who examine and deplore the effects of pornography on women might better "undertake the analysis that can tell us why men like porn (not, piously, why this or that exceptional man does *not*)" (Berg 185). The advent of gender criticism makes precisely that kind of analysis possible. Stephen H. Clark, who alludes to Ruby Rich's challenge, reads T. S. Eliot "as a man." Responding to "Eliot's implicit appeal to a specifically masculine audience—'"You! hypocrite lecteur!—mon semblable,—mon *frère!*"'—Clark concludes that poems like "Sweeney Among the Nightingales" and "Gerontion," rather than offering what they are usually said to offer—"a social critique into which a misogynistic language accidentally seeps"—instead articulate a masculine "psychology of sexual fear and desired retaliation" (Berg 173).

Some gender critics focusing on masculinity have analyzed "the anthropology of boyhood," a phrase coined by Mark Seltzer in an article in which he comparatively reads, among other things, Stephen Crane's *Red Badge of Courage,* Jack London's *White Fang,* and the first *Boy Scouts of America* handbook (Boone and Cadden 150).

Others have examined the fear men have that artistry is unmasculine, a guilty worry that surfaces perhaps most obviously in "The Custom-House," Hawthorne's lengthy preface to *The Scarlet Letter*. Still others have studied the representation in literature of subtly erotic disciple-patron relationships, relationships like the ones between Nick Carraway and Jay Gatsby, Charlie Marlow and Lord Jim, Doctor Watson and Sherlock Holmes, and any number of characters in Henry James's stories. Not all of these studies have focused on literary texts. Because the movies have played a primary role in gender construction during our lifetimes, gender critics have analyzed the dynamics of masculinity (vis-à-vis femininity and androgyny) in films from *Rebel Without a Cause* to *Tootsie* to last year's Best Picture. One of the "social technologies" most influential in (re)constructing gender, film is one of the media in which today's sexual politics is most evident.

Necessary as it is, in an introduction such as this one, to define the difference between feminist and gender criticism, it is equally necessary to conclude by unmaking the distinction, at least partially. The two topics just discussed (film theory and so-called "queer theory") give us grounds for undertaking that necessary deconstruction. The alliance I have been creating between gay and lesbian criticism on one hand and gender criticism on the other is complicated greatly by the fact that not all gay and lesbian critics are constructionists. Indeed, a number of them (Robert K. Martin included) share with many feminists the *essentialist* point of view; that is to say, they believe homosexuals and heterosexuals to be essentially different, different by nature, just as a number of feminists believe men and women to be different.

In film theory and criticism, feminist and gender critics have so influenced one another that their differences would be difficult to define based on any available criteria, including the ones outlined above. Cinema has been of special interest to contemporary feminists like Minh-ha (herself a filmmaker) and Spivak (whose critical eye has focused on movies including *My Beautiful Laundrette* and *Sammie and Rosie Get Laid*). Teresa de Lauretis, whose *Technologies of Gender* (1987) has proved influential in the area of gender studies, continues to publish film criticism consistent with earlier, unambiguously feminist works in which she argued that "the representation of woman as spectacle — body to be looked at, place of sexuality, and object of desire — so pervasive in our culture, finds in narrative cinema its most complex expression and widest circulation" (*Alice* 4).

Feminist film theory has developed alongside a feminist performance theory grounded in Joan Riviere's recently rediscovered essay "Womanliness as a Masquerade" (1929), in which the author argues that there is no femininity that is *not* masquerade. Marjorie Garber, a contemporary cultural critic with an interest in gender, has analyzed the constructed nature of femininity by focusing on men who have apparently achieved it—through the transvestism, transsexualism, and other forms of "cross-dressing" evident in cultural productions from Shakespeare to Elvis, from "Little Red Riding Hood" to *La Cage aux Folles*. The future of feminist and gender criticism, it would seem, is not one of further bifurcation but one involving a refocusing on femininity, masculinity, and related sexualities, not only as represented in poems, novels, and films but also as manifested and developed in video, on television, and along the almost infinite number of way-stations rapidly being developed on the information highways running through an exponentially expanding cyberspace.

Vicki Mahaffey begins the following essay on *Ulysses* by discussing Joyce's belief that "sexuality as it has been socially and historically defined" underlies numerous and "different failures of communication." In Joyce's view, which he expressed as early as *Dubliners* (1914), "rigidly heterosexual imperatives" have impeded relationships not only between persons of the same sex but also between men and women— for instance, by making heterosexual Platonic friendship difficult if not impossible.

A writer, Joyce realized, cannot easily change a culture's "gender imperatives." If a writer's "intentions are revisionary, those intentions can be derailed by the reader's wishes, which may not cooperate to produce the intended meaning." A writer *can*, however, resist and begin to revise those imperatives. In writing *Ulysses*, "Joyce first identified what the socially conditioned reader is most likely to want and expect from male and female characters of different ages" and then created characters that "frustrate" and "challenge" those expectations. By "composing characters who violate popular preconceptions of what makes men and women admirable," he revealed "the gender system" to be "arbitrary and inadequate."

The socially conditioned or "acculturated" Western reader, Mahaffey asserts, expects an epic or mythic hero to be brave, strong, handsome, and well-born; "Joyce counters that expectation with Stephen Dedalus," a "scrawny intellectual who is poor, physically dirty, periodically infested with vermin, and a coward. . . . [I]nstead of being optimistic, confident, and determined, he is morose and riddled with guilt." Leopold Bloom is "the next model of male heroism that Joyce proceeds to display and partly dismantle." Bloom's "caution, his propensity to delay action, and his distrust of reprisal" make him more unlike than like Homer's Odysseus, who slaughtered his wife's suitors and reclaimed his wife (along with all his other possessions) when he returned home after a ten-year absence.

Joyce uses both Stephen and Bloom to challenge Western conceptions of the hero and the heroic. Through Stephen, Mahaffey argues, Joyce forces us to see that we have trouble viewing as heroes young men facing the negativity of need, degradation, humility, hopelessness, and deprivation. Through Bloom, she maintains, Joyce contests "the traditions of epic and romance" by redefining the older male hero as one who is "neither brave nor vengeful" but, rather, "cautious, realistic, and slowly willing to contemplate the possibility that his relation to those he loves has inadvertently been hurtful."

Joyce's most positive and admirable male characters, Mahaffey suggests, are men with the "moral courage to imagine freshly the perspectives of people they have wronged," including women and people of other races, places, and religions. Conversely, Joyce's most negative and least admirable male characters—Blazes Boylan and the Citizen, for example—approximate the image of the epic or mythic hero as it is inscribed in Western culture. Thus, "the reader's expectation clashes loudly with the actual experience of reading *Ulysses*, and the cacophony that results brings the currency of our cultural definition of gender categories comically into question."

Joyce's women, Mahaffey goes on to argue, challenge the reader's culture-coded expectations as fully as do Joyce's men. Readers expect female characters to be attractive, innocent, virginal, and weak— "beauties" in search of some rough male beast who, in turn, views winsome young women as commodities to be acquired. *Ulysses* is not without such conventional heroines but, as Mahaffey shows through an extended analysis of the Gerty MacDowell episode, Joyce uses them to demonstrate that the beauty associated with such characters is a mirage and that, indeed, women who ascribe to the culture's conventional definitions of femininity are "defenseless against the pressure of natural desires"—their own and those of exploitative men.

By way of contrast, Joyce creates a different, unconventional kind of woman character in Molly Bloom, termed by Mahaffey an "anti-Gerty" who projects herself in a way that the culture would define as "aggressive" and, therefore, "masculine." Comfortable with all aspects and functions of her body, Molly is as different from the traditional ideal of womanhood as Stephen (who lacks her physicality and strength) is from the traditional ideal of manhood. "But neither Stephen nor Molly," Mahaffey argues, "is presented as a counter-ideal," for Joyce's "attack is on the unreality and counterproductive-ness of ideals in general, as well as on specific, mutually exclusive ideals for men and women, in particular."

Although several statements Mahaffey makes (about female power and sexuality, for instance) are feminist in their attitude and outlook, "*Ulysses* and the End of Gender" is not best described as a work of feminist criticism. It neither represents Joyce as a feminist (indeed, it admits that he dissociated himself from the feminist cause) nor offers a feminist critique of Joyce or of *Ulysses*. Instead, Mahaffey's essay is best understood as a work of gender criticism, for it interrogates not only those traditional restrictions that make women less than fully human but also the debilitating limits placed on men, male characters, and de-finitions of masculine *character*.

Without going so far as to suggest that men can write like women, "*Ulysses* and the End of Gender" effectively demonstrates how one male writer with a critical sensibility and an interest in resisting and re-vising literary conventions simultaneously resisted and revised those cultural stereotypes that simplistically (over)determine gender and gender difference. Mahaffey herself describes gender difference — increasingly a focus of gender criticism — as a "mirage," one of those "borders designed to be surpassed — not lightly, but at the appropriate time, to initiate new stages of cognitive and emotional development."

Ross C Murfin

FEMINIST AND GENDER CRITICISM: A SELECTED BIBLIOGRAPHY

French Feminist Theory

Cixous, Hélène. "The Laugh of the Medusa." Trans. Keith Cohen and Paula Cohen. *Signs* 1 (1976): 875–93.

Cixous, Hélène, and Catherine Clément. *The Newly Born Woman.* Trans. Betsy Wing. Minneapolis: U of Minnesota P, 1986.

Irigaray, Luce. *An Ethics of Sexual Difference.* Trans. Carolyn Burke and Gillian C. Gill. Ithaca: Cornell UP, 1993.

————. *This Sex Which Is Not One.* Trans. Catherine Porter. Ithaca: Cornell UP, 1985.

Jones, Ann Rosalind. "Inscribing Femininity: French Theories of the Feminine." *Making a Difference: Feminist Literary Criticism.* Ed. Gayle Green and Coppélia Kahn. London: Methuen, 1985. 80–112.

————. "Writing the Body: Toward an Understanding of *L'Écriture féminine*." Showalter, *The New Feminist Criticism* 361–77.

Kristeva, Julia. *Desire in Language: A Semiotic Approach to Literature and Art.* Ed. Leon S. Roudiez. Trans. Thomas Gora, Alice Jardine, and Roudiez. New York: Columbia UP, 1980.

Marks, Elaine, and Isabelle de Courtivron, eds. *New French Feminisms: An Anthology.* Amherst: U of Massachusetts P, 1980.

Moi, Toril, ed. *French Feminist Thought: A Reader.* Oxford: Basil Blackwell, 1987.

Feminist Theory: Classic Texts, General Approaches, Collections

Abel, Elizabeth, and Emily K. Abel, eds. *The "Signs" Reader: Women, Gender, and Scholarship.* Chicago: U of Chicago P, 1983.

Barrett, Michèle, and Anne Phillips. *Destabilizing Theory: Contemporary Feminist Debates.* Stanford: Stanford UP, 1992.

Beauvoir, Simone de. *The Second Sex.* 1953. Trans. and ed. H. M. Parshley. New York: Bantam, 1961.

Benstock, Shari. *Textualizing the Feminine: On the Limits of Genre.* Norman: U of Oklahoma P, 1991.

Butler, Judith. *Gender Trouble: Feminism and the Subversion of Identity.* New York: Routledge, 1990.

de Lauretis, Teresa, ed. *Feminist Studies/Critical Studies.* Bloomington: Indiana UP, 1986.

Felman, Shoshana. "Women and Madness: The Critical Phallacy." *Diacritics* 5 (1975): 2–10.

Fetterley, Judith. *The Resisting Reader: A Feminist Approach to American Fiction.* Bloomington: Indiana UP, 1978.

Fuss, Diana. *Essentially Speaking: Feminism, Nature and Difference.* New York: Routledge, 1989.

Gallop, Jane. *Around 1981: Academic Feminist Literary Theory.* New York: Routledge, 1992.

————. *The Daughter's Seduction: Feminism and Psychoanalysis.* Ithaca: Cornell UP, 1982.

hooks, bell. *Feminist Theory: From Margin to Center.* Boston: South End, 1984.

Kolodny, Annette. "Dancing Through the Minefield: Some Observations on the Theory, Practice, and Politics of a Feminist Literary Criticism." Showalter, *The New Feminist Criticism* 144–67.

———. "Some Notes on Defining a 'Feminist Literary Criticism.'" *Critical Inquiry* 2 (1975): 78.

Lovell, Terry, ed. *British Feminist Thought: A Reader.* Oxford: Basil Blackwell, 1990.

Meese, Elizabeth, and Alice Parker, eds. *The Difference Within: Feminism and Critical Theory.* Philadelphia: John Benjamins, 1989.

Miller, Nancy K., ed. *The Poetics of Gender.* New York: Columbia UP, 1986.

Millett, Kate. *Sexual Politics.* Garden City: Doubleday, 1970.

Rich, Adrienne. *On Lies, Secrets, and Silence: Selected Prose, 1966–1979.* New York: Norton, 1979.

Showalter, Elaine. "Toward a Feminist Poetics." Showalter, *The New Feminist Criticism* 125–43.

———, ed. *The New Feminist Criticism: Essays on Women, Literature, and Theory.* New York: Pantheon, 1985.

Stimpson, Catharine R. "Feminist Criticism." *Redrawing the Boundaries: The Transformation of English and American Literary Studies.* Ed. Stephen Greenblatt and Giles Gunn. New York: MLA, 1992. 251–70.

Warhol, Robyn, and Diane Price Herndl, eds. *Feminisms: An Anthology of Literary Theory and Criticism.* New Brunswick, NJ: Rutgers UP, 1991.

Weed, Elizabeth, ed. *Coming to Terms: Feminism, Theory, Politics.* New York: Routledge, 1989.

Woolf, Virginia. *A Room of One's Own.* New York: Harcourt, 1929.

Women's Writing and Creativity

Abel, Elizabeth, ed. *Writing and Sexual Difference.* Chicago: U of Chicago P, 1982.

Berg, Temma F., ed. *Engendering the Word: Feminist Essays in Psychosexual Poetics.* Co-ed. Anna Shannon Elfenbein, Jeanne Larsen, and Elisa Kay Sparks. Urbana: U of Illinois P, 1989.

DuPlessis, Rachel Blau. *The Pink Guitar: Writing as Feminist Practice.* New York: Routledge, 1990.

Finke, Laurie. *Feminist Theory, Women's Writing.* Ithaca: Cornell UP, 1992.

Gilbert, Sandra M., and Susan Gubar. *The Madwoman in the Attic: The Woman Writer and the Nineteenth-Century Literary Imagination.* New Haven: Yale UP, 1979.

Homans, Margaret. *Bearing the Word: Language and Female Experience in Nineteenth-Century Women's Writing.* Chicago: U of Chicago P, 1986.

Jacobus, Mary, ed. *Women Writing and Writing about Women.* New York: Barnes, 1979.

Miller, Nancy K. *Subject to Change: Reading Feminist Writing.* New York: Columbia UP, 1988.

Newton, Judith Lowder. *Women, Power and Subversion: Social Strategies in British Fiction, 1778–1860.* Athens: U of Georgia P, 1981.

Poovey, Mary. *The Proper Lady and the Woman Writer: Ideology as Style in the Works of Mary Wollstonecraft, Mary Shelley, and Jane Austen.* Chicago: U of Chicago P, 1984.

Showalter, Elaine. *A Literature of Their Own: British Women Novelists from Brontë to Lessing.* Princeton: Princeton UP, 1977.

Spacks, Patricia Meyer. *The Female Imagination.* New York: Knopf, 1975.

Feminism, Race, Class, and Nationality

Anzaldúa, Gloria. *Borderlands: La Frontera = The New Mestiza.* San Francisco: Spinsters/Aunt Lute, 1987.

Christian, Barbara. *Black Feminist Criticism: Perspectives on Black Women Writers.* New York: Pergamon, 1985.

hooks, bell. *Ain't I a Woman?: Black Women and Feminism.* Boston: South End, 1981.

———. *Black Looks: Race and Representation.* Boston: South End, 1992.

Kaplan, Cora. *Sea Changes: Essays on Culture and Feminism.* London: Verso, 1986.

Moraga, Cherríe, and Gloria Anzaldúa. *This Bridge Called My Back: Writings by Radical Women of Color.* New York: Kitchen Table, 1981.

Newton, Judith, and Deborah Rosenfelt, eds. *Feminist Criticism and Social Change: Sex, Class, and Race in Literature and Culture.* New York: Methuen, 1985.

Pryse, Marjorie, and Hortense Spillers, eds. *Conjuring: Black Women, Fiction, and Literary Tradition.* Bloomington: Indiana UP, 1985.

Robinson, Lillian S. *Sex, Class, and Culture.* 1978. New York: Methuen, 1986.

Smith, Barbara. "Towards a Black Feminist Criticism." Showalter, *The New Feminist Criticism* 168–85.

Feminism and Postcoloniality

Emberley, Julia. *Thresholds of Difference: Feminist Critique, Native Women's Writings, Postcolonial Theory.* Toronto: U of Toronto P, 1993.

Mohanty, Chandra Talpade, Ann Russo, and Lourdes Torres, eds. *Third World Women and the Politics of Feminism.* Bloomington: Indiana UP, 1991.

Schipper, Mineke, ed. *Unheard Words: Women and Literature in Africa, the Arab World, Asia, the Caribbean, and Latin America.* London: Allison, 1985.

Spivak, Gayatri Chakravorty. *In Other Worlds: Essays in Cultural Politics.* New York: Methuen, 1987.

———. *Outside in the Teaching Machine.* New York: Routledge, 1993.

Trinh T. Minh-ha. *Woman, Native, Other: Writing Postcoloniality and Feminism.* Bloomington: Indiana UP, 1989.

Wilson, Armit. *Finding a Voice: Asian Women in Britain.* 1979. London: Virago, 1980.

Women's Self-Representation and Personal Criticism

Benstock, Shari, ed. *The Private Self: Theory and Practice of Women's Autobiographical Writings.* Chapel Hill: U of North Carolina P, 1988.

Gilmore, Leigh. *Autobiographics: A Feminist Theory of Self-Representation.* Ithaca: Cornell UP, 1994.

Martin, Biddy, and Chandra Talpade Mohanty. "Feminist Politics: What's Home Got to Do with It?" *Life/Lines: Theorizing Women's Autobiography.* Ed. Bella Brodski and Celeste Schenck. Ithaca: Cornell UP, 1988.

Miller, Nancy K. *Getting Personal: Feminist Occasions and Other Autobiographical Acts.* New York: Routledge, 1991.

Smith, Sidonie. *A Poetics of Women's Autobiography: Marginality and the Fictions of Self-Representation.* Bloomington: Indiana UP, 1988.

Feminist Film Theory

de Lauretis, Teresa. *Alice Doesn't: Feminism, Semiotics, Cinema.* Bloomington: Indiana UP, 1986.

Doane, Mary Ann. *Re-vision: Essays in Feminist Film Criticism.* Frederick: U Publications of America, 1984.

Modleski, Tania. *Feminism without Women: Culture and Criticism in a "Postfeminist" Age.* New York: Routledge, 1991.

Mulvey, Laura. *Visual and Other Pleasures.* Bloomington: Indiana UP, 1989.

Penley, Constance, ed. *Feminism and Film Theory.* New York: Routledge, 1988.

Studies of Gender and Sexuality

Boone, Joseph A., and Michael Cadden, eds. *Engendering Men: The Question of Male Feminist Criticism.* New York: Routledge, 1990.

Butler, Judith. *Gender Trouble: Feminism and the Subversion of Identity.* New York: Routledge, 1990.

Chodorow, Nancy. *The Reproduction of Mothering: Psychoanalysis and the Sociology of Gender.* Berkeley: U of California P, 1978.

Claridge, Laura, and Elizabeth Langland, eds. *Out of Bounds: Male Writing and Gender(ed) Criticism.* Amherst: U of Massachusetts P, 1990.

de Lauretis, Teresa. *Technologies of Gender: Essays on Theory, Film, and Fiction.* Bloomington: Indiana UP, 1987.

Doane, Mary Ann. "Masquerade Reconsidered: Further Thoughts on the Female Spectator." *Discourse* 11 (1988–89): 42–54.

Eisenstein, Hester, and Alice Jardine, eds. *The Future of Difference.* Boston: G. K. Hall, 1980.

Flynn, Elizabeth A., and Patrocinio P. Schweickart, eds. *Gender and Reading: Essays on Readers, Texts, and Contexts.* Baltimore: Johns Hopkins UP, 1986.

Foucault, Michel. *The History of Sexuality: Volume I: An Introduction.* Trans. Robert Hurley. New York: Random, 1978.

Kamuf, Peggy. "Writing Like a Woman." *Women and Language in Literature and Society.* New York: Praeger, 1980. 284–99.

Laqueur, Thomas. *Making Sex: Body and Gender from the Greeks to Freud.* Cambridge: Harvard UP, 1990.

Riviere, Joan. "Womanliness as a Masquerade." 1929. Rpt. in *Formations of Fantasy.* Ed. Victor Burgin, James Donald, and Cora Kaplan. London: Methuen, 1986. 35–44.

Rubin, Gayle. "Thinking Sex: Notes for a Radical Theory of the Politics of Sexuality." Abelove et al., *The Lesbian and Gay Reader* 3–44.

———. "The Traffic in Women: Notes on the 'Political Economy' of Sex." *Toward an Anthropology of Women.* Ed. Rayna R. Reiter. New York: Monthly Review, 1975. 157–210.

Schor, Naomi. "Feminist and Gender Studies." *Introduction to Scholarship in Modern Languages and Literatures.* Ed. Joseph Gibaldi. New York: MLA, 1992. 262–87.

Sedgwick, Eve Kosofsky. *Between Men: English Literature and Male Homosocial Desire.* New York: Columbia UP, 1988.

———. "Gender Criticism." *Redrawing the Boundaries: The Transformation of English and American Literary Studies.* Ed. Stephen Greenblatt and Giles Gunn. New York: MLA, 1992. 271–302.

Lesbian and Gay Criticism

Abelove, Henry, Michèle Aina Barale, and David Halperin, eds. *The Lesbian and Gay Studies Reader.* New York: Routledge, 1993.

Butters, Ronald, John M. Clum, and Michael Moon, eds. *Displacing Homophobia: Gay Male Perspectives in Literature and Culture.* Durham: Duke UP, 1989.

Craft, Christopher. *Another Kind of Love: Male Homosexual Desire in English Discourse, 1850–1920.* Berkeley: U of California P, 1994.

de Lauretis, Teresa. *The Practice of Love: Lesbian Sexuality and Perverse Desire.* Bloomington: Indiana UP, 1994.

Dollimore, Jonathan. *Sexual Dissidence: Augustine to Wilde, Freud to Foucault.* Oxford: Clarendon, 1991.

Fuss, Diana, ed. *Inside/Out: Lesbian Theories, Gay Theories.* New York: Routledge, 1991.

Garber, Marjorie. *Vested Interests: Cross-Dressing and Cultural Anxiety.* New York: Routledge, 1992.

Halperin, David M. *One Hundred Years of Homosexuality and Other Essays on Greek Love.* New York: Routledge, 1990.

The Lesbian Issue. Special issue, *Signs* 9 (1984).

Martin, Robert K. *Hero, Captain, and Stranger: Male Friendship, Social Critique, and Literary Form in the Sea Novels of Herman Melville.* Chapel Hill: U of North Carolina P, 1986.

Munt, Sally, ed. *New Lesbian Criticism: Literary and Cultural Readings.* New York: Harvester Wheatsheaf, 1992.

Rich, Adrienne. "Compulsory Heterosexuality and Lesbian Existence." Elizabeth Abel and Emily K. Abel, *The "Signs" Reader,* 139–68.

Stimpson, Catherine R. "Zero Degree Deviancy: The Lesbian Novel in English." *Critical Inquiry* 8 (1981): 363–79.

Weeks, Jeffrey. *Sexuality and Its Discontents: Meanings, Myths, and Modern Sexualities.* London: Routledge, 1985.

Wittig, Monique. "The Mark of Gender." Miller, *The Poetics of Gender,* 63–73.

———. "One Is Not Born a Woman." *Feminist Issues* 1.2 (1981): 47–54.

———. *The Straight Mind and Other Essays.* Boston: Beacon, 1992.

Queer Theory

Butler, Judith. *Bodies That Matter: On the Discursive Limits of "Sex."* New York: Routledge, 1993.

Cohen, Ed. *Talk on the Wilde Side: Towards a Genealogy of Discourse on Male Sexualities.* New York: Routledge, 1993.

de Lauretis, Teresa, ed. Issue on Queer Theory, *differences* 3.2 (1991).

Sedgwick, Eve Kosofsky. *Epistemology of the Closet.* Berkeley: U of California P, 1991.

———. *Tendencies.* Durham: Duke UP, 1993.

Sinfield, Alan. *Cultural Politics—Queer Reading.* Philadelphia: U of Pennsylvania P, 1994.

———. *The Wilde Century: Effeminacy, Oscar Wilde, and the Queer Moment.* New York: Columbia UP, 1994.

Warner, Michael, ed. *Fear of a Queer Planet: Queer Politics and Social Theory.* Minneapolis: U of Minnesota P, 1993.

Feminist and Gender Approaches to Joyce

Boheemen, Christine van. *The Novel as Family Romance: Language, Gender, and Authority from Fielding to Joyce.* Ithaca: Cornell UP, 1987.

Brivic, Sheldon. *Joyce's Waking Women*. Madison: U of Wisconsin P, 1995.

Henke, Suzette A. *James Joyce and the Politics of Desire*. New York: Routledge, 1990.

Henke, Suzette, and Elaine Unkeless, eds. *Women in Joyce*. Urbana: U of Illinois P, 1982.

Jones, Ellen Carol, guest co-ed. *Modern Fiction Studies* 35 (Autumn 1989). "Feminist Readings of Joyce" issue.

Lawrence, Karen. "Joyce and Feminism." *The Cambridge Companion to James Joyce*. Ed. Derek Attridge. New York: Cambridge UP, 1990. 237–58.

Mahaffey, Vicki. *Reauthorizing Joyce*. New York: Cambridge UP, 1988.

Norris, Margot. *Joyce's Web: The Social Unraveling of Modernism*. Austin: U of Texas P, 1992.

Pearce, Richard, ed. *Molly Blooms: A Polylogue on "Penelope" and Cultural Studies*. Madison: U of Wisconsin P, 1994.

Scott, Bonnie Kime. *Joyce and Feminism*. Bloomington: Indiana UP, 1984.

Valente, Joseph. *James Joyce and the Problem of Justice: Negotiating Sexual and Colonial Difference*. Cambridge: Cambridge UP, 1995.

A GENDER PERSPECTIVE

VICKI MAHAFFEY

Ulysses and the End of Gender

It is easiest to begin a discussion of Joyce's gender politics in *Ulysses* by identifying the positions he does not adopt: his is not an activist stance, nor is he an advocate for disenfranchised groups—whether women or the Irish. Joyce disavows that he is a feminist; as he playfully employs the term in the "Circe" episode of *Ulysses*, feminism is concerned primarily with action (as opposed to thought) and with a desire to appropriate (rather than redistribute) male privilege. When Bloom is being hailed as the world's greatest reformer, a group of women whisper his praises in such a way as to highlight not his but their own attributes: a millionairess appreciates him "richly," a

noblewoman lauds him "nobly," and a feminist commends his numerous accomplishments "masculinely" (*U* 15.1461–66). Joyce here presents feminism as a paradoxically masculine, action-oriented position,
from which he implicitly differentiates his own practices.

To say, however, that Joyce dissociates himself from the feminist
movements of his time does not mean that Joyce was unconcerned
with the social construction of gender and its subtle ramifications. On
the contrary, he repeatedly traces many apparently different failures of
communication—between Irish and English, between men and men,
between women and men, between women and women, between parents and children—to the fault line of sexuality as it has been socially
and historically defined. His characters discover again and again that
there is no sexual, textual, or parental relation;[1] that the call of desire
evokes only fantasy and despair. As early as *Dubliners* Joyce links the
paralysis of desire to society's insistence on the commodification of
the beloved, which he associates with the sin of simony, and on the
rigidly heterosexual imperatives that turn characters such as Father
Flynn of "The Sisters" and the stranger in "An Encounter" into
"gnomons," geometrical figures of spiritual and sexual incompleteness.
As Mr. Duffy writes after breaking off his relation with Mrs. Sinico in
"A Painful Case," "Love between man and man is impossible because
there must not be sexual intercourse and friendship between man and
woman is impossible because there must be sexual intercourse" (*D* 112).

If *Dubliners* records the longing of isolated individuals for meaningful connection, counterpointing their poignant but futile yearning
against the rules of a social system that effectively (if not intentionally)
prohibits relation in favor of idealized admiration, manipulation, and
competition, *Ulysses* takes a lighter attitude towards the impossibility
of communication. If *Dubliners* aims to expose the vision of human
connection as a mirage, precluded by the very social mechanisms that
promote it, *Ulysses* begins with the literally utopian conviction that
there is no place (*u-topia*) where such connection can happen because
there is no discursive or conceptual space free from the implied rules of
gendered (non)relation. Writing is an address, a letter from writer to
reader, and from one time and place to another; one writer alone cannot rewrite the play of social interaction and communication because
he or she is always writing against a background of expectation and de-

---

[1]I am echoing Jacques Lacan's famous assertion that there is no sexual relation. He
first makes this argument in Seminar XX, *Encore* (1972–1973); see *Feminine Sexuality:
Jacques Lacan and the école freudienne*, ed. Juliet Mitchell and Jacqueline Rose (New
York: Norton, 1982), 138. He then repeats the claim several times in his seminars.

sire that is socially programmed and often unconscious. Even if the writer's own intentions are revisionary, those intentions can be derailed by the reader's wishes, which may not cooperate to produce the intended meaning. In designing *Ulysses*, Joyce first identified what the socially conditioned reader is most likely to want and expect from male and female characters of different ages, and then he provides his readers with characters who frustrate and implicitly challenge that desire. The bewildering friction that results is designed to expose the gender system itself as an arbitrary and inadequate fiction, to measure its isolating mechanisms against the urgent complexity of personal desire. Joyce turns the threnody of nonrelation in *Dubliners* into the stuff of comedy in *Ulysses* by composing characters who violate popular preconceptions of what makes men and women admirable.[2]

Joyce begins his dialogue with the acculturated reader by offering an anti-portrait of the young male "hero." Even a cursory review of the epic tradition confirms that the young male hero is defined by courage and physical strength; Joyce counters that expectation with Stephen Dedalus, who fears dogs, thunderstorms, and drowning and is easily felled by a drunken British soldier. If the frame were mythological instead of epic, the hero would be a fearless, brawny, handsome prince, heir to a just and well-managed kingdom. Joyce evokes the dream of the charming prince through the twin shadows of

---

[2]Compare the project proposed by Lieutenant Puddock and Captain Devereux in Sheridan Le Fanu's *The House by the Churchyard*, which Joyce would later use as a point of reference in *Finnegans Wake*. Puddock suggests that he and Devereux devise an Irish variation upon the plays of Shakespeare:

> Seriously, by sometimes changing an old person to a young, sometimes a comical to a melancholy, or the reverse, sometimes a male for a female, or a female for a male—I assure you, you can so entirely disguise the piece, and yet produce situations so new and surprising—

Devereux responds by proposing a new version of *Othello*, in which

> [a] gay young Venetian nobleman, of singular beauty, charmed by her tales of "anthropophagites and men whose heads do grow beneath their shoulders," is seduced from his father's house and married by a middle-aged, somewhat hard-featured black woman, Juno, or Dido.

Sheridan Le Fanu, *The House by the Churchyard*, intro. by Thomas Kilroy (Belfast: Appletree, 1992), 135.

Joyce's project in *Ulysses*, although it is a variation on not one but two literary works (the *Odyssey* and *Hamlet*), resembles that of Puddock and Devereux in its comic design to expose the hero as a gendered construction, defined not only by sex but also by age, race, and class. The different roles in a Shakespeare play or in a Homeric epic are not reversible without dramatic alterations in meaning, for the simple reason that the meanings of sex, age, and class inhere in the culture; the text merely plays against them.

Telemachus and Hamlet, only to puncture it by presenting his readers with a scrawny intellectual who is poor, physically dirty, periodically infested with vermin, and a coward. Even Stephen's disposition violates generic expectations; instead of being optimistic, confident, and determined, he is morose and riddled with guilt. Unlike Telemachus in the *Odyssey*, who resolves to perform whatever feats are necessary to gain information about his father, confronting Nestor and appealing to Menelaus in his determined effort to gain control of his home, Stephen, depressed by the crass "wisdom" of Mr. Deasy, struggles blindly with the sea-changes of language and philosophy, only to drink himself into a stupor and go berserk in a whorehouse. As a troubled protagonist, Stephen is most temperamentally akin to Shakespeare's Hamlet, who *is* a prince, but a prince who disdains the corruption he is heir to. Joyce darkens the portrait of disaffected youth still further in his portrayal of Stephen, whose indulgence in obscure thought is more oblique than Hamlet's affected madness, and who—as a freethinking Irish Catholic youth in a poor, colonized country—occupies a dramatically reduced economic and social position.

The portrait of Stephen, offered as a replacement for that of the conventional young male hero, is not a narcissistic celebration of Joyce's own vulgarity, as some early readers charged. On the contrary, its function is to provoke a reappraisal of the criteria for heroism in Western culture. Why admire young men whose courage is due partly to the accident of age and health and partly to a rash refusal to assess danger realistically? Why privilege the accident of class and social position, which insulates young "heroes" from more lethal dangers that spring from need, hopelessness, and deprivation? Why is the avoidance of humiliation and degradation (through birth, appearance, and youth) valued more highly than the experience and survival of injustice? Joyce's depiction of Stephen against a grain of expectation makes him an ugly duckling from the perspective of what we were prepared to admire, but at the same time it exposes the hidden basis of our admiration. It becomes clear in retrospect that what makes a young male hero in the popular sense is not bravery, but luck. The hero does not *earn* admiration at all; he merely makes use of the blessings of strength and riches. Moreover, valuing luck gives us no way of differentiating between heroes and villains, since a successful—or lucky—villain is indistinguishable from a hero.[3] When Joyce presents

[3]In Le Fanu's *The House by the Churchyard*, the villain, whom everyone had taken for a powerful and successful man, declares his "heroic" faith when he is unmasked: "I believe in luck, Sir, and there's the sum of my creed." He argues, with coldly logical so-

us with "twin" heroes at the beginning of *Ulysses* in the characters of Stephen and Buck Mulligan, he uses them to make just such a point. Buck is the conventional hero—not only does he have the sunny disposition, good health, and financial solvency of the hero, but he is also clean, well-groomed, and has saved a man from drowning. Stephen uncertainly tries to determine whether he could do what Buck did:

> He saved men from drowning and you shake at a cur's yelping. But the courtiers who mocked Guido in Or san Michele were in their own house. House of . . . We don't want any of your medieval abstrusiosities. Would you do what he did? A boat would be near, a lifebuoy. *Natuerlich*, put there for you. Would you or would you not? . . . The truth, spit it out. I would want to. I would try. I am not a strong swimmer . . . If I had land under my feet. I want his life still to be his, mine to be mine. A drowning man. His human eyes scream to me out of horror of his death. I . . . With him together down. . . . I could not save her. Waters: bitter death: lost. (*U* 3.317–30).

Set against Buck's animal health, Stephen's honest interrogation of his strengths ("I am not a strong swimmer") and his memory of failure at saving others, especially his mother ("I could not save her"), emerge as thoughtful and realistic. His values are less competitive than egalitarian ("I want his life still to be his, mine to be mine"). Instead of idealizing the feat of salvation, Stephen tries to focus on the reality of support ("A boat would be near, a lifebuoy"). Very gradually, as Joyce explained to Frank Budgen, the reader should begin to appreciate the slow discipline of Stephen's ethics, contrasting it to the easier panache of Buck's.

The next model of male heroism that Joyce proceeds to display and partly dismantle is that of the mature man, epitomized by Ulysses. The heroism of an older man is more complex than that of a younger one, but ultimately it still depends on the exercise of ruthless physical strength. The *Odyssey* suggests that the mature male hero is cunning, patient, and adept at lying and disguise. He has the capacity to sustain hardships for a very long time, but ultimately he too gathers his resources for a violent, merciless confrontation in which he slaughters

---

cial criticism, that his actions were perpetrated in the name of the same principle that his accusers evoke in putting him to death, "justice, which means only the collective selfishness of my fellow-creatures" (412). The book builds to the climactic and significant revelation that the much-admired Paul Dangerfield and the villainous Charles Archer are the same man.

his opponents and reclaims his possessions (which include his wife).
Joyce endows Bloom with Odysseus' more unconventional characteristics—his adaptability, his taste for disguise, and above all his capacity
for survival—but he translates Odysseus' bloody slaughter of the suitors into Bloom's rational dismissal of his scruples in "Ithaca."[4] Moreover, he stretches Odysseus' talent for deception to include a tendency
toward self-deception.

In a powerful critique of the ethos of manly heroism (in *Finnegans
Wake* Joyce renames the hero a "zero," or "belowes hero," *FW*
343.17), Joyce intimates that it is the powerful and subtle temptation
to deceive oneself, to which everyone is susceptible, that renders self-
righteous confrontation and retribution suspect rather than heroic. By
building his complex verbal structure around a protagonist who tries
to avoid the knowledge that his wife has a sexual assignation with another man on that very day, Joyce implicitly challenges two of the
most common assumptions about heroism: that the hero is fully aware
of his motives for acting, and that those motives are simple, uncon-
flicted, and completely endorsed by the society he epitomizes. In contrast to the stock hero, Bloom is as suspicious of himself as he is of
others. Bloom's caution, his propensity to delay action, and his distrust of reprisal make him a different kind of hero, one who will never
be guilty of violent abuse. Like Stephen, Bloom aims not to "be master of others or their slave" (*U* 3.295–96), a goal that prods him to
question—half unconsciously—his own complicity in his wife's desire
for other men. Bloom's bipartisan refusal of mastery and enslavement
prevents him from becoming like Farrington in "Counterparts,"
driven to deny his sociopolitical impotence by ignobly beating a child.
Moreover, Bloom's half-conscious preoccupation with the painful
knowledge he is trying to disown also signals his refusal to detach himself from Molly by employing the easy, self-congratulatory mechanisms
of contempt. His rejection of detachment as a solution to the problems of relation is what differentiates him from cold and haunted characters such as Mr. Duffy in "A Painful Case."

Defying the traditions of epic and romance, Joyce redefines a male
hero as neither brave nor vengeful, but as cautious, realistic, and slowly
willing to contemplate the possibility that his relation to those he loves

---

[4]In the schema he gave Stuart Gilbert, Joyce suggests that instead of violently
slaughtering Molly's suitors, like Odysseus, Bloom uses reason to destroy his scruples.
Under "Correspondences" for the "Ithaca" episode, Joyce identifies the suitors as
"scruples" and the bow with which Ulysses slaughters them as "reason." See Don Gifford, with Robert J. Seidman, "*Ulysses*" *Annotated: Notes for James Joyce's "Ulysses,"* rev.
ed. (Berkeley: U of California P, 1988), 566.

has inadvertently been hurtful. Joyce's most sympathetic male characters see themselves, painfully, as fallible; their heroism grows not out of boundless confidence in the rightness of physical might, but out of what might be called the moral courage to imagine freshly the perspectives of people they have wronged. Although Stephen is unable to change his relations with his dead mother and unwilling to show gratitude to Bloom for Bloom's tactful solicitude, his appreciation of Jewish merchants as patient and knowing (*U* 2.364–73), and his vision of Muslim and Jewish intellectuals as "dark men in mien and movement, flashing in their mocking mirrors the obscure soul of the world, a darkness shining in brightness which brightness could not comprehend (*U* 2.158–60)," suggest that he feels an empathy with other races and other times that he is not yet capable of experiencing in the present at the level of individual relations. Stephen's view of woman is also sympathetic, if abstract. Stephen sees her as irresistible, lonely, overburdened, and weary; he calls her the handmaid of the moon, journeying ever westward, "followed by the sun's flaming sword" (*U* 3.391–92), pulling the tide in her wake. Stephen also sees tides within woman—blood, "a winedark sea"—a red flood that attracts man, in his role of vampire, toward her (*U* 3.397–98). As the moon, she wearily gathers and releases the waves in splendid isolation; in her perpetual toil, she (like the harp in "Two Gallants") cares nothing for her lovers: "Weary too in sight of lovers, lascivious men, a naked woman shining in her courts, she draws a toil of waters" (*U* 3.468–69).

Although Stephen romanticizes and denigrates woman by turns,[5] he is also able to picture to himself her loneliness, toil, pain, and even indifference. Bloom, too, is led by "ruth": "Woman's woe with wonder pondering" (*U* 14.186); "Ruth red him, love led on with will to wander, loth to leave" (*U* 14.201). Bloom is sensitive not only to the travail of woman in childbirth, but also to the deprivation and creeping despair of Josie Breen, caring for a crazed husband: Bloom notes with compassion her worn clothes, the lines around her mouth, the cruel eye of a passing woman upon her (*U* 8.265–69). He is also quick to sympathize with Gerty MacDowell when he realizes she is lame, "Poor girl!" (*U* 13.772), and he even imagines how difficult rejection must be for whores-in-training: "Aho! If you don't answer when they solicit must be horrible for them till they harden" (*U* 13.869–70). Most important, Bloom is able to sympathize with woman's hardships

---

[5]He expresses disgust at "woman's unclean loins, of man's flesh made not in God's likeness, the serpent's prey" (*U* 1.421–22).

without sentimentalizing them; he stops short of condescending to woman as an innocent (and therefore childlike) victim of brutal male desire. He knows, for example, that Gerty solicits his gaze, that she is driven by powerful yearnings that she cannot identify to herself as sexual. Bloom is quick to adopt the woman's perspective in a variety of situations, but in his awareness of the manifold compromises of relation, he is wary of delivering definitive judgments. He imagines the feelings of a woman who is married to a drunk:

> Husband rolling in drunk, stink of pub off him like a polecat. Have that in your nose in the dark, whiff of stale boose. Then ask in the morning: was I drunk last night? Bad policy however to fault the husband. Chickens come home to roost. They stick by one another like glue. Maybe the women's fault also. (*U* 13.964–68)

Bloom sees woman as capable and possibly culpable, but his reluctance to judge never prevents him from imagining himself vividly in her place: "Have that in your nose in the dark, whiff of stale boose."

The image of male heroism embedded in Western culture is emphatically physical; as the male hero ages, his courage is supplemented by cunning, but the basis of his appeal is the power of brute force and a willingness to use that force to protect (and simultaneously to restrict) women in particular and the community in general. In *Ulysses*, Joyce constructs a verbal edifice that promises to house popular epic heroes, but what the reader finds within it instead are thinking, caring men who—like most people—are prone to self-deception and error. The only men in the novel who pride themselves on their physical prowess are an adulterer and a bigot: the exaggeratedly hot Blazes Boylan and the hypocritical Citizen. The reader's expectation clashes loudly with the actual experience of reading *Ulysses*, and the cacophony that results brings the currency of our cultural definition of gender categories comically into question.

Given the premium placed on physical strength in men, it is perhaps surprising that cultural prescriptions for women demand an erasure or concealment of the body and of sexual power. If male heroes should be strong and active, female heroes must be aesthetically pleasing and passive; moreover, they should be immature, the innocent cause and reward of man's desire. The ideal role of the female heroine is to serve as an inspirational icon who is also the prize in a patriarchal contest, as Joyce suggests in *Finnegans Wake* by rendering "beauty" as "booty" (*FW* 560.20). In a typically compressed fashion, Joyce suggests that romantic love, in the popular imagination, is epitomized by

the story of "booty with the bedst" (Beauty and the Beast), a tale of
rapine in which the brawny man—simultaneously identified as "best"
and "beast"—aims to land his "booty" in bed.[6]

Joyce's critique of popular culture's objectification of the young
"heroine"—who learns to see herself from the outside and to adver-
tise herself even in her thoughts as a desirable commodity on the marriage market—is perhaps his most trenchant exposé of the ludicrous
cultural prescriptions for women. (As Issy notes in *Finnegans Wake*, in
partial response to her name: "I sold/Isolde"—"One must sell it to
some one, the sacred name of love," *FW* 268 n. 1.) In "Nausicaa,"
Joyce introduces us to the thoughts of Gerty MacDowell, who is so
thoroughly indoctrinated by the image of the culturally desirable young
woman that she cannot own or realize her own desires, revealing them
by indirection, cloaking them with narrative fantasies, burying them in
the sand on which she sits. From Gerty we learn that a heroine should
be an inanimate *objet d'art*, "ivorylike . . . Greekly perfect . . . hands
were of finely veined alabaster" (*U* 13.88–89), and that she resembles
a fairytale heroine. Like Cinderella, she has small feet: "Edy Boardman
prided herself that she was very *petite* but she never had a foot like Gerty
MacDowell, a five, and never would ash, oak or elm" (*U* 13.165–67).[7]
Also like Cinderella, her inborn qualities reveal her as belonging to a
more privileged class from which an unkind fate has exiled her:

> There was an innate refinement, a languid queenly *hauteur* about
> Gerty which was unmistakably evidenced in her delicate hands
> and higharched instep. Had kind fate but willed her to be born a
> gentlewoman of high degree in her own right and had she only re-
> ceived the benefit of a good education Gerty MacDowell might
> easily have held her own beside any lady in the land. (*U* 13.96–102)

Most poignantly, we observe that although Gerty is careful to deck her
body for constant display, she herself is discouraged from inhabiting it:
she cannot refer to bodily functions or even the place where they
occur. She is uncomfortable both with eating ("she didn't like the
eating part when there were any people that made her shy and often

---

[6]"Booty" is also a boot, or a glass slipper, a fetish that represents the hero's desire
for her to contain his foot (or *foutre*), while remaining inert.

[7]In *Finnegans Wake*, Joyce stresses the relation between Cinderella and her ashes,
which signify the mortality her story denies, more emphatically than he does here by issuing a warning to Cinderella in language that echoes that of the Ash Wednesday service: "Remember, maid, thou dust art powder but Cinderella thou must return" (*FW*
440.26–27).

she wondered why you couldn't eat something poetical like violets or roses," *U* 13.228–30) and with elimination. When Cissy refers to a part of the body, "the beeoteetom," Gerty "bent down her head and crimsoned at the idea of Cissy saying an unladylike thing like that out loud she'd be ashamed of her life to say" (*U* 13.263–66). And when she goes to "that place where she never forgot every fortnight the chlorate of lime" (*U* 13.332–33), she distracts herself from what she is doing by gazing at a

> picture of halcyon days where a young gentleman in the costume they used to wear then with a threecornered hat was offering a bunch of flowers to his ladylove with oldtime chivalry . . . She often looked at them dreamily when she went there for a certain purpose and felt her own arms that were white and soft just like hers. (*U* 13.334–41)

Although Gerty is physically mature, she is unable to realize that maturity and accept the complexity of physical being because she must constantly identify herself in her own mind with beauty. Even in the outhouse she must block out her surroundings by staring at a picture of old-fashioned gallantry. Gerty relentlessly censors her thoughts and perceptions, vigilantly replacing them with sentimental pictures: of herself as a model in a fashion magazine decked out in "a neat blouse of electric blue . . . and a navy threequarter skirt cut to the stride" (*U* 13.150–55); of herself as rescued by "a manly man with a strong quiet face who had not found his ideal, perhaps his hair slightly flecked with grey, and who would understand, take her in his sheltering arms, strain her to him in all the strength of his deep passionate nature and comfort her with a long long kiss" (*U* 13.210–14). She paints a highly touched-up picture of marriage, complete with "a beautifully appointed drawingroom with pictures and engravings" and "that silver toastrack in Clery's summer jumble sales" (*U* 13.231–34), where her tall husband with broad shoulders and "glistening white teeth under his carefully trimmed sweeping moustache" (*U* 13.236–37) has "brekky" with her every morning, "simple but perfectly served." "[B]efore he went out to business he would give his dear little wifey a good hearty hug and gaze for a moment deep down into her eyes" (*U* 13.240–42).

In accordance with what Joyce identified as the meaning of this episode, "The Projected Mirage,"[8] Gerty has replaced herself with a

---

[8]According to the Linati schema, the "Sense (Meaning)" of the episode is "The Projected Mirage," and its Symbol is "Onanism: Female: Hypocrisy." See Gifford *Ulysses Annotated* 384.

series of aesthetically pleasing pictures, or mirages, that serve the function of advertisements (and that are in fact modeled on advertisements). Gerty has read the signs of popular culture accurately, and she has done as directed by turning herself into something to be seen, like a painting (the "Art" of the episode is "painting"). Gerty has fashioned herself quite literally into a heroine, "as fair a specimen of winsome Irish girlhood as one could wish to see" (*U* 13.80–81), and she seems to epitomize the most admirable aspects of her age and gender: virginity, innocence, a deep longing to minister to the needs of men, aesthetic appeal enhanced by the judicious and thrifty use of clothes and cosmetics, religious faith, and "sweet girlish shyness" (*U* 13.121). One of her favorite poems is called *"Art thou real, my ideal?"* by Louis J Walsh, Magherafelt (*U* 13.645–46), and she has constructed herself as an answer to that question. Gerty represents the Irish feminine ideal that Irish audiences so hotly defended in their protests against W. B. Yeats's *The Countess Cathleen* (1899) and J. M. Synge's *The Playboy of the Western World* (1907),[9] but Joyce examines the implications of this ideal more carefully than did the nationalist protesters; he exposes its pathetic limitations, reducing a real, potentially complex woman into a lonely caricature and common cliché, although one that is tremendously exciting to men at a distance.

Moreover, Joyce uses Gerty to show that an icon of purity carries within it the seeds of a necessary defilement; this is what Joyce somewhat imprecisely refers to in his schema as the hypocrisy equivalent to female onanism: "Onanism: Female: Hypocrisy." What is hypocritical is not women but the feminine ideal, which in "Circe" is represented by the immortal nymph (*U* 15.3232). The nymph advertises

---

[9]The *Playboy* riots erupted after Christy Mahon, the playboy, tells the Widow Quin, "It's Pegeen I'm seeking only, and what'd I care if you brought me a drift of chosen females, standing in their shifts itself, maybe, from this place to the Eastern World?" J. M. Synge, *The Playboy of the Western World*, act 3, *Modern Irish Drama*, ed. John P. Harrington (New York: Norton, 1991), 115. Joseph Holloway, in a theater journal entry for Thursday, January 31, 1907, refers to this as filth and libel of the Irish peasant girl on the stage. *Modern Irish Drama*, 459. In a letter to the *Freeman's Journal* on January 28, 1907, an Irishwoman writes,

in no part of Ireland are the women so wanting in modesty as to make advances to a total stranger, much less to a criminal.

Cited in James Kilroy, *The Playboy Riots* (Dublin: Dolmen, 1971), 10. Interestingly, *The Playboy of the Western World* takes as its subject the difference between the *image* of heroism and its ugly realities. The townspeople in Synge's play celebrate Christy's heroic pose as a man who killed his father but revile him when they see actual evidence of the attempt, much as a reader might expect Gerty to remain a picture but express shock when she is actually looked at with desire.

herself as "stonecold and pure" (*U* 15.3393) as she castigates Bloom for his furtive indecencies, but then she begins to undergo a transformation. She first turns into an eyeless nun, intoning "No more desire . . . Only the ethereal" (*U* 15.3436–37), then she starts showing stains, and finally "her plaster cast" cracks, emitting a cloud of stench (*U* 15.3457, 3469–70). The ideal is itself corrupt, and it cannot hide that corruption indefinitely.

Like the nymph-nun in "Circe," Gerty, by constructing herself as pure and by censoring any indelicate thoughts, renders herself defenseless against the pressure of natural desires. As the ideal female, Gerty is a "sleeping beauty," which Joyce translates in *Finnegans Wake* as a "slipping beauty" (*FW* 477.23); Gerty's unawareness of her own desires is precisely what makes her vulnerable to the penetration of Bloom's gaze.[10] What Joyce shows, by having Gerty swing her shoe buckle and then her leg for Bloom, leaning far back until "he had a full view high up above her knee where no-one ever not even on the swing or wading and she wasn't ashamed and he wasn't either to look in that immodest way" (*U* 13.728–30), is that her behavior is totally consistent with her cultural definition as something to be looked at. Although "from everything in the least indelicate her finebred nature instinctively recoiled" (*U* 13.660–61), Gerty can picture her self-display as a romantic dream-encounter:

> She had to go but they would meet again, there, and she would dream of that till then, tomorrow, of her dream of yester eve . . . Their souls met in a last lingering glance and the eyes that reached her heart, full of a strange shining, hung enraptured on her sweet flowerlike face. She half smiled at him wanly, a sweet forgiving smile, a smile that verged on tears, and then they parted. (*U* 13.760–65)

Even her image of physical perfection is unveiled as a mirage, when she is revealed as lame.

The attitude that *Ulysses* takes toward female beauty is exuberantly unconventional. Joyce depicts beauty as a sleight-of-hand, a trick of

---

[10]Joyce's insistence on the interdependence of "sleeping" and "slipping" is reinforced by different variants of the "Sleeping Beauty" tale that portray sleeping as an end to innocence. In an Irish version, "The Queen of Tubber Tintye," or "The King of Erin and the Queen of the Lonesome Island," the queen is not only impregnated but also gives birth while sleeping (she awakens when her son is six years old). And in the version from *The Pentamerone of Giambattista Basile*, "Sole, Luna, e Talia," Sleeping Beauty is again raped while sleeping, whereupon she gives birth to two children, Sun and Moon. See P. L. Travers, *About the Sleeping Beauty* (London: Collins, 1975), 96–123.

costume, an accident of lighting, a byproduct of style, designed to make women feel less ordinary and to provoke sexual desire in men. The language of beauty is rooted in the language of magic; as Gerty amply demonstrates, the desired transformation is risibly, poignantly transitory. However, those who counsel women in the deception of beauty do so, unethically, in the name of truth:

> Time was when those brows were not so silkily seductive. It was Madame Vera Verity [true truth], directress of the Woman Beautiful page of the Princess Novelette, who had first advised her to try eyebrowleine which gave that haunting expression to the eyes, so becoming in leaders of fashion. (U 13.108–12)

Beauty traffics in the illusion that a woman's body may transcend "those discharges she used to get and that tired feeling" (U 13.86–87), that she may be transformed into a spiritual, young, and virginal vision of unstained perfection, a lady whose "innate refinement" refutes the indignities of her present station (U 13.97).

By humorously dissecting the magic of cosmetic transformation and by exposing the purposes that the cult of beauty serves for men and women, Joyce derails the reader's desire for a beautiful, faithful heroine and spotlights its implied misogyny. If what we want is a heroine with a "waxen pallor . . . almost spiritual in its ivorylike purity" (U 13.87–88), then we are simultaneously expressing a distaste for real women, with the physical afflictions and imperfections that make them long for the magical transformations promised by cosmetics.

Joyce's exposure of the ideal that Gerty worships and imitates as both false and blind (her "little strangled cry" aligns her with the blind bat that flies out at dusk "with a tiny lost cry," U 13.735, 13.626–27) helps to contextualize his decision to design his mature female heroine along radically unpopular lines. Joyce rejects "beauty parlous" (beauty parlors, parlous beauty, FW 454.19–20) as the source of Molly Bloom's attractiveness. Molly is not beautiful in the cosmetic sense, although she is powerfully attractive in the gravitational sense. Moreover, part of what makes her attractive is precisely what prevents her from being conventionally beautiful in fairytale terms: her large mass. Attractive not beautiful, Molly exercises considerable sexual power instead of becoming "booty."

Molly was never designed to "represent" Joyce's idea of womanhood, which would indeed make her a problematic character;[11]

[11]See, for example, Karen Lawrence's discussion of Sandra Gilbert and Susan Gubar's attack on Joyce's "misogyny" in "Joyce and Feminism," *The Cambridge*

instead, her character is a supplement, an antiphonal answer to the popular (and risibly anemic) idea of a heroine. She is, in a sense, an anti-Gerty, if Gerty is understood to typify someone who, under strong cultural pressure, has replaced herself as she is in biological reality with a picture of what a young woman should be. If Gerty's introjected ideal image is feminine, Joyce has Molly project herself as aggressive and even masculine ("the missus is master," *U* 15.2759). If Gerty airbrushes her body out of consciousness, clothing her body parts in a conscientious effort to deny and replace them,[12] Molly takes pleasure in her ample flesh and consciously registers all aspects of her physical existence—from sexual arousal and climax to urination and menstruation ("wait O Jesus wait yes that thing has come on me yes now wouldnt that afflict you of course all the poking and rooting and ploughing he had up in me," *U* 18.1104–06). If Gerty is defined by the clothes she uses simultaneously to reveal and conceal herself, Molly is either minimally clothed or nude, like the picture of *The Bath of the Nymph* over the bed that reminds Bloom of her: "Not unlike her with her hair down: slimmer . . . Naked nymphs" (*U* 4.371–73). Instead of looking at her clothes, Bloom looks through Molly's clothes to appreciate her "ample bedwarmed flesh" (*U* 4.238–39): "He looked calmly down on her bulk and between her large soft bubs, sloping within her nightdress like a shegoat's udder" (*U* 4.304–05). All we see

---

Companion to James Joyce, ed. Derek Attridge (New York: Cambridge UP, 1990), 237–58. Gilbert and Gubar object that Joyce identifies woman too completely with "matter"; Lawrence lends some credence to this view by pointing out Joyce's expressions of guilt over his treatment of women in his fiction and his dreams, but then she goes on to argue that "a catalogue of misogynistic images or female stereotypes in Joyce's work fails to account for his undermining of the grounds of representation" (240). She suggests that "woman in writing is beyond [Joyce's] control and might stand for a play of language that always exceeds the writer's intention" (240), and that woman "becomes the figure for illegitimacy, errancy, and forgery rather than patriarchal signature" (241). My own emphasis is somewhat different, in that I see Molly less as a principle of excess than as an embodiment of physical realities that are conspicuously missing from what might be called the compound cultural self-image that all women are called on to measure themselves against.

[12]Interestingly, what Gerty "reveals" to Bloom is not her body but her underclothing, the fetishized substitute for her body that corresponds to the picture she has substituted for herself. To allow the reader a glimpse of what Gerty fears about the body, the narrator (speaking in Gerty's idiom) refers to underwear as "undies," thereby highlighting not only Gerty's taste for common diminutives but also underscoring the fact that clothes, unlike the body, don't die. "As for undies they were Gerty's chief care and who that knows the fluttering hopes and fears of sweet seventeen (though Gerty would never see seventeen again) can find it in his heart to blame her?" (*U* 13.171–73). Gerty is exceptionally conscious of the passing of time, since she has passed the most marriageable age. "Then they could talk about her till they went blue in the face, Bertha Supple too, and Edy, little spitfire, because she would be twentytwo in November" (*U* 13.220–22).

of Molly in "Wandering Rocks" is "a plump bare generous arm" shining "from a white petticoatbodice and taut shiftstraps" (*U* 10.251–52). Molly is presented in a shift, that item of clothing that it was controversial for actors even to name in *The Playboy of the Western World*; an Irishwoman in a letter to the *Freeman's Journal* declared that the word used to indicate this "essential item of female attire" was one that a "lady would probably never utter in ordinary circumstances, even to herself."[13]

Unlike Gerty, Molly is triumphantly, painfully presented as "a nature full and volatile in its free state" that is naturally the agent and reagent of attraction (*U* 17.2163–64). In sharp contrast to Gerty's self-advertising picture of feminine underwear, the last image we are given of Molly before she begins to speak is an unprecedentedly alluring image of her nude breasts and rump,

> adipose anterior and posterior female hemispheres, redolent of milk and honey and of excretory sanguine and seminal warmth, reminiscent of secular families of curves of amplitude, insusceptible of moods of impression or of contrarieties of expression, expressive of mute immutable mature animality. (*U* 17.2232–36)

Joyce refuses to reduce Molly to the fat tissue of her rump, but where else in literature or culture can we find a comparable instance of appreciation for female corporeality? To a culture that protested raucously against the use of the *word* shift as a libel upon womanhood, Joyce offers an image of Bloom kissing "the plump mellow yellow smellow melons of [a woman's] rump, on each plump melonous hemisphere, in their mellow yellow furrow" (*U* 17.2241–42). Which is the more misogynist stance, the one that celebrates the full experience of female flesh, or the one that censors even the mention of intimate articles of female clothing? In a culture in which thousands of anorectic young women are trying to melt the flesh off their bodies, amenorrheal from the attempt to eat nothing but "violets and roses," how can a representation of ample female flesh as something more beautiful than any work of art, something as vital as the earth itself, be considered misogynist? And when Molly starts to speak, the reader learns that she is far more than the "2 lumps of lard" to which she fears Bloom has reduced her (*U* 18.1404): she is full of memory and desire, sensation and longing, poetry and dross. Unlike so many women who think of themselves even in the third person, she speaks for herself—powerfully, lyrically, sometimes crudely, and without inhibition. Unlike

[13]Kilroy, *The Playboy Riots* 10.

Gerty, who has so pitifully suppressed hers, Molly has a voracious appetite for life, and as a result she sometimes cannot find "this mortal world enough."[14] But her famous affirmation with which the book ends expresses her willed acceptance of life *and* loss, her resistance to attenuation and despair, to being turned to stone by a realistic sight of the world as it is, and not in the romantic world of faery.

Even Nora, Joyce's wife, was not immune to the shock of being asked to read against the grain of glossy fashion images by seeing Molly as a female hero. When asked if she was a model for Molly Bloom, Nora denied it, claiming with some vanity that Molly was fatter than she was.[15] Although men have long appreciated the proportional relation of size and power (a relation that made small men like Napoleon famously anxious), women as a rule do not interrogate the possible correlation of a petite figure and powerlessness. Although Joyce certainly could have made Molly more intellectual (more like her namesake Molly Ivors in "The Dead"), the role of resistant intellectual had already been assigned to Stephen as a way of countering the expectation that heroes *must be* physical. The characters of Stephen and Molly were designed to violate cultural prescriptions insisting that men must be physical and women may not be physical, a prescription that seems to preclude any meaningful heterosexual connection. But neither Stephen nor Molly is presented as a counter-ideal; Joyce's attack is on the unreality and counterproductiveness of ideals in general, as well as on specific, mutually exclusive ideals for men and women, in particular.

Joyce sees woman as powerful; where he differs radically from the culture at large is that he does not brand female sexual power as evil.[16] *Ulysses* is shot through with references to powerful female figures: Ann Hathaway, Helen of Troy, Kitty O'Shea, "naked Eve": "She had no navel. Gaze. Belly without blemish, bulging big, a buckler of taut vellum, no, whitcheaped corn, orient and immortal, standing from ever-

[14]W. H. Auden, "Lullaby." *The Norton Anthology of English Literature.* 4th Edition. Vol. 2. (New York: W. W. Norton & Company, Inc., 1979), 2397.

[15]Brenda Maddox, *Nora: A Biography of Nora Joyce* (New York: Fawcett Columbine, 1988), 198.

[16]There are very few representations of mature female sexual power that are not demonized as evil. Shakespeare's portrait of Cleopatra in *Antony and Cleopatra* may be one, although Cleopatra is far from triumphant at the end; Queen Elizabeth consolidated her political power by refusing to allow it to be interpreted as sexual, billing herself as "The Virgin Queen." The notion of the femme fatale sums up the prevailing sense that female sexual power is dangerous, at best, and fatal, at worst, and there are almost no examples of good-intentioned, successful women who are physically strong and resistant to oppression (even Joan of Arc was martyred).

lasting to everlasting" (*U* 3.41–44). Although men like Garrett Deasy blame women for our "many errors and many sins" (*U* 2.389–90), Joyce dismisses such bigotry as an insidiously disguised personal complaint (Deasy's wife is an unpredictable alcoholic), focusing instead on women's loneliness, a loneliness enhanced by a legacy of shame. Although *Ulysses* is built around a single decisive event, Molly's adultery, Joyce refuses to categorize Molly as an evil or corrupt woman; like Thomas Hardy, who controversially described Tess of the d'Urbervilles as "A Pure Woman," Joyce levels his criticism not at the individual but at the institutions that ravage her, reminding the reader that "from outrage (matrimony) to outrage (adultery) there arose nought but outrage (copulation)" (*U* 17.2196–97). Joyce makes it clear that the "debility of the female" has been "fallaciously inferred" (*U* 17.2215–16) and, along with Bloom, he asserts "the futility of triumph or protest or vindication," spurning "the inanity of extolled virtue" (*U* 17.2224–25).

Ulysses is unusual in that it expresses neither fear nor denigration nor denial of the power of female sexuality. The burden of Stephen's theory of Shakespeare is that Shakespeare's productivity grew out of his encounter with a sexually powerful woman, a woman whose capacity for desire—like that of Queen Gertrude in *Hamlet*—is read by others as faithlessness.[17] Stephen tells his listeners that Ann Hathaway was no mere mistake of Shakespeare's youth; she was the portal of discovery through which he passed without ever really learning the significance of what his writing everywhere reveals, the central importance of his early receptivity to an older, assured woman: "he passes on towards eternity in undiminished personality, untaught by the wisdom he has written or by the laws he has revealed" (*U* 9.476–79). The "events which cast their shadow over the hell of time of *King Lear, Othello, Hamlet, Troilus and Cressida*," are the events that surrounded Shakespeare's seduction by Ann Hathaway, who tumbled "in a cornfield a lover younger than herself" (*U* 9.260). What his experience of a sexually powerful, physically alive woman produces in Shakespeare is—crucially—ambivalence, an ambivalence that makes him "Ravisher and ravished," pursuing "what he would but would not" (*U* 9.472–73); "Belief in himself has been untimely killed" (*U* 9.455–56), and his ego is splintered in painfully productive ways. He has lost the assured ease of judgmental condemnation but gained the capacity to find himself in

[17]Compare Virginia Woolf's famous imaginary account of Shakespeare's "sister" in *A Room of One's Own* (1929; New York and London: Harcourt, 1957).

all his characters, finding "in the world without as actual what was in his world within as possible" (*U* 9.1041–42). It is not Ann Hathaway's beauty that produces such a harvest (as "beautifulinsadness Best" says to "ugling Eglinton," "The sense of beauty leads us astray," *U* 9.735), but her vivid reality, the physical and erotic strength that society would debar to women.

Cultural stereotypes, ideals, even gender differences themselves (insofar as they prescribe differences in thought and behavior) are attempts to contain and sterilize the contaminating power of a reality that, like mortality itself, ultimately destroys all categories. Joyce's war with convention in *Ulysses* highlights the vitality of eschewing judgment and embracing the catalytic force of change. Perhaps Joyce is mistaken in his view that woman, having been sharply forbidden fleshly indulgence for at least a millennium, has a capacity to experience physical life exceeding that of men. Virginia Woolf certainly thought that Joyce underestimated the effects on women of centuries of repression. But what Joyce systematically attacks throughout *Ulysses* are those compound cultural images that crowd out individual apprehension, experimentation, and thought, the products and prescriptions of what Gerty calls "Society with a big ess" (*U* 13.666). Gender difference is one such debilitating mirage; boundaries, as Joyce describes them, are heuristic borders designed to be surpassed—not lightly, but at the appropriate time, to initiate new stages of cognitive and emotional development. *Ulysses* is designed to inculcate "heterodox resistance" to simplistic cultural constructions (*U* 17.23); it both protests and mourns the increasing "restriction of the . . . domain of interindividual relations" (*U* 17.64–65). Instead of feminine young women and masculine young men, it offers its readers the fuller, surer touch of a "firm full masculine feminine passive active hand" (*U* 17.289–90). Its categories are mixed, controversial, changing, and alive; its stance is a feminist one in the sense that it prefers "sins of excess" to "sins of denial."[18] Like Bloom, Joyce expresses in *Ulysses* a desire "to amend many social conditions, the product of inequality and avarice and international animosity" (*U* 17.990–92), and in *Ulysses*, he commits himself fully to the "convulsions of metamorphosis, from infancy through maturity to decay" (*U* 17.1005–06). *Ulysses* affirms "the fact of vital growth" (*U* 17.1005), not artificial categories such as gender, a word with an "end" in it.

---

[18]Jeanette Winterson, *Sexing the Cherry* (New York: Random-Vintage, 1989), 70.

Psychoanalytic Criticism
and
Ulysses

WHAT IS PSYCHOANALYTIC CRITICISM?

It seems natural to think about literature in terms of dreams. Like dreams, literary works are fictions, inventions of the mind that, although based on reality, are by definition not literally true. Like a literary work, a dream may have some truth to tell, but, like a literary work, it may need to be interpreted before that truth can be grasped. We can live vicariously through romantic fictions, much as we can through daydreams. Terrifying novels and nightmares affect us in much the same way, plunging us into an atmosphere that continues to cling, even after the last chapter has been read—or the alarm clock has sounded.

The notion that dreams allow such psychic explorations, of course, like the analogy between literary works and dreams, owes a great deal to the thinking of Sigmund Freud, the famous Austrian psychoanalyst who in 1900 published a seminal text, *The Interpretation of Dreams*. But is the reader who feels that Emily Brontë's *Wuthering Heights* is dreamlike—who feels that Mary Shelley's *Frankenstein* is nightmarish—necessarily a Freudian literary critic? To some extent the answer has to be yes. We are all Freudians, really, whether or not we have read a single work by Freud. At one time or another, most of us have referred to ego, libido, complexes, unconscious desires, and sexual repression. The premises of Freud's thought have changed the way the

Western world thinks about itself. Psychoanalytic criticism has influenced the teachers our teachers studied with, the works of scholarship and criticism they read, and the critical and creative writers *we* read as well.

What Freud did was develop a language that described, a model that explained, a theory that encompassed human psychology. Many of the elements of psychology he sought to describe and explain are present in the literary works of various ages and cultures, from Sophocles' *Oedipus Rex* to Shakespeare's *Hamlet* to works being written in our own day. When the great novel of the twenty-first century is written, many of these same elements of psychology will probably inform its discourse as well. If, by understanding human psychology according to Freud, we can appreciate literature on a new level, then we should acquaint ourselves with his insights.

Freud's theories are either directly or indirectly concerned with the nature of the unconscious mind. Freud didn't invent the notion of the unconscious; others before him had suggested that even the supposedly "sane" human mind was conscious and rational only at times, and even then at possibly only one level. But Freud went further, suggesting that the powers motivating men and women are *mainly* and *normally* unconscious.

Freud, then, powerfully developed an old idea: that the human mind is essentially dual in nature. He called the predominantly passional, irrational, unknown, and unconscious part of the psyche the *id*, or "it." The *ego*, or "I," was his term for the predominantly rational, logical, orderly, conscious part. Another aspect of the psyche, which he called the *superego*, is really a projection of the ego. The superego almost seems to be outside of the self, making moral judgments, telling us to make sacrifices for good causes even though self-sacrifice may not be quite logical or rational. And, in a sense, the superego *is* "outside," since much of what it tells us to do or think we have learned from our parents, our schools, or our religious institutions.

What the ego and superego tell us *not* to do or think is repressed, forced into the unconscious mind. One of Freud's most important contributions to the study of the psyche, the theory of repression, goes something like this: much of what lies in the unconscious mind has been put there by consciousness, which acts as a censor, driving underground unconscious or conscious thoughts or instincts that it deems unacceptable. Censored materials often involve infantile sexual desires, Freud postulated. Repressed to an unconscious state, they emerge only in disguised forms: in dreams, in language (so-called Freudian slips), in creative activity that may produce art (including literature), and in neurotic behavior.

According to Freud, all of us have repressed wishes and fears; we all have dreams in which repressed feelings and memories emerge disguised, and thus we are all potential candidates for dream analysis. One of the unconscious desires most commonly repressed is the childhood wish to displace the parent of our own sex and take his or her place in the affections of the parent of the opposite sex. This desire really involves a number of different but related wishes and fears. (A boy—and it should be remarked in passing that Freud here concerns himself mainly with the male—may fear that his father will castrate him, and he may wish that his mother would return to nursing him.) Freud referred to the whole complex of feelings by the word *oedipal,* naming the complex after the Greek tragic hero Oedipus, who unwittingly killed his father and married his mother.

Why are oedipal wishes and fears repressed by the conscious side of the mind? And what happens to them after they have been censored? As Roy P. Basler puts it in *Sex, Symbolism, and Psychology in Literature* (1975), "from the beginning of recorded history such wishes have been restrained by the most powerful religious and social taboos, and as a result have come to be regarded as 'unnatural,'" even though "Freud found that such wishes are more or less characteristic of normal human development":

> In dreams, particularly, Freud found ample evidence that such
> wishes persisted. . . . Hence he conceived that natural urges, when
> identified as "wrong," may be repressed but not obliterated. . . .
> In the unconscious, these urges take on symbolic garb, regarded
> as nonsense by the waking mind that does not recognize their
> significance. (14)

Freud's belief in the significance of dreams, of course, was no more original than his belief that there is an unconscious side to the psyche. Again, it was the extent to which he developed a theory of how dreams work—and the extent to which that theory helped him, by analogy, to understand far more than just dreams—that made him unusual, important, and influential beyond the perimeters of medical schools and psychiatrists' offices.

The psychoanalytic approach to literature not only rests on the theories of Freud; it may even be said to have *begun* with Freud, who was interested in writers, especially those who relied heavily on symbols. Such writers regularly cloak or mystify ideas in figures that make sense only when interpreted, much as the unconscious mind of a neurotic disguises secret thoughts in dream stories or bizarre actions that need to be interpreted by an analyst. Freud's interest in literary artists led him to make some unfortunate generalizations about creativity; for example, in the twenty-third lecture in *Introductory Lectures on Psycho-Analysis* (1922), he defined the artist as "one urged on by instinctive needs that are too clamorous" (314). But it also led him to write creative literary criticism of his own, including an influential essay on "The Relation of a Poet to Daydreaming" (1908) and "The Uncanny" (1919), a provocative psychoanalytic reading of E. T. A. Hoffmann's supernatural tale "The Sandman."

Freud's application of psychoanalytic theory to literature quickly caught on. In 1909, only a year after Freud had published "The Relation of a Poet to Daydreaming," the psychoanalyst Otto Rank published *The Myth of the Birth of the Hero*. In that work, Rank subscribes to the notion that the artist turns a powerful, secret wish into a literary fantasy, and he uses Freud's notion about the "oedipal" complex to explain why the popular stories of so many heroes in literature are so similar. A year after Rank had published his psychoanalytic account of heroic texts, Ernest Jones, Freud's student and eventual biographer, turned his attention to a tragic text: Shakespeare's *Hamlet*. In an essay first published in the *American Journal of Psychology*, Jones, like Rank, makes use of the oedipal concept: he suggests that Hamlet is a victim of strong feelings toward his mother, the queen.

Between 1909 and 1949, numerous other critics decided that psychological and psychoanalytic theory could assist in the understanding of literature. I. A. Richards, Kenneth Burke, and Edmund Wilson were among the most influential to become interested in the new approach. Not all of the early critics were committed to the approach; neither were all of them Freudians. Some followed Alfred Adler, who believed that writers wrote out of inferiority complexes, and others applied the ideas of Carl Gustav Jung, who had broken with Freud over Freud's emphasis on sex and who had developed a theory of the *collective* unconscious. According to Jungian theory, a great work of literature is not a disguised expression of its author's personal, repressed wishes; rather, it is a manifestation of desires once held by the whole human race but now repressed because of the advent of civilization.

It is important to point out that among those who relied on Freud's models were a number of critics who were poets and novelists as well. Conrad Aiken wrote a Freudian study of American literature, and poets such as Robert Graves and W. H. Auden applied Freudian insights when writing critical prose. William Faulkner, Henry James, James Joyce, D. H. Lawrence, Marcel Proust, and Toni Morrison are only a few of the novelists who have either written criticism influenced by Freud or who have written novels that conceive of character, conflict, and creative writing itself in Freudian terms. The poet H.D. (Hilda Doolittle) was actually a patient of Freud's and provided an account of her analysis in her book *Tribute to Freud*. By giving Freudian theory credibility among students of literature that only they could bestow, such writers helped to endow earlier psychoanalytic criticism with a largely Freudian orientation that has begun to be challenged only in the last two decades.

The willingness, even eagerness, of writers to use Freudian models in producing literature and criticism of their own consummated a relationship that, to Freud and other pioneering psychoanalytic theorists, had seemed fated from the beginning; after all, therapy involves the close analysis of language. René Wellek and Austin Warren included "psychological" criticism as one of the five "extrinsic" approaches to literature described in their influential book *Theory of Literature* (1942). Psychological criticism, they suggest, typically attempts to do at least one of the following: provide a psychological study of an individual writer; explore the nature of the creative process; generalize about "types and laws present within works of literature"; or theorize about the psychological "effects of literature upon its readers" (81). Entire books on psychoanalytic criticism began to appear, such as Frederick J. Hoffman's *Freudianism and the Literary Mind* (1945).

Probably because of Freud's characterization of the creative mind as "clamorous" if not ill, psychoanalytic criticism written before 1950 tended to psychoanalyze the individual author. Poems were read as fantasies that allowed authors to indulge repressed wishes, to protect themselves from deep-seated anxieties, or both. A perfect example of author analysis would be Marie Bonaparte's 1933 study of Edgar Allan Poe. Bonaparte found Poe to be so fixated on his mother that his repressed longing emerges in his stories in images such as the white spot on a black cat's breast, said to represent mother's milk.

A later generation of psychoanalytic critics often paused to analyze the characters in novels and plays before proceeding to their authors. But not for long, since characters, both evil and good, tended to be seen by these critics as the author's potential selves or projections of various repressed aspects of his or her psyche. For instance, in *A Psychoanalytic Study of the Double in Literature* (1970), Robert Rogers begins with the view that human beings are double or multiple in nature. Using this assumption, along with the psychoanalytic concept of "dissociation" (best known by its result, the dual or multiple personality), Rogers concludes that writers reveal instinctual or repressed selves in their books, often without realizing that they have done so.

In the view of critics attempting to arrive at more psychological insights into an author than biographical materials can provide, a work of literature is a fantasy or a dream—or at least so analogous to daydream or dream that Freudian analysis can help explain the nature of the mind that produced it. The author's purpose in writing is to gratify secretly some forbidden wish, in particular an infantile wish or desire that has been repressed into the unconscious mind. To discover what the wish is, the psychoanalytic critic employs many of the terms and procedures developed by Freud to analyze dreams.

The literal surface of a work is sometimes spoken of as its "manifest content" and treated as a "manifest dream" or "dream story" would be treated by a Freudian analyst. Just as the analyst tries to figure out the "dream thought" behind the dream story—that is, the latent or hidden content of the manifest dream—so the psychoanalytic literary critic tries to expose the latent, underlying content of a work. Freud used the words *condensation* and *displacement* to explain two of the mental processes whereby the mind disguises its wishes and fears in dream stories. In condensation, several thoughts or persons may be condensed into a single manifestation or image in a dream story; in displacement, an anxiety, a wish, or a person may be displaced onto the image of another, with which or whom it is loosely connected through a string of associations that only an analyst can untangle. Psychoanalytic critics treat metaphors as if they were dream condensations; they treat metonyms—figures of speech based on extremely loose, arbitrary associations—as if they were dream displacements. Thus figurative literary language in general is treated as something that evolves as the writer's conscious mind resists what the unconscious tells it to picture or describe. A symbol is, in Daniel Weiss's words, "a meaningful concealment of truth as the truth promises to emerge as some frightening or forbidden idea" (20).

In a 1970 article entitled "The 'Unconscious' of Literature," Norman Holland, a literary critic trained in psychoanalysis, succinctly sums up the attitudes held by critics who would psychoanalyze authors, but without quite saying that it is the *author* that is being analyzed by the psychoanalytic critic. "When one looks at a poem psychoanalytically," he writes, "one considers it as though it were a dream or as though some ideal patient [were speaking] from the couch in iambic pentameter."

One "looks for the general level or levels of fantasy associated with the language. By level I mean the familiar stages of childhood development—oral [when desires for nourishment and infantile sexual desires overlap], anal [when infants receive their primary pleasure from defecation], urethral [when urinary functions are the locus of sexual pleasure], phallic [when the penis or, in girls, some penis substitute is of primary interest], oedipal." Holland continues by analyzing not Robert Frost but Frost's poem "Mending Wall" as a specifically oral fantasy that is not unique to its author. "Mending Wall" is "about breaking down the wall which marks the separated or individuated self so as to return to a state of closeness to some Other"—including and perhaps essentially the nursing mother ("'Unconscious'" 136, 139).

While not denying the idea that the unconscious plays a role in creativity, psychoanalytic critics such as Holland began to focus more on the ways in which authors create works that appeal to *our* repressed wishes and fantasies. Consequently, they shifted their focus away from the psyche of the author and toward the psychology of the reader and the text. Holland's theories, which have concerned themselves more with the reader than with the text, have helped to establish another school of critical theory: reader-response criticism. Elizabeth Wright explains Holland's brand of modern psychoanalytic criticism in this way: "What draws us as readers to a text is the secret expression of what we desire to hear, much as we protest we do not. The disguise must be good enough to fool the censor into thinking that the text is respectable, but bad enough to allow the unconscious to glimpse the unrespectable" (117).

Holland is one of dozens of critics who have revised Freud significantly in the process of revitalizing psychoanalytic criticism. Another such critic is R. D. Laing, whose controversial and often poetical writings about personality, repression, masks, and the double or "schizoid" self have (re)blurred the boundary between creative writing and psychoanalytic discourse. Yet another is D. W. Winnicott, an "object relations" theorist who has had a significant impact on literary criticism. Critics influenced by Winnicott and his school have questioned the tendency to see reader/text as an either/or construct; instead, they have seen reader and text (or audience and play) in terms of a *relationship* taking place in what Winnicott calls a "transitional" or "potential" space—space in which binary terms such as *real* and *illusory, objective* and *subjective,* have little or no meaning.

Psychoanalytic theorists influenced by Winnicott see the transitional or potential reader/text (or audience/play) space as being *like* the space entered into by psychoanalyst and patient. More important, they also see it as being similar to the space between mother and infant: a space characterized by trust in which categorizing terms such as *knowing* and *feeling* mix and merge and have little meaning apart from one another.

Whereas Freud saw the mother-son relationship in terms of the son and his repressed oedipal complex (and saw the analyst-patient relationship in terms of the patient and the repressed "truth" that the analyst could scientifically extract), object-relations analysts see both relationships as *dyadic*—that is, as being dynamic in both directions. Consequently, they don't depersonalize analysis or their analyses. It is hardly surprising, therefore, that contemporary literary critics who apply object-relations theory to the texts they discuss don't depersonalize critics or categorize their interpretations as "truthful," at least not in any objective or scientific sense. In the view of such critics, interpretations are made of language—itself a transitional object—and are themselves the mediating terms or transitional objects of a relationship.

Like critics of the Winnicottian school, the French structuralist theorist Jacques Lacan focused on language and language-related issues. He treated the unconscious *as* a language and, consequently, viewed the dream not as Freud did (that is, as a form and symptom of repression) but rather as a form of discourse. Thus we may study dreams psychoanalytically to learn about literature, even as we may study literature to learn more about the unconscious. In Lacan's seminar on Poe's "The Purloined Letter," a pattern of repetition like that used by psychoanalysts in their analyses is used to arrive at a reading of the story. According to Wright, "the new psychoanalytic structural approach to literature" employs "analogies from psychoanalysis . . . to explain the workings of the text as distinct from the workings of a particular author's, character's, or even reader's mind" (125).

Lacan, however, did far more than extend Freud's theory of dreams, literature, and the interpretation of both. More significantly, he took Freud's whole theory of psyche and gender and added to it a crucial third term—that of language. In the process, he both used and significantly developed Freud's ideas about the oedipal stage and complex.

Lacan pointed out that the pre-oedipal stage, in which the child at first does not even recognize its independence from its mother, is also a pre*verbal* stage, one in which the child communicates without the medium of language, or—if we insist on calling the child's communications a language—in a language that can only be called *literal*. ("Coos," certainly, cannot be said to be figurative or symbolic.) Then, while still in the pre-oedipal stage, the child enters the *mirror* stage.

During the mirror period, the child comes to view itself and its mother, later other people as well, *as* independent selves. This is the stage in which the child is first able to fear the aggressions of another, to desire what is recognizably beyond the self (initially the mother), and, finally, to want to compete with another for the same desired object. This is also the stage at which the child first becomes able to feel sympathy with another being who is being hurt by a third, to cry when another cries. All of these developments, of course, involve projecting beyond the self and, by extension, constructing one's own self (or "ego" or "I") as others view one—that is, as *another*. Such constructions, according to Lacan, are just that: constructs, products, artifacts—fictions of coherence that in fact hide what Lacan called the "absence" or "lack" of being.

The mirror stage, which Lacan also referred to as the *imaginary* stage, is fairly quickly succeeded by the oedipal stage. As in Freud, this stage begins when the child, having come to view itself as self and the father and mother as separate selves, perceives gender and gender differences between its parents and between itself and one of its parents. For boys, gender awareness involves another, more powerful recognition, for the recognition of the father's phallus as the mark of his difference from the mother involves, at the same time, the recognition that his older and more powerful father is also his rival. That, in turn, leads to the understanding that what once seemed wholly his and even indistinguishable from himself is in fact someone else's: something properly desired only at a distance and in the form of socially acceptable *substitutes*.

The fact that the oedipal stage roughly coincides with the entry of the child into language is extremely important for Lacan. For the linguistic order is essentially a figurative or "Symbolic" order; words are not the things they stand for but are, rather, stand-ins or substitutes for those things. Hence boys, who in the most critical period of their development have had to submit to what Lacan called the "Law of the Father"—a law that prohibits direct desire for and communicative intimacy with what has been the boy's whole world—enter more easily into the realm of language and the Symbolic order than do girls, who have never really had to renounce that which once seemed continuous with the self: the mother. The gap that has been opened up for boys, which includes the gap between signs and what they substitute—the gap marked by the phallus and encoded with the boy's sense of his maleness—has not opened up for girls, or has not opened up in the same way, to the same degree.

For Lacan, the father need not be present to trigger the oedipal stage; nor does his phallus have to be seen to catalyze the boy's (easier) transition into the Symbolic order. Rather, Lacan argued, a child's recognition of its gender is intricately tied up with a growing recognition of the system of names and naming, part of the larger system of substitutions we call language. A child has little doubt about who its mother is, but who is its father, and how would one know? The father's claim rests on the mother's *word* that he is in fact the father; the father's relationship to the child is thus established through language and a system of marriage and kinship—names—that in turn is basic to rules of everything from property to law. The name of the father (*nom du père,* which in French sounds like *non du père*) involves, in a sense, nothing of the father—nothing, that is, except his word or name.

Lacan's development of Freud has had several important results. First, his sexist-seeming association of maleness with the Symbolic order, together with his claim that women cannot therefore enter easily into the order, has prompted feminists not to reject his theory out of hand but, rather, to look more closely at the relation between language and gender, language and women's inequality. Some feminists have gone so far as to suggest that the social and political relationships between male and female will not be fundamentally altered until language itself has been radically changed. (That change might begin dialectically, with the development of some kind of "feminine language" grounded in the presymbolic, literal-to-imaginary communication between mother and child.)

Second, Lacan's theory has proved of interest to deconstructors and other poststructuralists, in part because it holds that the ego (which in Freud's view is as necessary as it is natural) is a product or construct. The ego-artifact, produced during the mirror stage, *seems* at once unified, consistent, and organized around a determinate center. But the unified self, or ego, is a fiction, according to Lacan. The yoking together of fragments and destructively dissimilar elements takes its psychic toll, and it is the job of the Lacanian psychoanalyst to "deconstruct," as it were, the ego, to show its continuities to be contradictions as well.

Kimberly J. Devlin's psychoanalytic approach to *Ulysses* begins with an epigraph from Freud's *The Ego and the Id* (1923). Freud, after defining a "word" as "the mnemic residue" (memory trace) of "a word that has been heard," speaks of an "optical" mnemic residue, that is, the memory trace of a thing that has been seen. He then contends that this sort of visual as opposed to verbal thinking, this sort of "thinking in pictures . . . , stands nearer to unconscious processes than does thinking in words." As a result, he maintains, it is possible to bring previously unconscious thought processes to consciousness "through a reversion to visual residues." In Devlin's words, "pictorial thought" can be "a mediating aid . . . in enabling unconscious thoughts to return."

In an earlier case history of his so-called Wolf Man patient, an essay entitled "From the History of an Infantile Neurosis" (1918), Freud asserted even more strongly the claims that visual thought mediates between what can and cannot be verbally expressed. His analysis of the Wolf Man suggests that optic images (for example, dream images of wolves) can simultaneously represent not only unconscious thoughts and wishes but also "the regulatory agencies that attempt to overpower unconscious thoughts" (for example, the "vigilant gaze" of the mind's "dream censor"). Using Freud's insight as a starting point, Devlin proceeds to analyze *Ulysses* and, more particularly, the psyche of Leopold Bloom. What she demonstrates is that Bloom's pictorial thought reveals an unconscious desire for optical surveillance and subsequent control, what Devlin calls "scopic power."

Like "Freud's analysand," the Wolf Man, Bloom "emerges as an individual with a highly sensitive visual psyche." He is pleased by particular sights and displeased by others; for instance, he notices that a woman's "stockings are loose over her ankles" and thinks: "I detest that: so tasteless." Bloom, however, is also a man of words, words that lead him from thought to (subtly related) thought. A critically important feature of what Devlin calls "opticality" in *Ulysses* is "the way Joyce interweaves a strand of Bloom's pictorial thinking" with a specific and "richly symptomatic" verbal signifier, namely, "the common feminine forename of 'Mary.'" This name interwoven with a strand of images, this verbal thinking embedded in visual thinking, enables Devlin to consider auditory *and* optical mnemic residues—words *and* things, signifiers in general—and their relation to unconscious thought in the world of Joyce's novel.

In the first part of her essay, Devlin discusses "the contexts in which 'Mary' surfaces in Bloom's psyche." It first enters Bloom's consciousness in "Lotus-Eaters," where a pin that Martha Clifford has used to attach a flower to a letter reminds Bloom of a song he once heard some "sluts" singing about a "Mairy" who "lost the pin of her drawers." At this point, Devlin points out, Bloom "produces what will turn out to be a visual symptom—a recollection of a specific painting of Jesus with the sisters of Lazarus," Mary and Martha. ("Martha, Mary. I saw that picture somewhere I forget now old master or faked for money.") He then associates the two women in the picture with "the two sluts in the Coombe" because, as Devlin points out, Mary the sister of Lazarus "is sometimes confused with Mary Magdalene," the prostitute who became one of Jesus' followers and friends.

The signifier "Mary" recurs in "Lotus-Eaters" as Bloom associates Martha Clifford with a fantasy woman named Mary, whom he pictures confessing her sins to a priest. "Bloom's fantasy here," Devlin maintains, "symptomatizes an unconscious phobia inherent in his relationship with Martha," the fear "that she has confessed her epistolary affair to the counterpart of the clergy, the local police force." In Devlin's view, the optical image of the confessional as a soundbooth enabling "spousal eavesdropping" also reflects Bloom's desire to scrutinize his wife Molly's "flirtations," his desire for "surveillance" that would lead to "a masterful sense" of scopic "power-knowledge."

Devlin analyzes a number of other scenes, such as the one in "Lestrygonians" in which Bloom, on seeing some constables, remembers an unpleasant encounter he once had with the police, speculates about police spies, and has a fantasy— "both visual and auditory"—in which a servant girl named Mary is asked about the clothes she is ironing by a "hotblooded young student" who pretends to be courting her. Devlin suggests that the student is connected in Bloom's mind with plainclothed policemen who might pry out of household servants, or "slaveys," information about the families employing them. Thus, the female servant in possession of family secrets is also subject to surveillance by officials who would have her "confess" all she knows.

The Mary of this fantasy, Devlin asserts, is connected in Bloom's psyche to a servant girl named Mary Driscoll, whom he employed and toward whom he once made sexual advances. (In "Circe," Devlin suggests, the fantasy of Mary Driscoll testifying that Bloom entered her quarters while Molly was out shopping on the pretense of needing a safety pin "retrospectively explains why the pin in Martha's letter unconsciously evokes a ditty about a 'Mairy.'") Devlin also views Mary Driscoll as the "latent subtext" of Bloom's reaction to the sweet, high voice of the acolyte singing at Paddy Dignam's funeral service. Hearing the Latin word "*tentationem*" (temptation) sung by a "soprano and hence feminized voice," Bloom's mind turns to images of domestic servants. It does so "symptomatically," in Devlin's view, because of Bloom's "association of the signifier 'Mary' with personal temptation."

The scenes in *Ulysses* analyzed by Devlin show how "the scopic powers" Bloom exercises over the bodies of young women associated with the signifier "Mary" reveal "unconscious thoughts" about "personal temptation of a sexual nature." Ultimately, however, the threat posed to Bloom's psyche by the "two types of exploited women in *Ulysses*—the slavey and the prostitute, merged under the signifier of 'Mary'"—is not merely or perhaps even predominantly sexual. Such women also have a "definite power in Bloom's psyche, on account of their access to taboo secrets." Devlin speculates that "Molly's dismissal of Mary from live-in maid service is motivated not only by the slavey's unwanted status as sexual rival, but also by her equally unwanted status as domestic countergaze, as inevitable witness to marital rifts and disharmonies (and finally, of course, their fallguy)."

In concluding her essay, Devlin summarizes but also extends her argument by suggesting that images called forth by and associated with the signifier "Mary" in *Ulysses* signify one character's but also a patriarchal culture's "desire for control over particular female *bodies*." Beyond that, they signify an even deeper wish to "regulate" not only those bodies but also the "*speech* of a specific subculture of exploited women. . . . Submerged beneath its masochistic surface, this fantasy scenario bespeaks a phobic need to control the discourse of those perversely privileged female subjectivities who constitute a countergaze, a countergaze that knows the dirty secrets hidden in many a male Dubliner's bottom drawer."

Ross C Murfin

PSYCHOANALYTIC CRITICISM:
A SELECTED BIBLIOGRAPHY

Some Short Introductions to Psychological and Psychoanalytic Criticism

Holland, Norman. "The 'Unconscious' of Literature: The Psychoanalytic Approach." *Contemporary Criticism.* Ed. Malcolm Bradbury and David Palmer. Stratford-upon-Avon Studies 12. New York: St. Martin's, 1971. 131–53.

Natoli, Joseph, and Frederik L. Rusch, comps. *Psychocriticism: An Annotated Bibliography*. Westport: Greenwood, 1984.

Scott, Wilbur. *Five Approaches to Literary Criticism*. London: Collier-Macmillan, 1962. See the essays by Burke and Gorer as well as Scott's introduction to the section "The Psychological Approach: Literature in the Light of Psychological Theory."

Wellek, René, and Austin Warren. *Theory of Literature*. New York: Harcourt, 1942. See the chapter "Literature and Psychology" in pt. 3, "The Extrinsic Approach to the Study of Literature."

Wright, Elizabeth. "Modern Psychoanalytic Criticism." *Modern Literary Theory: A Comparative Introduction*. Ed. Ann Jefferson and David Robey. Totowa: Barnes, 1982. 113–33.

Freud, Lacan, and Their Influence

Basler, Roy P. *Sex, Symbolism, and Psychology in Literature*. New York: Octagon, 1975. See especially 13–19.

Bowie, Malcolm. *Lacan*. Cambridge: Harvard UP, 1991.

Clément, Catherine. *The Lives and Legends of Jacques Lacan*. Trans. Arthur Goldhammer. New York: Columbia UP, 1983.

Freud, Sigmund. *Introductory Lectures on Psycho-Analysis*. Trans. Joan Riviere. London: Allen, 1922.

Gallop, Jane. *Reading Lacan*. Ithaca: Cornell UP, 1985.

Hoffman, Frederick J. *Freudianism and the Literary Mind*. Baton Rouge: Louisiana State UP, 1945.

Hogan, Patrick Colm, and Lalita Pandit, eds. *Lacan and Criticism: Essays and Dialogue on Language, Structure, and the Unconscious*. Athens: U of Georgia P, 1990.

Kazin, Alfred. "Freud and His Consequences." *Contemporaries*. Boston: Little, 1962. 351–93.

Lacan, Jacques. *Écrits: A Selection*. Trans. Alan Sheridan. New York: Norton, 1977.

———. *Feminine Sexuality: Lacan and the École Freudienne*. Ed. Juliet Mitchell and Jacqueline Rose. Trans. Rose. New York: Norton, 1985.

———. *The Four Fundamental Concepts of Psychoanalysis*. Trans. Alan Sheridan. London: Penguin, 1980.

Macey, David. *Lacan in Contexts*. New York: Verso, 1988.

Meisel, Perry, ed. *Freud: A Collection of Critical Essays*. Englewood Cliffs: Prentice, 1981.

Muller, John P., and William J. Richardson. *Lacan and Language: A Reader's Guide to "Écrits."* New York: International UP, 1982.

Porter, Laurence M. *"The Interpretation of Dreams": Freud's Theories Revisited.* Twayne's Masterwork Studies Ser. Boston: G. K. Hall, 1986.

Reppen, Joseph, and Maurice Charney. *The Psychoanalytic Study of Literature.* Hillsdale: Analytic, 1985.

Schneiderman, Stuart. *Jacques Lacan: The Death of an Intellectual Hero.* Cambridge: Harvard UP, 1983.

———. *Returning to Freud: Clinical Psychoanalysis in the School of Lacan.* New Haven: Yale UP, 1980.

Selden, Raman. *A Reader's Guide to Contemporary Literary Theory.* 2nd ed. Lexington: U of Kentucky P, 1989. See "Jacques Lacan: Language and the Unconscious."

Sullivan, Ellie Ragland. *Jacques Lacan and the Philosophy of Psychoanalysis.* Champaign: U of Illinois P, 1986.

Sullivan, Ellie Ragland, and Mark Bracher, eds. *Lacan and the Subject of Language.* New York: Routledge, 1991.

Trilling, Lionel. "Art and Neurosis." *The Liberal Imagination.* New York: Scribner's, 1950. 160–80.

Wilden, Anthony. "Lacan and the Discourse of the Other." In *Lacan, Speech and Language in Psychoanalysis.* Trans. Wilden. Baltimore: Johns Hopkins UP, 1981. (Published as *The Language of the Self* in 1968.) 159–311.

Žižek, Slavoj. *Looking Awry: An Introduction to Jacques Lacan through Popular Culture.* Cambridge: MIT P, 1991.

Psychoanalysis, Feminism, and Literature

Chodorow, Nancy. *The Reproduction of Mothering: Psychoanalysis and the Sociology of Gender.* Berkeley: U of California P, 1978.

Gallop, Jane. *The Daughter's Seduction: Feminism and Psychoanalysis.* Ithaca: Cornell UP, 1982.

Garner, Shirley Nelson, Claire Kahane, and Madelon Sprengnether. *The (M)other Tongue: Essays in Feminist Psychoanalytic Interpretation.* Ithaca: Cornell UP, 1985.

Grosz, Elizabeth. *Jacques Lacan: A Feminist Introduction.* New York: Routledge, 1990.

Irigaray, Luce. *The Speculum of the Other Woman.* Trans. Gillian C. Gill. Ithaca: Cornell UP, 1985.

———. *This Sex Which Is Not One.* Trans. Catherine Porter. Ithaca: Cornell UP, 1985.

Jacobus, Mary. "Is There a Woman in This Text?" *New Literary History* 14 (1982): 117–41.

Kristeva, Julia. *The Kristeva Reader.* Ed. Toril Moi. New York: Columbia UP, 1986. See especially the selection from *Revolution in Poetic Language,* 89–136.

Mitchell, Juliet. *Psychoanalysis and Feminism.* New York: Random, 1974.

Mitchell, Juliet, and Jacqueline Rose. "Introduction I" and "Introduction II." Lacan, *Feminine Sexuality: Jacques Lacan and the École Freudienne.* New York: Norton, 1985. 1–26, 27–57.

Sprengnether, Madelon. *The Spectral Mother: Freud, Feminism, and Psychoanalysis.* Ithaca: Cornell UP, 1990.

Psychological and Psychoanalytic Studies of Literature

Bettelheim, Bruno. *The Uses of Enchantment: The Meaning and Importance of Fairy Tales.* New York: Knopf, 1976. Although this book is about fairy tales instead of literary works written for publication, it offers model Freudian readings of well-known stories.

Crews, Frederick C. *Out of My System: Psychoanalysis, Ideology, and Critical Method.* New York: Oxford UP, 1975.

———. *Relations of Literary Study.* New York: MLA, 1967. See the chapter "Literature and Psychology."

Diehl, Joanne Feit. "Re-Reading *The Letter:* Hawthorne, the Fetish, and the (Family) Romance." *Nathaniel Hawthorne, The Scarlet Letter.* Ed. Ross C Murfin. Case Studies in Contemporary Criticism Ser. Ed. Ross C Murfin. Boston: Bedford–St. Martin's, 1991. 235–51.

Hallman, Ralph. *Psychology of Literature: A Study of Alienation and Tragedy.* New York: Philosophical Library, 1961.

Hartman, Geoffrey, ed. *Psychoanalysis and the Question of the Text.* Baltimore: Johns Hopkins UP, 1978. See especially the essays by Hartman, Johnson, Nelson, and Schwartz.

Hertz, Neil. *The End of the Line: Essays on Psychoanalysis and the Sublime.* New York: Columbia UP, 1985.

Holland, Norman N. *Dynamics of Literary Response.* New York: Oxford UP, 1968.

———. *Poems in Persons: An Introduction to the Psychoanalysis of Literature.* New York: Norton, 1973.

Kris, Ernest. *Psychoanalytic Explorations in Art.* New York: International, 1952.

Lucas, F. L. *Literature and Psychology.* London: Cassell, 1951.

Natoli, Joseph, ed. *Psychological Perspectives on Literature: Freudian Dissidents and Non-Freudians: A Casebook.* Hamden: Archon Books–Shoe String, 1984.

Phillips, William, ed. *Art and Psychoanalysis.* New York: Columbia UP, 1977.

Rogers, Robert. *A Psychoanalytic Study of the Double in Literature.* Detroit: Wayne State UP, 1970.

Skura, Meredith. *The Literary Use of the Psychoanalytic Process.* New Haven: Yale UP, 1981.

Strelka, Joseph P. *Literary Criticism and Psychology.* University Park: Pennsylvania State UP, 1976. See especially the essays by Lerner and Peckham.

Weiss, Daniel. *The Critic Agonistes: Psychology, Myth, and the Art of Fiction.* Ed. Eric Solomon and Stephen Arkin. Seattle: U of Washington P, 1985.

Lacanian Psychoanalytic Studies of Literature

Collings, David. "The Monster and the Imaginary Mother: A Lacanian Reading of *Frankenstein.*" *Mary Shelley, Frankenstein.* Ed. Johanna M. Smith. Case Studies in Contemporary Criticism. Ser. Ed. Ross C Murfin. Boston: Bedford–St. Martin's, 1992. 245–58.

Davis, Robert Con, ed. *The Fictional Father: Lacanian Readings of the Text.* Amherst: U of Massachusetts P, 1981.

———. "Lacan and Narration." *Modern Language Notes* 5 (1983): 848–59.

Felman, Shoshana, ed. *Jacques Lacan and the Adventure of Insight: Psychoanalysis in Contemporary Culture.* Cambridge: Harvard UP, 1987.

———. *Literature and Psychoanalysis: The Question of Reading: Otherwise.* Baltimore: Johns Hopkins UP, 1982.

Froula, Christine. "When Eve Reads Milton: Undoing the Canonical Economy." *Canons.* Ed. Robert von Hallberg. Chicago: U of Chicago P, 1984. 149–75.

Homans, Margaret. *Bearing the Word: Language and Female Experience in Nineteenth-Century Women's Writing.* Chicago: U of Chicago P, 1986.

Mellard, James. *Using Lacan, Reading Fiction.* Urbana: U of Illinois P, 1991.

Muller, John P., and William J. Richardson, eds. *The Purloined Poe: Lacan, Derrida, and Psychoanalytic Reading.* Baltimore: Johns Hopkins UP, 1988. Includes Lacan's seminar on Poe's "The Purloined Letter."

Psychoanalytic Approaches to Joyce

Brivic, Sheldon. *The Veil of Signs: Joyce, Lacan, and Perception.* Urbana: U of Illinois P, 1985.

Brivic, Sheldon, with Ellie Ragland-Sullivan, guest co-eds. *James Joyce Quarterly* 29 (Fall 1991). "Joyce Between Genders: Lacanian Views" issue.

Devlin, Kimberly J. *Wandering and Return in "Finnegans Wake": An Integrative Approach to Joyce's Fictions.* Princeton: Princeton UP, 1991.

Ferrer, Daniel. "Circe, Regret and Regression." *Post-structuralist Joyce.* Ed. Derek Attridge and Daniel Ferrer. Cambridge: Cambridge UP, 1984.

Friedman, Susan Stanford, ed. *Joyce: The Return of the Repressed.* Ithaca: Cornell UP, 1993.

Kimball, Jean. "Freud, Leonardo, and Joyce: The Dimensions of a Childhood Memory." *James Joyce Quarterly* 17:2 (Winter 1980): 165–82.

Leonard, Garry M. *Reading "Dubliners" Again: A Lacanian Perspective.* Syracuse: Syracuse UP, 1993.

Restuccia, Frances L. *Joyce and the Law of the Father.* New Haven: Yale UP, 1989.

Shechner, Mark. *Joyce in Nighttown: A Psychoanalytic Inquiry into "Ulysses."* Berkeley: U of California P, 1974.

A PSYCHOANALYTIC PERSPECTIVE

KIMBERLY J. DEVLIN

"I saw that picture somewhere":
Tracking the Symptom of the Sisters of Lazarus

Verbal residues are derived primarily from auditory perceptions, so
that the system *Pcs.* [preconscious] has, as it were, a special sensory
source. The visual components of word-presentations are secondary, acquired through reading. . . . In essence a word is after
all the mnemic residue of a word that has been heard.

We must not be led, in the interests of simplification perhaps,
to forget the importance of optical mnemic residues, when they
are of *things*, or to deny that it is possible for thought-processes to
become conscious through a reversion to visual residues, and that
in many people this seems to be the favoured method. The study of
dreams and of preconscious phantasies as shown in Varendonck's
observations can give us an idea of the special character of this visual thinking. We learn that what becomes conscious in it is as a
rule only the concrete subject-matter of the thought, and that the
relations between the various elements of this subject-matter,
which is what specially characterizes thoughts, cannot be given visual expression. Thinking in pictures is, therefore, only a very incomplete form of becoming conscious. In some way, too, it stands
nearer to unconscious processes than does thinking in words, and
it is unquestionably older than the latter both ontogenetically and
phylogenetically. (Freud 10–11)

This comment from *The Ego and Id*, published in 1923, is
excerpted from Freud's theorization of how unconscious thoughts become preconscious or latent by attaching themselves to mnemic
residues to emerge—potentially—into consciousness. The passage
contains a slight ambivalence about visual thinking. On the one hand,
it acknowledges the limitations of "thinking in pictures," hinting that
such ideation eliminates crucial details, specifically "the relations between the various elements" in the subject-matter of the repressed
thought being retrieved through memory traces. But on the other
hand, it simultaneously insists at the outset that "the importance of
optical mnemic residues" must not be forgotten and concludes by noting that "thinking in pictures" is the primal mode of ideation for both
individuals and species. Pictorial thought becomes a potential crux of

psychic development, as well as a mediating aid—albeit a limited one —in enabling unconscious thoughts to return, in allowing them to outwit the regulatory psychic agencies of repression.

A case history Freud published five years earlier, "From the History of an Infantile Neurosis" (1918), is much less equivocal about the pivotal role of visuality in translating unconscious thoughts into conscious ones. To be sure, as in all of Freud's works, "verbal residues . . . derived primarily from auditory perceptions" play a crucial part in this particular record of a psychoanalytic treatment and recovery. In Freud's analysis of the Wolf Man's symptoms,[1] for instance, the concrete sounds of names recurrently provide associative clues in unraveling the logic of the neurosis. When his sister rejects his sexual advances, the Wolf Man "at once turned away from her to a little peasant girl who was a servant in the house and had the same name as his sister" (178). Later a recollection of a pear and the Russian word for it, *grusha*, lead the analysand to a repressed memory of his nursery maid, whose forename occupied the exact same signifier. An auditory parapraxis—the Wolf Man's mispronunciation of *Wespe* (German for *wasp*) as *Espe*—reveals his own initials (S. P.) and emerges as his unconscious figuration of himself as a castrated being, as a signifier lacking a certain part, symbolized in its missing letter. This verbal play runs throughout the case history to reveal the acoustic ingenuity of the unconscious in its moving of ideas into latency; but this auditory dimension is overshadowed by a visual one that Freud, curiously, never explicitly comments on. The strong visual matrix of the analysis may lie behind Freud's later concession in 1923 of "the importance of optical mnemic residues."

The Wolf Man's castration complex originates from a phantasmic visual disturbance, an imagined visual absence, and expresses itself in mediating symptoms that have marked visual keys—memories of a chopped up snake, for instance, or a phallicized woman ("[the governess] had said to the people coming behind her: 'Do look at my little tail!'" [175]). The analysand also exhibits what Stephen Dedalus would characterize as "kinetic" responses to various sights: a desirous compulsion to kiss the holy pictures in his room or a phobic flight from a butterfly opening and shutting its wings, a flight motivated by its mnemic visual residue of a woman opening and shutting her legs. The laborious construction of the unconscious primal scene hinges on

---

[1]The patient in the case is often informally referred to as the Wolf Man because of his intense phobia of wolves.

many clues and details, but two visual images are foregrounded as central: a recalled illustration of an upright wolf from a childhood book, the sight of which produced extreme anxiety in the analysand when he was young, and a contrasting optical configuration of a being on all fours, the animal-like position that, when assumed by women, aroused in him sudden feelings of inexplicable desire. The major breakthrough of the analysis, of course, follows the remembered mediating dream of the wolves and its translation into its numerous unconscious referents: the dream involves a scenario about watching and being watched and is so vividly pictorial that the patient draws it for Freud. The dreamtext becomes oddly self-reflexive insofar as the staring wolves, screen images of the father and his law, figure forth the regulatory agencies that attempt to overpower unconscious thoughts; but in their over-determined encoded messages, the wolves operate on behalf of the unconscious, outwitting the dream censor and slipping by its vigilant gaze. The strong visual axis of the case history has its origins in the neurosis's own origins in the Wolf Man's infancy: the primal scene occurs during his preverbal state where thinking in pictures predominates. Significantly, however, the hegemonic visual symptomology perdures long after the analysand's entry into orality. Freud's study of the Wolf Man illustrates that the forces of repression are subverted by optical as well as auditory clues. The regulatory regimes of the psyche loose their control over the patient's secrets through the insistence of visual symptoms, of latent optical images and impulses that facilitate the entrance of unconscious ideas into consciousness.

Like Freud's analysand, Joyce's protagonist in *Ulysses* emerges as an individual with a highly sensitive visual psyche. Leopold Bloom is attuned to particular optical pleasures ("To catch up and walk behind her if she went slowly, behind her moving hams. Pleasant to see first thing in the morning" [*U* 4.171–73]) as well as to decided optical distastes ("Her stockings are loose over her ankles. I detest that: so tasteless" [*U* 8.542]). The sight of a blind young man causes Bloom to ponder how one survives without recourse to optic perception, and his meditation concludes on a note of restrained anguish that betrays an assumptional equation of the visual with reality itself: "Poor fellow! Quite a boy. Terrible. Really terrible. What dreams would he have, not seeing? Life a dream for him. Where is the justice being born that way?" (*U* 8.1144–46).

What interests me in this essay about opticality in *Ulysses* is the way Joyce interweaves a strand of Bloom's pictorial thinking with a specific signifier that emerges—retrospectively in the "Circe" episode—as richly symptomatic. The specific signifier is the common feminine forename of "Mary"—perhaps *the* most common feminine forename in a mariolatrous culture. But psychoanalytic inquiry is precisely interested in the ways in which an individual psyche appropriates ordinary signifiers (a name, a fairytale, an illustration) and cathects them with unique meanings. It explores the ways in which the unconscious charges everyday discourse with personal connotations that work to overturn the regulatory forces of repression. The initial part of this essay will discuss the contexts in which "Mary" surfaces in Bloom's psyche to speculate, ultimately, about what exactly this symptomatic signifier betrays. I hope also to delineate in the process a paradox about visuality when used within a psychoanalytic framework. On the one hand, vision—particularly scrutinizing or surveillant vision—is often aligned with regulatory agencies (such as the superego, the law of the father, the police, the clergy, omniscient deity, and what Jacques Lacan calls "the gaze"); but on the other hand, visions—optical memories and necessarily interpretive ways of seeing—work against regulatory agencies in that they often record latent thoughts, pressing for articulation against psychic resistances.

The signifier "Mary" enters Bloom's consciousness in "Lotus-Eaters," where it is triggered by the pin Martha Clifford has used to attach the flower to her letter. The pin reminds him of a street ditty he heard sung by "two sluts that night in the Coombe" about a woman who finds herself by accident in an exhibitionist pose: "*O, Mairy lost the pin of her drawers. / She didn't know what to do / To keep it up, / To keep it up*" (*U* 5.279–84). Bloom then produces what will turn out to be a visual symptom—a recollection of a specific painting of Jesus with the sisters of Lazarus:

> Martha, Mary. I saw that picture somewhere I forget now old master or faked for money. He is sitting in their house, talking. Mysterious. Also the two sluts in the Coombe would listen.
> *To keep it up.*
> Nice kind of evening feeling. No more wandering about. Just loll there: quiet dusk: let everything rip. Forget. Tell about the places you have been, strange customs. The other one, jar on her head, was getting the supper: fruit, olives, lovely cool water out of a well, stonecold like the hole in the wall at Ashtown. Must carry a paper goblet next time I go to the trottingmatches. She listens with big dark soft eyes. Tell her: more and more: all. Then a sigh: silence. Long long long rest. (*U* 5.289–99)

The two women in the picture are associated with "the two sluts in the Coombe," in part because Mary, the sister of Lazarus, is sometimes confused with Mary Magdalene (Gifford 90). This dyad of women, in other words, is ambivalently coded, as Bloom's psyche traverses a range of moral markings: the two fallen women ("the two sluts") are conflated with the virtuous ones (the sisters of Lazarus) through the hybrid combination created by the misrecognition of one of the figures as the former prostitute among Christ's followers. After recalling this particular pictorial text, Bloom unconsciously enters it by identifying with the figure of Jesus. He can feel the temperature of the water one of the women draws from the well, for example, and he imagines himself producing a narrative for the other female figure ("Tell about the places you have been, strange customs") that turns into a confession ("She listens with big dark soft eyes. Tell her: more and more: all")—a fantasy based in Martha Clifford's epistolary request ("Please write me a long letter and tell me more" [U 5.251]). It is also worth noting, for later associative purposes, that in the recalled picture one of the sisters is in a position of servitude ("The other one, jar on her head, was getting the supper"); in its biblical pretext, which Bloom may have heard in the course of his piecemeal exposure to Catholicism, this sister complains that she "was cumbered about such serving" and is called "careful and troubled about many things" (Luke 10: 38–42). The Bible story also clarifies which woman is Mary and which one is Martha, but Bloom's recollective vision fails to identify either woman with a specific name, marking them instead in terms of two roles: the female server, preparing food, and the female confessor, hearing the wanderings of a weary Christ.

The signifier "Mary" resurfaces again later in "Lotus-Eaters" when Bloom envisions a female confessant, thus inverting one of the sister's roles in the recalled picture. The recurrence of a phrase from Martha's letter ("Then I will tell you all" [U 5.254]) within the scenario suggests that Bloom is recalling her promise to share her secrets with him in their mutually confessional correspondence. It also hints that he subliminally identifies her with the fantasy woman spilling her sins to her priest:

> Glorious and immaculate virgin. Joseph, her spouse. Peter and Paul. More interesting if you understood what it was all about. Wonderful organisation certainly, goes like clockwork. Confession. Everyone wants to. Then I will tell you all. Penance. Punish me, please. Great weapon in their hands. More than doctor or solicitor. Woman dying to. And I schschschschsch. And did you chachachachacha? And why did you? Look down at her ring to

find an excuse. Whispering gallery walls have ears. Husband learn
to his surprise. God's little joke. Then out she comes. Repentance
skindeep. Lovely shame. Pray at an altar. Hail Mary and Holy
Mary. Flowers, incense, candles melting. Hide her blushes. Salvation army blatant imitation. Reformed prostitute will address the
meeting. How I found the Lord. (*U* 5.423–34)

Bloom characterizes Catholicism as a well-regulated organization,
catering perfectly in its rituals to common psychic needs. But within
the supposedly hermetic regime of confession, he envisions potential
leaks: first a priest who could use his knowledge of various sins for
blackmail ("Great weapon in their hands") and then a confession
booth strategically placed to produce a whispering gallery, allowing
the husband of the confessant (and, of course, others) to hear the
details of the woman's transgressive dalliances. Bloom's fantasy here
symptomatizes an unconscious phobia inherent in his relationship with
Martha, a phobia made transparent in "Circe": namely, that she has
confessed her epistolary affair to the counterpart of the clergy, the
local police force.[2] The whimsical image of the confessional as a devi-
ous sound trap that facilitates spousal eavesdropping simultaneously
records an ongoing desire that inflects his relationship with his wife: a
desire for surveillance over her flirtations that aims to produce a masterful sense of power-knowledge. The associative logic of Bloom's
thinking, moving from Catholic ritual to the Salvation Army, is motivated by the shared confessional outlets of the two institutions; but his
vision earlier in the hour of the ambiguous biblical "Mary" (Mary,
sister of Lazarus, conflated with Mary Magdalene) operates as a secondary impetus for the psychic juxtaposition of the Blessed Virgin
Mary and the reformed prostitute.

Bloom's next explicitly visual symptom featuring the signifier
"Mary" appears toward the beginning of "Aeolus" and is structured
around a tripled textual mediation of William Brayden, the editor of
the *Freeman's Journal*. After noting this figure ascending the staircase,
"steered by an umbrella, a solemn beardframed face" (*U* 7.45–46),

---

[2]Joyce doubles these two regulatory forces explicitly in Stephen's retort to the nationalist Madden in *Stephen Hero*:

—We remain true to the Church because it is our national Church, the
Church our people have suffered for and would suffer for again. The police are different. We look upon them as aliens, traitors, oppressors of the people.

—The old peasant down the country doesn't seem to be of your opinion
when he counts over his greasy notes and says "I'll put the priest on Tom an' I'll
put the polisman on Mickey." (64)

Bloom hears Red Murray's question, "—Don't you think his face is like Our Saviour?," and responds to reveal his own visual associations:

> Our Saviour: beardframed oval face: talking in the dusk. Mary, Martha. Steered by an umbrella sword to the footlights: Mario the tenor.
> —Or like Mario, Mr Bloom said.
> —Yes, Red Murray agreed. But Mario was said to be the picture of Our Saviour.
> Jesusmario with rougy cheeks, doublet and spindle legs. Hand on his heart. In *Martha*.
> *Co-ome thou lost one,*
> *Co-ome thou dear one!* (*U* 7.52–60)

The allusion to an image of Christ reminds Bloom of the picture he visualized after reading Martha's letter, as the fragment "talking in the dusk" reveals: it refers back to the atmosphere of "quiet dusk" (*U* 5.294) he envisions earlier. The picture in turn reminds him of *Mario* the tenor, through the verbal associative link of *Mary* and *Martha*. This link is reinforced, of course, by Mario's performance of the role of Lionel in the light opera entitled *Martha* and by Mario's uncanny resemblance to a traditional image in the visual iconography of Christ. Because Mario gave his last stage appearance in 1871 when Bloom was only five years old, Bloom is probably remembering a picture of the tenor, just as surely as Red Murray is remembering a picture of "Our Saviour."[3] In this passage, Brayden's appearance is filtered through three textual screens (Christ, Mario, and Lionel), but by the end of it, Bloom once again unconsciously positions himself within the overdetermined representational image by silently singing Mario/Lionel's song (*"Co-ome thou lost one, / Co-ome thou dear one!"*). His earlier subliminal fantasy of himself as the pictorialized Christ facilitates the identification here. The "Mary, Martha" in Bloom's associative train refers back not only to the picture of the sisters of Lazarus, with its ambivalent moral inflections of the two female figures, but also to the light opera itself. *Martha* centers around two women who are hired at a fair as servant girls by well-to-do farmers. The ambivalent code in this operatic pretext is tied to class identity: the two female servants are in fact a queen and her maid of honor, who assume lower-class disguises out of boredom with court life (Gifford 129).

[3]This speculation about what Bloom is recalling in the above passage appeared in a recent issue of the *James Joyce Broadsheet*. The issue also features on its cover an illustrative portrait of Mario the tenor that makes patent his visual similarities to certain representations of Christ (see Bekker and Brown 4).

Yet another symptomatic "Mary" in Bloom's psychic meanderings emerges in "Lestrygonians," in the context of the most visible regulatory regime at work in Dublin. Seeing a squad of constables returning to their beats after their lunch, Bloom recalls a frightening encounter he had with the Dublin Metropolitan Police during a pro-Boer demonstration and its perduring unsettling affects: "Police whistle in my ears still" (U 8.431), he thinks to himself. This memory leads to speculations about the network of police spies that aids the workings of this particular disciplinary regime and, subsequently, a fantasy—both visual and auditory—that centers on a servant girl named "Mary":

> Never know who you're talking to. Corny Kelleher he has
> Harvey Duff in his eye. Like that Peter or Denis or James Carey
> that blew the gaff on the invincibles. Member of the corporation
> too. Egging raw youths on to get in the know all the time drawing
> secret service pay from the castle. Drop him like a hot potato. Why
> those plainclothes men are always courting slaveys. Easily twig a
> man used to uniform. Squarepushing up against a backdoor. Maul
> her a bit. Then the next thing on the menu. And who is the gentle-
> man does be visiting there? Was the young master saying any-
> thing? Peeping Tom through the keyhole. Decoy duck. Hot-
> blooded young student fooling round her fat arms ironing.
> —Are those yours, Mary?
> —I don't wear such things. . . . Stop or I'll tell the missus on you.
> Out half the night.
> —There are great times coming, Mary. Wait till you see.
> —Ah, gelong with your great times coming. (U 8.441–55)

Although the politics of this imagined scenario are not unambiguous, its context suggests that the "young student" flirting with "Mary" may be an example of one of the "plainclothes men" employed by the police and the castle to milk unsuspecting slaveys for information about the households where they work. The "great times coming" may refer to the improved economic situation the young man anticipates as a consequence of his unofficial new job. The servant girl "Mary" in this fantasy is represented as a resistant but potential leak within a domestic enclosure. She is familiar not only with the family undergarments, which she is ironing, but also with the family's politics, its visitors, and—by inference—its internal dynamics. She is psychically connected to the other female maid Bloom imagines at the outset of "Lestrygonians" and codes as the repository of compromising knowledge, as the potential witness to her priestly employer's excesses and lapses:

> I'd like to see them do the black fast Yom Kippur. Crossbuns. One meal and a collation for fear he'd collapse on the altar. A house-keeper of one of those fellows if you could pick it out of her. Never pick it out of her. Like getting L. s. d. out of him. Does himself well. No guests. All for number one. Watching his water. Bring your own bread and butter. His reverence: mum's the word. (*U* 8.35–40)

In both these fantasies, the confined space of the domicile remains in-violate, but only precariously so, much like the confession box in "Lotus-Eaters." The plainclothes deputy puts pressure on "Mary" to talk, and the hypothetical priest takes pains to swear his domestic to secrecy. Within the regulated unit known as the house*hold* (with its implicit suggestion of containment), the female servant may function as a barely visible countergaze and epistemological pore, potentially exploitable by larger regulatory structures.

In the stylistic parody in "Cyclops" that opens with "Love loves to love love," we find within the listed affairs of the heart, "Constable 14A loves Mary Kelly" (*U* 12.1493–94). This comic clue, read in con-junction with Bloom's fantasy about the servant "Mary" fondled by a secret agent of the police force, leads me to speculate that the first but unnamed "Mary" figure is actually "the nextdoor girl" Bloom ogles at the porkbutcher's in "Calypso," for he phantasmically pairs this ser-vant with a policeman as well:

> The porkbutcher snapped two sheets from the pile, wrapped up her prime sausages and made a red grimace.
> —Now, my miss, he said.
> She tendered a coin, smiling boldly, holding her thick wrist out.
> —Thank you, my miss. And one shilling threepence change. For you, please?
> Mr Bloom pointed quickly. To catch up and walk behind her if she went slowly, behind her moving hams. Pleasant to see first thing in the morning. Hurry up, damn it. Make hay while the sun shines. She stood outside the shop in sunlight and sauntered lazily to the right. He sighed down his nose: they never understand. Sodachapped hands. Crusted toenails too. Brown scapulars in tat-ters, defending her both ways. The sting of disregard glowed to

weak pleasure within his breast. For another: a constable off duty cuddling her in Eccles lane. They like them sizeable. Prime sausage. O please, Mr Policeman, I'm lost in the wood. (*U* 4.165–79)

A visual symptom can be located in the psychic appearance of the police force — the regulatory gaze of the metropolis — after an instance of actual and then fantasized voyeurism. The scopic powers that Bloom exercises over the young woman's body are checked by a more powerful source of visual surveillance: "*They* like them sizeable" refers to the Dublin Metropolitan Police, who had a minimum height requirement for jobs on the force (Gifford 73). The servant girl's fantasized lament to the enforcer of law — "O please, Mr Policeman, I'm lost in the *wood*" — contains a parapraxis, for shortly before Bloom thinks, "*Woods* his name is. Wonder what he does. Wife is oldish. New blood. No followers allowed" (*U* 4.148–50, my emphasis).[4] Bloom imagines a relationship between the older male employer and his female domestic, and one can residually hear in her complaint of helplessness to the policeman her protest against her sexual exploitation. In "Sirens" Bloom psychically pairs this young woman (linked to the phantasmic "Mary" of "Lestrygonians") with his penpal Martha, by calling up a memory of her in Woods's backyard while he writes to his mystery correspondent: "P. S. The rum tum tum. How will you pun? You punish me? Crooked skirt swinging, whack by. Tell me I want to. Know" (*U* 11.890–92). In "Nausicaa" the female dyad resurfaces in its original form as the sisters of Lazarus, recalled by Bloom for the timelessness of their apparel and revealingly contextualized in ruminations about women-on-the-market: "Dressed up to the nines for somebody. Fashion part of their charm. Just changes except when you're on the track of the secret. Except the east: Mary, Martha: now as then. No reasonable offer refused" (*U* 13.804–06).

The "Circe" episode reveals many of the unconscious thoughts that lie behind Bloom's latent visions and associations. It exposes the repressed referent behind the anonymous signifier "Mary," for instance, as a specific and real young woman, Mary Driscoll, the Blooms' former slavey and victim of the husband's unwanted sexual advances. Bloom allows this psychically troubling figure from his past to enter his consciousness very obliquely in "Hades" in a suggestive

---

[4]This parapraxis was pointed out to me by James Mitchell, a student of mine in an undergraduate course on *Ulysses* at the University of California, Riverside, in Spring 1995.

but significantly truncated thought. Mary Driscoll is more than likely the latent subtext of his response to the high voice of the acolyte at Paddy Dignam's funeral service: "*Et ne nos inducas in tentationem.* / The server piped the answer in the treble. I often thought it would be better to have boy servants. Up to fifteen or so. After that, of course . . ." (*U* 6.618–20, Joyce's ellipsis). Recognizing the word *temptation* in the Latinate phrase ("And lead us not into temptation") and hearing the soprano and hence feminized voice of the priest's server, Bloom's mind symptomatically turns to domestic servants. His tendency to sexualize the Blessed Virgin Mary ("By Bassi's blessed virgins Bloom's dark eyes went by. Bluerobed, white under, come to me. . . . That brings those rakes of fellows in: her white" [*U* 11.151–55]) may not be merely an example of desublimated mariolatry but also a function of his association of the signifier "Mary" with personal temptation. In the hint in "Hades" that mature male servants might offer a temptation to Molly and be vulnerable to her lustful overtures, the Blooms' household offers perverse equal opportunities for sexual harassment.

It is not difficult to trace the signifiers in Bloom's Circean fantasies that trigger Mary Driscoll's appearance, which allow the repressed referent of the waking visual symptoms to surface. The first mnemonic triggers are the two police agents (the First and Second Watch) whom Bloom earlier suspects of using female slaveys for inside information. The second is Signor Maffei's announced introduction of "Mademoiselle Ruby, the pride of the ring" (*U* 15.716), the abused indentured servant of circus reform fiction. The third is the accusation of "unlawfully watching and besetting" (*U* 15.733–34), Bloom's crime against his former employee. The fourth is the witness Martha, recurrently paired with Mary in Bloom's thoughts on account of the recalled picture of Lazarus's sisters. The fifth is a voice that recalls Bloom's participation in the pro-Boer demonstration ("Turncoat! Up the Boers! Who booed Joe Chamberlain?" [*U* 15.791]), the political event that generates the fantasy of the Mary pressured to reveal household secrets. The resisting domestic leak of Bloom's imagined scenario in "Lestrygonians" becomes in "Circe" the all too willing witness for the prosecution. Mary's testimony about Bloom's pathetic pretense for his sexual advances—"He surprised me in the rere of the premises, Your honour, when the missus was out shopping one morning with a request for a safety pin" (*U* 15.885–86)—retrospectively explains why the pin in Martha's letter unconsciously evokes a ditty about a "Mairy." The two working-class female witnesses are succeeded by accusatory upper-class women: this transformation may be motivated in part by Bloom's earlier association of Martha and Mary with the two servant women in the light opera *Martha*, who are in fact a queen and her maid of honor in disguise.

The regional specificity of Mary's accusation ("He surprised me in the rere of the premises") hints that Bloom assaulted her in a domestic zone he was supposed to steer clear of while she worked; the charge also resonates unmistakably of attempted anal rape. Indeed, the Circean context in which Mary Driscoll appears suggests that Bloom understands his attempted sexual exploits as a territorial violation. The fantasy sequence containing Mary includes as well Sir Philip Beaufoy, accusing Bloom of appropriating his works ("A plagiarist. A soapy sneak masquerading as a *littérateur*" [*U* 15.822–23]); Bloom himself, pretending to be pro-colonialist ("I'm as staunch a Britisher as you are, sir. I fought with the colours for king and country in the absent-minded war" [*U* 15.794–95])—as if "legitimized" military boundary assaults are an adequate defense against unauthorized private ones; and the society ladies, claiming Bloom has overstepped class lines ("This plebeian Don Juan observed me from behind a hackney car and sent me in double envelopes an obscene photograph, such as are sold after dark on Paris boulevards, insulting to any lady. I have it still" [*U* 15.1064–67]). Bloom allegedly responds to Mary's remonstrations with the command "keep it quiet" (*U* 15.893); according to her testimony, he has defensively requested either that she not report his territorial advances to Molly or that she keep her voice down, perhaps for fear that the neighbors—or, more specifically, that the neighbors' servant—will hear. Earlier in the day when he walks out to the jakes, he is warily self-conscious of the potential presence of the Woods's slavey: "He went out through the backdoor into the garden: stood to listen towards the next garden. No sound. Perhaps hanging clothes out to dry. The maid was in the garden" (*U* 4.472–74); he may be checking for her again when "before sitting down he peered through a chink up at the nextdoor windows. The king was in his countinghouse. Nobody" (*U* 4.497–99). Mary Driscoll's allegations against Bloom add a new psychological dimension to his conscious thoughts about garters and oysters. The former are his figurative attempted bribe for her sexual compliance, while the latter provide the trumped-up charges a jealous Molly uses as a pretext for firing the girl. In his waking thoughts, Bloom associates oysters with Boylan and his own imminent cuckolding ("Fizz and Red bank oysters. Effect on the sexual. Aphrodis. He was in the Red Bank this morning. Was he oysters old fish at table perhaps he young flesh in bed no June has no ar no oysters" [*U* 8.865–68]); in the unconscious phantasmagoria of "Circe," he betrays that they also have a referent to a sexual scenario in which he is not the victim but rather the victimizer. Perhaps the most disturbing and revealing element of Mary's testimony resides in the policeman's opening question to her: "Are you of the unfortunate class?" (*U* 15.865). Mary indignantly assures him that she is not, but the very possibility raised in the inquiry suggests that psychically Bloom fears that his former slavey has had to turn to prostitution for alternative employment. The victim of Bloom's failure to regulate his lusts becomes the victim of Molly's corrective ousting and, in the nightmarish question of one of his psychic watchmen, the possible victim, in turn, of the Dublin sex trade.

The policeman's imagined inquiry may explain why Bloom, out of the forty-four responses to his ad, chooses to establish a confessionary sado-masochistic correspondence with a woman named Martha. Having potentially ruined Mary, he seeks punishment—through a patent transference—from her figurative sister and *Doppelgänger* in his psychic economy. He moves, in other words, from the female server to the female confessor, substituting one figure in the pictorial text for the other. Bloom's unconscious fears about Mary's plight may motivate the vicarious and distanced forms his sexual pleasures take: his one direct extramarital dalliance backfired surely beyond his expectations in its victimizing fallout, perhaps explaining why in the present he opts for the relative safety of fantasy, voyeurism, scripted "dirty talk" from prostitutes, or the controlled erotic correspondence. Significantly, the ditty of "*O, Mairy lost the pin of her drawers*" enters Bloom's thoughts in "Lotus-Eaters" immediately after he dismisses the possibility of Martha's requested meeting ("Could meet one Sunday after the rosary. Thank you: not having any. Usual love scrimmage" [*U* 5.270–71]): the rejection of personal contact with his penpal reminds him in a latent image of the young woman whom he did indeed risk touching. The policeman's disturbing question to Mary Driscoll also hints at why the dual female figures of Mary and Martha are coded ambiguously in his mind—as virgins, as prostitutes, as a virgin and a prostitute. When one reads his early visual symptom—the recalled painting of the biblical sisters—retrospectively from the vantage point of "Circe," one can speculate that he unconsciously enters the image as a thoroughly unholy and inverse Christ-figure: as a man who turns respectable women into prostitutes, rather than the other way around. This is Bloom's dreaded counter-conversionary power.

He symptomatically enacts this perverse role in the sexgame he plays with his weary wife: "who is in your mind now tell me who are you thinking of who is it tell me his name who tell me who the german Emperor is it yes imagine Im him think of him can you feel him trying to make a whore of me what he never will" (*U* 18.94–97).

The wording of the police constable's question—"Are you of the unfortunate *class*?" (my emphasis)—implies that Bloom's sense of guilt stems primarily from the economic consequences of his lapse. Indeed, the sexual dimension of the scenario (as in most couplings in Joyce's fictions, be they successful or merely attempted) borders on the ludicrous, the comical—in the very mundanity of the setting, in the clumsiness of the encounter, and in the shabbiness of the would-be seducer's attire (*"housejacket of ripplecloth, flannel trousers, heelless slippers, unshaven, his hair rumpled"* [*U* 15.875–76]). But the economic implications of the Circean fantasy cannot be included within the comedy of the scene, simply because we know from Bloom's waking thoughts that he takes economic issues seriously and that potential impoverishment is never a laughing matter for him. After all, Bloom's main critique of Irish nationalism, as it manifested itself in 1904, is that the movement does not place preeminent emphasis on pragmatic economic concerns ("That the language question should take precedence of the economic question" [*U* 8.466–67], he thinks with exasperation in "Lestrygonians," a chapter that addresses Dublin's economic plight through contrasting images of dietary abundance and scarcity, gluttony and starvation). The phantasm of Mary Driscoll suggests that he fears he has committed what is ultimately a class-based crime: an implicit coercion of a laborer from a lower-class position that is nonetheless respectable and relatively secure to an even "lower" means of employment that is disreputed, physically hazardous, and economically unreliable. Joyce hints at the potential psychological tolls of prostitution through the sad figure of "the whore of the lane" (*U* 11.1250–51), who appears to be suffering from dementia.

These two types of exploited women in *Ulysses*—the slavey and the prostitute, merged under the signifier of "Mary"—have a definite power in Bloom's psyche, on account of their access to taboo secrets. One can speculate that Molly's dismissal of Mary from live-in maid service is motivated not only by the slavey's unwanted status as sexual rival, but also by her equally unwanted status as domestic counter-gaze, as inevitable witness to marital rifts and disharmonies (and finally, of course, their fallguy). The Blooms' one remaining domestic assistant—Mrs. Fleming, the cleaning woman—works for the couple only part-time ("Mrs Fleming is in to clean," Bloom thinks in "Hades" [*U* 6.237]) and, from Molly's account of her, sounds conveniently short-sighted ("that old Mrs Fleming you have to be walking round after her putting the things into her hands" [*U* 18.1081–83]). In retaliation for his flirtation with their nubile maid, Molly fantasizes about pairing her husband off with this older employee ("a picnic suppose we all gave 5/- each and or let him [Boylan] pay it and invite some other woman for him [Bloom] who Mrs Fleming" [*U* 18.946–47]).

Like the full-time domestic, the prostitute, too, becomes a sort of countergaze by default, a figure whose very economic disempowerment forces her into positions of epistemic power. Suggestively, the "whore of the lane" wearing the black straw sailor hat—whose appearances in both "Sirens" and "Eumaeus" make Bloom noticeably uneasy because she knows who his wife is—earns her income not only through sex but also laundering, another trade that necessarily implicates the worker in potentially compromising knowledge of others' intimate affairs. At the close of "Sirens," Bloom notes of this unnamed woman, "Off her beat here" (*U* 11.1255), turning her into a sort of policeman with a demarcated part of the city to patrol. And the "Circe" episode indeed hints—both in Bella's threat to call the police and in the provocative appearance of Corny Kelleher, the police tout—that the police and the prostitutes, at least in some circumstances, have a collaborative rather than an adversarial relationship. Bloom desires a more conventional antagonistic positioning of the police station and the brothel, as is made clear in his professed belief that the bodies of prostitutes should be subjected to a regime of mandatory inspections, regulated by an intrusive governmental gaze. This desire for control over particular female *bodies* may mask a deeper wish and express it only in displaced form. This deeper wish is disguised and symptomatized in one of Bloom's remnant sexual pleasures, in his interaction with Martha's other *Doppelgänger*, the young prostitute he pays to speak his particular language of desire (as he does his penpal, through his pecuniary gifts): "Girl in Meath street that night. All the dirty things I made her say. All wrong of course. My arks she called it. . . . And kissed my hand when I gave her the extra two shillings. Parrots. Press the button and the bird will squeak. Wish she hadn't called me sir" (*U* 13.867–72). On the surface, of course, Bloom's pleasure may appear masochistic, insofar as the girl's mispronunciation of "arse" hints that she speaks to him (or at least tries to speak to him) in a punitive discourse of flagellation. But if we read the structure of this attempted enactment of fantasy as opposed to its content, an alternate wish emerges, a wish in which Bloom is not the abject penitent, but rather the domineering master. As his insistence on the prostitute's verbal mimicry implies, Bloom secretly desires to regulate not merely the *bodies,* but also the *speech* of a specific subculture of exploited women. In his psyche, the young prostitute is not only the orally mimetic parrot but also a mechanical toy, encodings that doubly desubjectify and silence her point of view. Bloom is clearly irritated when she departs from his script — "Wish she hadn't called me sir" — in such a way that emphasizes his real position of power beneath his fantasized role of abjection. Submerged beneath its masochistic surface, this fantasy scenario bespeaks a phobic need to control the discourse of those perversely privileged female subjectivities who constitute a countergaze, a countergaze that knows the dirty secrets hidden in many a male Dubliner's bottom drawer.

WORKS CITED

Bekker, Pieter, and Richard Brown, eds. *James Joyce Broadsheet* 19 (Feb. 1986): 1–4.

Freud, Sigmund. *The Ego and the Id.* Trans. Joan Riviere. Ed. James Strachey. New York: Norton, 1962.

———. "From the History of an Infantile Neurosis." *Three Case Histories.* Ed. Philip Rieff. New York: Collier, 1993. 161–280.

Gifford, Don, with Robert J. Seidman. *"Ulysses" Annotated: Notes for James Joyce's "Ulysses."* Rev. ed. Berkeley: U of California P, 1988.

Joyce, James. *Stephen Hero.* New York: New Directions, 1963.

Lacan, Jacques. "Of the Gaze as *Objet Petit a.*" *The Four Fundamental Concepts of Psycho-Analysis.* Ed. Jacques-Alain Miller. Trans. Alan Sheridan. New York: Norton, 1981.

Marxist Criticism
and
Ulysses

WHAT IS MARXIST CRITICISM?

To the question "What is Marxist criticism?" it may be tempting to respond with another question: "What does it matter?" In light of the rapid and largely unanticipated demise of Soviet-style communism in the former USSR and throughout Eastern Europe, it is understandable to suppose that Marxist literary analysis would disappear too, quickly becoming an anachronism in a world enamored with full-market capitalism.

In fact, however, there is no reason why Marxist criticism should weaken, let alone disappear. It is, after all, a phenomenon distinct from Soviet and Eastern European communism, having had its beginnings nearly eighty years before the Bolshevik revolution and having thrived, since the 1940s, mainly in the West—not as a form of communist propaganda but rather as a form of critique, a discourse for interrogating *all* societies and their texts in terms of certain specific issues. Those issues—including race, class, and the attitudes shared within a given culture—are as much with us as ever, not only in contemporary Russia but also in the United States.

The argument could even be made that Marxist criticism has been strengthened by the collapse of Soviet-style communism. There was a time, after all, when few self-respecting Anglo-American journals would use Marxist terms or models, however illuminating, to analyze Western issues or problems. It smacked of sleeping with the enemy. With the collapse of the Kremlin, however, old taboos began to give way. Even the staid *Wall Street Journal* now seems comfortable using phrases like "worker alienation" to discuss the problems plaguing the American business world.

The assumption that Marxist criticism will die on the vine of a moribund political system rests in part on another mistaken assumption, namely, that Marxist literary analysis is practiced only by people who would like to see society transformed into a Marxist-communist state, one created through land reform, the redistribution of wealth, a tightly and centrally managed economy, the abolition of institutionalized religion, and so on. In fact, it has never been necessary to be a communist political revolutionary to be classified as a Marxist literary critic. (Many of the critics discussed in this introduction actually *fled* communist societies to live in the West.) Nor is it necessary to like only those literary works with a radical social vision or to dislike books that represent or even reinforce a middle-class, capitalist world-view. It is necessary, however, to adopt what most students of literature would consider a radical definition of the purpose and function of literary criticism.

More traditional forms of criticism, according to the Marxist critic Pierre Macherey, "set . . . out to deliver the text from its own silences by coaxing it into giving up its true, latent, or hidden meaning." Inevitably, however, non-Marxist criticism "intrude[s] its own discourse between the reader and the text" (qtd. in Bennett 107). Marxist critics, by contrast, do not attempt to discover hidden meanings in texts. Or if they do, they do so only after seeing the text, first and foremost, as a material product to be understood in broadly historical terms. That is to say, a literary work is first viewed as a product *of* work (and hence of the realm of production and consumption we call economics). Second, it may be looked upon as a work that *does* identifiable work of its own. At one level, that work is usually to enforce and reinforce the prevailing ideology, that is, the network of conventions, values, and opinions to which the majority of people uncritically subscribe.

This does not mean that Marxist critics merely describe the obvious. Quite the contrary: the relationship that the Marxist critic Terry Eagleton outlines in *Criticism and Ideology* (1978) among the soaring cost of books in the nineteenth century, the growth of lending libraries, the practice of publishing "three-decker" novels (so that three borrowers could be reading the same book at the same time), and the changing *content* of those novels is highly complex in its own way. But the complexity Eagleton finds is not that of the deeply buried meaning of the text. Rather, it is that of the complex web of social and economic relationships that were prerequisite to the work's production. Marxist criticism does not seek to be, in Eagleton's words, "a passage from text to reader." Indeed, "its task is to show the text as it cannot know itself, to manifest those conditions of its making (inscribed in its very letter) about which it is necessarily silent" (43).

As everyone knows, Marxism began with Karl Marx, the nineteenth-century German philosopher best known for writing *Das Kapital,* the seminal work of the communist movement. What everyone doesn't know is that Marx was also the first Marxist literary critic (much as Sigmund Freud, who psychoanalyzed E. T. A. Hoffmann's supernatural tale "The Sandman," was the first Freudian literary critic). During the 1830s Marx wrote critical essays on writers such as Goethe and Shakespeare (whose tragic vision of Elizabethan disintegration he praised).

The fact that Marxist literary criticism began with Marx himself is hardly surprising, given Marx's education and early interests. Trained in the classics at the University of Bonn, Marx wrote literary imitations, his own poetry, a failed novel, and a fragment of a tragic drama (*Oulanem*) before turning to contemplative and political philosophy. Even after he met Friedrich Engels in 1843 and began collaborating on works such as *The German Ideology* and *The Communist Manifesto,* Marx maintained a keen interest in literary writers and their works. He and Engels argued about the poetry of Heinrich Heine, admired Hermann Freiligrath (a poet critical of the German aristocracy), and faulted the playwright Ferdinand Lassalle for writing about a reactionary knight in the Peasants' War rather than about more progressive aspects of German history.

As these examples suggest, Marx and Engels would not—indeed, could not—think of aesthetic matters as being distinct and independent from such things as politics, economics, and history. Not surprisingly, they viewed the alienation of the worker in industrialized, capitalist societies as having grave consequences for the arts. How can people mechanically stamping out things that bear no mark of their producer's individuality (people thereby "reified," turned into things themselves) be expected to recognize, produce, or even consume things of beauty? And if there is no one to consume something, there will soon be no one to produce it, especially in an age in which production (even of something like literature) has come to mean *mass* (and therefore profitable) production.

In *The German Ideology* (1846), Marx and Engels expressed their sense of the relationship between the arts, politics, and basic economic reality in terms of a general social theory. Economics, they argued, provides the "base" or "infrastructure" of society, but from that base emerges a "superstructure" consisting of law, politics, philosophy, religion, and art.

Marx later admitted that the relationship between base and superstructure may be indirect and fluid: every change in economics may not be reflected by an immediate change in ethics or literature. In *The Eighteenth Brumaire of Louis Bonaparte* (1852), he came up with the word *homology* to describe the sometimes unbalanced, often delayed, and almost always loose correspondence between base and superstructure. And later in that same decade, while working on an introduction to his *Political Economy,* Marx further relaxed the base–superstructure relationship. Writing on the excellence of ancient Greek art (versus the primitive nature of ancient Greek economics), he conceded that a gap sometimes opens up between base and superstructure—between economic forms and those produced by the creative mind.

Nonetheless, *at* base the old formula was maintained. Economics remained basic and the connection between economics and superstructural elements of society was reaffirmed. Central to Marxism and Marxist literary criticism was and is the following "materialist" insight: consciousness, without which such things as art cannot be produced, is not the source of social forms and economic conditions. It is, rather, their most important product.

Marx and Engels, drawing upon the philosopher G. W. F. Hegel's theories about the dialectical synthesis of ideas out of theses and antitheses, believed that a revolutionary class war (pitting the capitalist class against a proletarian, antithetical class) would lead eventually to the synthesis of a new social and economic order. Placing their faith not in the idealist Hegelian dialectic but, rather, in what they called "dialectical materialism," they looked for a secular and material salvation of humanity—one in, not beyond, history—via revolution and not via divine intervention. And they believed that the communist society eventually established would be one capable of producing new forms of consciousness and belief and therefore, ultimately, great art.

The revolution anticipated by Marx and Engels did not occur in their century, let alone lifetime. When it finally did take place, it didn't happen in places where Marx and Engels had thought it might be successful: the United States, Great Britain, and Germany. It happened, rather, in 1917 Russia, a country long ruled by despotic czars but also enlightened by the works of powerful novelists and playwrights, including Chekhov, Pushkin, Tolstoy, and Dostoyevsky.

Perhaps because of its significant literary tradition, Russia produced revolutionaries like V.I. Lenin, who shared not only Marx's interest in literature but also his belief in literature's ultimate importance. But it was not without some hesitation that Lenin endorsed the significance of texts written during the reign of the czars. Well before 1917 he had questioned what the relationship should be between a society undergoing a revolution and the great old literature of its bourgeois past.

Lenin attempted to answer that question in a series of essays on Tolstoy that he wrote between 1908 and 1911. Tolstoy—the author of *War and Peace* and *Anna Karenina*—was an important nineteenth-century Russian writer whose views did not accord with all of those of young Marxist revolutionaries. Continuing interest in a writer like Tolstoy may be justified, Lenin reasoned, given the primitive and unenlightened economic order of the society that produced him. Since superstructure usually lags behind base (and is therefore usually *more* primitive), the attitudes of a Tolstoy were relatively progressive when viewed in light of the monarchical and precapitalist society out of which they arose.

Moreover, Lenin also reasoned, the writings of the great Russian realists would *have* to suffice, at least in the short run. Lenin looked forward, in essays like "Party Organization and Party Literature," to the day in which new artistic forms would be produced by progressive writers with revolutionary political views and agendas. But he also knew that a great proletarian literature was unlikely to evolve until a thoroughly literate proletariat had been produced by the educational system.

Lenin was hardly the only revolutionary leader involved in setting up the new Soviet state who took a strong interest in literary matters. In 1924 Leon Trotsky published a book called *Literature and Revolution,* which is still acknowledged as a classic of Marxist literary criticism.

Trotsky worried about the direction in which Marxist aesthetic theory seemed to be going. He responded skeptically to groups like Proletkult, which opposed tolerance toward pre- and nonrevolutionary writers, and which called for the establishment of a new, proletarian culture.

Trotsky warned of the danger of cultural sterility and risked unpopularity by pointing out that there is no necessary connection between the quality of a literary work and the quality of its author's politics.

In 1927 Trotsky lost a power struggle with Josef Stalin, a man who believed, among other things, that writers should be "engineers" of "human souls." After Trotsky's expulsion from the Soviet Union, views held by groups like Proletkult and the Left Front of Art (LEF), and by theorists such as Nikolai Bukharin and A. A. Zhdanov, became more prevalent. Speaking at the First Congress of the Union of Soviet Writers in 1934, the Soviet author Maxim Gorky called for writing that would "make labor the principal hero of our books." It was at the same writers' congress that "socialist realism," an art form glorifying workers and the revolutionary State, was made Communist party policy and the official literary form of the USSR.

Of those critics active in the USSR after the expulsion of Trotsky and the unfortunate triumph of Stalin, two critics stand out. One, Mikhail Bakhtin, was a Russian, later a Soviet, critic who spent much of his life in a kind of internal exile. Many of his essays were written in the 1930s and not published in the West or translated until the late 1960s. His work comes out of an engagement with the Marxist intellectual tradition as well as out of an indirect, even hidden, resistance to the Soviet government. It has been important to Marxist critics writing in the West because his theories provide a means to decode submerged social critique, especially in early modern texts. He viewed language—especially literary texts—in terms of discourses and dialogues. Within a novel written in a society in flux, for instance, the narrative may include an official, legitimate discourse, plus another infiltrated by challenging comments and even retorts. In a 1929 book on Dostoyevsky and a 1940 study titled *Rabelais and His World*, Bakhtin examined what he calls "polyphonic" novels, each characterized by a multiplicity of voices or discourses. In Dostoyevsky the independent status of a given character is marked by the difference of his or her language from that of the narrator. (The narrator's voice, too, can in fact be a dialogue.) In works by Rabelais, Bakhtin finds that the (profane) language of the carnival and of other popular festivals plays against and parodies the more official discourses, that is, of the king, church, or even socially powerful intellectuals. Bakhtin influenced modern cultural criticism by showing, in a sense, that the conflict between "high" and "low" culture takes place not only between classic and popular texts but also between the "dialogic" voices that exist within many books—whether "high" or "low."

The other subtle Marxist critic who managed to survive Stalin's dictatorship and his repressive policies was Georg Lukács. A Hungarian who had begun his career as an "idealist" critic, Lukács had converted to Marxism in 1919; renounced his earlier, Hegelian work shortly thereafter; visited Moscow in 1930–31; and finally emigrated to the USSR in 1933, just one year before the First Congress of the Union of Soviet Writers met. Lukács was far less narrow in his views than the most strident Stalinist Soviet critics of the 1930s and 1940s. He disliked much socialist realism and appreciated prerevolutionary, realistic novels that broadly reflected cultural "totalities"—and were populated with characters representing human "types" of the author's place and time. (Lukács was particularly fond of the historical canvasses painted by the early nineteenth-century novelist Sir Walter Scott.) But like his more rigid and censorious contemporaries, he drew the line at accepting nonrevolutionary, modernist works like James Joyce's *Ulysses*. He condemned movements like expressionism and symbolism, preferring works with "content" over more decadent, experimental works characterized mainly by "form."

With Lukács its most liberal and tolerant critic from the early 1930s until well into the 1960s, the Soviet literary scene degenerated to the point that the works of great writers like Franz Kafka were no longer read, either because they were viewed as decadent, formal experiments or because they "engineered souls" in "nonprogressive" directions. Officially sanctioned works were generally ones in which artistry lagged far behind the politics (no matter how bad the politics were).

Fortunately for the Marxist critical movement, politically radical critics *outside* the Soviet Union were free of its narrow, constricting policies and, consequently, able fruitfully to develop the thinking of Marx, Engels, and Trotsky. It was these non-Soviet Marxists who kept Marxist critical theory alive and useful in discussing all *kinds* of literature, written across the entire historical spectrum.

Perhaps because Lukács was the best of the Soviet communists writing Marxist criticism in the 1930s and 1940s, non-Soviet Marxists tended to develop their ideas by publicly opposing those of Lukács. German dramatist and critic Bertolt Brecht countered Lukács by arguing that art ought to be viewed as a field of production, not as a container of "content." Brecht also criticized Lukács for his attempt to enshrine realism at the expense not only of other "isms" but also of poetry and drama, both of which had been largely ignored by Lukács.

Even more outspoken was Brecht's critical champion Walter Benjamin, a German Marxist who, in the 1930s, attacked those conventional and traditional literary forms conveying a stultifying "aura" of culture. Benjamin praised dadaism and, more important, new forms of art ushered in by the age of mechanical reproduction. Those forms—including radio and film—offered hope, he felt, for liberation from capitalist culture, for they were too new to be part of its stultifyingly ritualistic traditions.

But of all the anti-Lukácsians outside the USSR who made a contribution to the development of Marxist literary criticism, the most important was probably Theodor Adorno. Leader since the early 1950s of the Frankfurt school of Marxist criticism, Adorno attacked Lukács for his dogmatic rejection of nonrealist modern literature and for his belief in the primacy of content over form. Art does not equal science, Adorno insisted. He went on to argue for art's autonomy from empirical forms of knowledge and to suggest that the interior monologues of modernist works (by Beckett and Proust) reflect the fact of modern alienation in a way that Marxist criticism ought to find compelling.

In addition to turning against Lukács and his overly constrictive canon, Marxists outside the Soviet Union were able to take advantage of insights generated by non-Marxist critical theories being developed in post–World War II Europe. One of the movements that came to be of interest to non-Soviet Marxists was structuralism, a scientific approach to the study of humankind whose proponents believed that all elements of culture, including literature, could be understood as parts of a system of signs. Using modern linguistics as a model, structuralists like Claude Lévi-Strauss broke down the myths of various cultures into "mythemes" in an attempt to show that there are structural correspondences, or homologies, between the mythical elements produced by various human communities across time.

Of the European structuralist Marxists, one of the most influential was Lucien Goldmann, a Rumanian critic living in Paris. Goldmann combined structuralist principles with Marx's base–superstructure model in order to show how economics determines the mental structures of social groups, which are reflected in literary texts. Goldmann rejected the idea of individual human genius, choosing to see works, instead, as the "collective" products of "trans-individual" mental structures. In early studies, such as *The Hidden God* (1955), he related seventeenth-century French texts (such as Racine's *Phèdre*) to the ideology of Jansenism. In later works, he applied Marx's base–superstructure model even more strictly, describing a relationship between economic conditions and texts unmediated by an intervening, collective consciousness.

In spite of his rigidity and perhaps because of his affinities with structuralism, Goldmann came to be seen in the 1960s as the proponent of a kind of watered-down, "humanist" Marxism. He was certainly viewed that way by the French Marxist Louis Althusser, a disciple not of Lévi-Strauss and structuralism but rather of the psychoanalytic theorist Jacques Lacan and of the Italian communist Antonio Gramsci, famous for his writings about ideology and "hegemony." (Gramsci used the latter word to refer to the pervasive, web-like system of assumptions and values that shapes the way things look, what they mean, and therefore what reality *is* for the majority of people within a culture.)

Like Gramsci, Althusser viewed literary works primarily in terms of their relationship to ideology, the function of which, he argued, is to (re)produce the existing relations of production in a given society. Dave Laing, in *The Marxist Theory of Art* (1978), has attempted to explain this particular insight of Althusser by saying that ideologies, through the "ensemble of habits, moralities, and opinions" that can be found in any literary text, "ensure that the work-force (and those responsible for re-producing them in the family, school, etc.) are maintained in their position of subordination to the dominant class" (91). This is not to say that Althusser thought of the masses as a brainless multitude following only the dictates of the prevailing ideology: Althusser followed Gramsci in suggesting that even working-class people have some freedom to struggle against ideology and to change history. Nor is it to say that Althusser saw ideology as being a coherent, consistent force. In fact, he saw it as being riven with contradictions that works of literature sometimes expose and even widen. Thus Althusser followed Marx and Gramsci in believing that although literature must be seen in *relation* to ideology, it—like all social forms—has some degree of autonomy.

Althusser's followers included Pierre Macherey, who in *A Theory of Literary Production* (1978) developed Althusser's concept of the relationship between literature and ideology. A realistic novelist, he argued, attempts to produce a unified, coherent text, but instead ends up producing a work containing lapses, omissions, gaps. This happens because within ideology there are subjects that cannot be covered, things that cannot be said, contradictory views that aren't recognized as contradictory. (The critic's challenge, in this case, is to supply what the text cannot say, thereby making sense of gaps and contradictions.)

But there is another reason why gaps open up and contradictions become evident in texts. Works don't just reflect ideology (which Goldmann had referred to as "myth" and which Macherey refers to as a system of "illusory social beliefs"); they are also "fictions," works of art, *products* of ideology that have what Goldmann would call a "world-view" to offer. What kind of product, Macherey implicitly asks, is identical to the thing that produced it? It is hardly surprising, then, that Balzac's fiction shows French peasants in two different lights, only one of which is critical and judgmental, only one of which is baldly ideological. Writing approvingly on Macherey and Macherey's mentor Althusser in *Marxism and Literary Criticism* (1976), Terry Eagleton says: "It is by giving ideology a determinate form, fixing it within certain fictional limits, that art is able to distance itself from [ideology], thus revealing . . . [its] limits" (19).

A follower of Althusser, Macherey is sometimes referred to as a "post-Althusserian Marxist." Eagleton, too, is often described that way, as is his American contemporary Fredric Jameson. Jameson and Eagleton, as well as being post-Althusserians, are also among the few Anglo-American critics who have closely followed and significantly developed Marxist thought.

Before them, Marxist interpretation in English was limited to the work of a handful of critics: Christopher Caudwell, Christopher Hill, Arnold Kettle, E. P. Thompson, and Raymond Williams. Of these, Williams was perhaps least Marxist in orientation: he felt that Marxist critics, ironically, tended too much to isolate economics from culture; that they overlooked the individualism of people, opting instead to see them as "masses"; and that even more ironically, they had become an elitist group. But if the least Marxist of the British Marxists, Williams was also by far the most influential. Preferring to talk about "culture" instead of ideology, Williams argued in works such as *Culture and Society 1780–1950* (1958) that culture is "lived experience" and, as such, an interconnected set of social properties, each and all grounded in and influencing history.

Terry Eagleton's *Criticism and Ideology* (1978) is in many ways a response to the work of Williams. Responding to Williams's statement in *Culture and Society* that "there are in fact no masses; there are only ways of seeing people as masses" (289), Eagleton writes:

> That men and women really are now unique individuals was
> Williams's (unexceptionable) insistence; but it was a proposition
> bought at the expense of perceiving the fact that they must mass

and fight to achieve their full individual humanity. One has only to adapt Williams's statement to "There are in fact no classes; there are only ways of seeing people as classes" to expose its theoretical paucity. (*Criticism* 29)

Eagleton goes on, in *Criticism and Ideology*, to propose an elaborate theory about how history—in the form of "general," "authorial," and "aesthetic" ideology—enters texts, which in turn may revivify, open up, or critique those same ideologies, thereby setting in motion a process that may alter history. He shows how texts by Jane Austen, Matthew Arnold, Charles Dickens, George Eliot, Joseph Conrad, and T. S. Eliot deal with and transmute conflicts at the heart of the general and authorial ideologies behind them: conflicts between morality and individualism, and between individualism and social organicism and utilitarianism.

As all this emphasis on ideology and conflict suggests, a modern British Marxist like Eagleton, even while acknowledging the work of a British Marxist predecessor like Williams, is more nearly developing the ideas of Continental Marxists like Althusser and Macherey. That holds, as well, for modern American Marxists like Fredric Jameson. For although he makes occasional, sympathetic references to the works of Williams, Thompson, and Hill, Jameson makes far more *use* of Lukács, Adorno, and Althusser as well as non-Marxist structuralist, psychoanalytic, and poststructuralist critics.

In the first of several influential works, *Marxism and Form* (1971), Jameson takes up the question of form and content, arguing that the former is "but the working out" of the latter "in the realm of superstructure" (329). (In making such a statement Jameson opposes not only the tenets of Russian formalists, for whom content had merely been the fleshing out of form, but also those of so-called vulgar Marxists, who tended to define form as mere ornamentation or window-dressing.) In his later work *The Political Unconscious* (1981), Jameson uses what in *Marxism and Form* he had called "dialectical criticism" to synthesize out of structuralism and poststructuralism, Freud and Lacan, Althusser and Adorno, a set of complex arguments that can only be summarized reductively.

The fractured state of societies and the isolated condition of individuals, he argues, may be seen as indications that there originally existed an unfallen state of something that may be called "primitive communism." History—which records the subsequent divisions and alienations—limits awareness of its own contradictions and of that lost,

Better State, via ideologies and their manifestation in texts whose strategies essentially contain and repress desire, especially revolutionary desire, into the collective unconscious. (In Conrad's *Lord Jim,* Jameson shows, the knowledge that governing classes don't *deserve* their power is contained and repressed by an ending that metaphysically blames Nature for the tragedy and that melodramatically blames wicked Gentleman Brown.)

As demonstrated by Jameson in analyses like the one mentioned above, textual strategies of containment and concealment may be discovered by the critic, but only by the critic practicing dialectical criticism, that is to say, a criticism aware, among other things, of its *own* status as ideology. All thought, Jameson concludes, is ideological; only through ideological thought that knows itself as such can ideologies be seen through and eventually transcended.

Patrick McGee begins the following essay, "'Heavenly Bodies': *Ulysses* and the Ethics of Marxism," in a somewhat unusual, autobiographical mode, recounting his involvement in a radical Marxist group, the Spartacists, during the early 1970s. He also recalls the close questioning he endured from the group when he read *Ulysses;* in fact, his fellow revolutionaries questioned him not only about the appropriateness and value of Joyce's work but also of other books and movies they perceived as "bourgeois." McGee, a self-described housepainter's son, dropped out of the Spartacist League shortly thereafter and commenced the study of literary and cinematic art. He admits that, in so doing, he abandoned one world of illusion for another, but he also points out the difference between the consciously intended illusions of art and the unwitting ones embraced and perpetuated by political dogma.

McGee proceeds by quoting German Marxist Walter Benjamin's claim that "discretion concerning one's own existence, once an aristocratic virtue, has become more and more an affair of petty-bourgeois parvenus." Benjamin, McGee maintains, "saw a link between a Marxist vision of the world and certain monumental acts of indiscretion," that is, artistic works that "collapse the boundary between the personal and the social, the private and the public, the individual and the collective." McGee argues that Joyce produced just such a monumental act in *Ulysses,* "disclos[ing] with shocking indifference" everything from family secrets to bodily functions. In doing so, Joyce, though not a Maxist himself, placed art in the context of social and economic reality; to use broader and, more specifically, Marxist terminology, Joyce presented superstructure in terms of the economic base and prevailing means of production. Joyce also accomplished, in a radically creative way, what McGee hopes to accomplish critically by beginning and ending his reading of *Ulysses* with details of his own personal political history. McGee's "Heavenly Bodies" may not be the "monumental act of indiscretion" that *Ulysses* is, but its author does seek to be indiscreet in the Benjaminian sense of avoiding the "petty-bourgeois parvenus" of supposedly impersonal and objective political discourse.

McGee uses the Marxist notion that art mediates between the material and social world on one hand and the realm of the ideal on the other to explain that Joyce's *Ulysses* mediates "between bodily social existence and aesthetic form" by disclosing the relationship between the two. The body is explored or even rediscovered through linguistic mediation; conversely, language is shown to be invested with the imaginary value of bodily sensation. For instance, orgasmic delight pervades Gerty MacDowell's statement: "O so lovely, O, soft, sweet, soft!" And Stephen, McGee asserts, "speaks and writes in an effort to rediscover the body as a thing-in-itself, a thing that would be the ground of social change and that he identifies with the mother's womb as its point of origin."

McGee contrasts Stephen, who seeks to know the body through language, with Leopold Bloom, who "takes [the body] for granted and is much more interested in experiencing its different pleasures than in knowing its essence." For the "melancholic Stephen, art centers on the ego and makes the body—in this case, Stephen's body—into a symptom, the signifier of what it lacks in order to be whole." Bloom, by contrast, "subordinates his symbolic demand for love to his own physical needs and to the needs of those around him." The contrast McGee draws between the two characters is *not* meant to imply that "Bloom's relation to the body is natural, while Stephen's is unnatural or ideological." Rather, McGee seeks to show how "every character in *Ulysses* represents a limited vision of the social totality, whether it takes the form of Bloom's utopian fantasies in 'Circe' or Stephen's elitist disavowal of his sister's poverty in 'Wandering Rocks.'"

McGee's discussion of ideology is indebted not only to Terry Eagleton but, more significantly, to Louis Althusser's definition of ideology as "the imaginary relation of . . . individuals to the real relations in which they live" (165). In subsequently discussing the relation of the "imaginary" to the "real," McGee turns to the thought of French psychoanalytic theorist Jacques Lacan, who defined the imaginary and the real as two of the three "orders of subjectivity" (the third being the "symbolic"). Later, McGee applies Antonio Gramsci's concept of hegemony and, still later, Theodor Adorno's thought. He argues that "*Ulysses* is structured" by "a contradiction between the ideology of the aesthetic and the ideology of the body." Although "formally" the novel "is a pure expression of aesthetic ideology in so far as it posits itself as an autonomous work of art, what Adorno calls the 'windowless monad,'" it is "precisely as an autonomous whole, as an aesthetic body, that *Ulysses* manifests its materiality and reveals its commodity form as the form of its historical existence. *Ulysses* is what Adorno would call an absolute commodity, a social product which 'rids itself of the ideology inherent in the commodity form.'"

Unlike those Marxists who view Joyce ultimately as a traditionalist whose main interest is in literary forms and styles, McGee argues for the radical nature of Joyce's accomplishment. "There is no contradiction," he writes, "between Joyce's 'naturalism,' if you will, and his experiments with style. Joyce always insists on representing the unrepresentable, including the body's processes that have been disavowed by the norms of traditional literature and conventional culture." What makes Joyce's representations so revolutionary, McGee maintains, is the way they celebrate the pleasure Bloom takes in his bowel movement or that Gerty's language manifests rather than simply describing naturalistically "the process that would find its ideal version in a biology textbook." ("Joyce," McGee writes, "does not try to efface the gap between language and Gerty's 'real' orgasm (whatever that would be) in the manner of [D. H.] Lawrence. It isn't the orgasm that is Joyce's object of representation but the language that becomes charged with pleasure as its imaginary value.") Thus, "the styles of *Ulysses* and all of its technical innovations articulate the body not as something outside but immanent to representation," indeed, as the very "material basis of representation."

McGee concludes "Heavenly Bodies" by saying, "I don't know if it is appropriate for me to call myself a Marxist critic." He goes on to say, however, that he has "tried to model" his form of criticism on "the work of . . . Benjamin and Adorno"—not on their critical styles but, rather, on the "concept of constellation" that lies behind their work. According to that concept, the critic's job is to dismantle and reconfigure the components of a given text, thereby representing—and, in Eagleton's words, "redeeming"—the work's meaning and value.

But the appropriateness of referring to McGee as a Marxist critic is perhaps best belied by another statement, namely, that "Marxist or any other form of political criticism is not a substitute for political action:

it is a form of political action. . . . Critical practice occupies a position in a historical constellation of forces that must involve many other political and social positions. Within that constellation, there are many forms of action in which decisions have to be made—political decisions with implications for the lives of 'real' human beings. Even criticism requires a decision, and it is never simply an act of inconsequential free play."

Ross C Murfin

MARXIST CRITICISM: A SELECTED BIBLIOGRAPHY

Marx, Engels, Lenin, and Trotsky

Engels, Friedrich. *The Condition of the Working Class in England.* Ed. and trans. W. O. Henderson and W. H. Chaloner. Stanford: Stanford UP, 1968.

Lenin, V. I. *On Literature and Art.* Moscow: Progress, 1967.

Marx, Karl. *Selected Writings.* Ed. David McLellan. Oxford: Oxford UP, 1977.

Trotsky, Leon. *Literature and Revolution.* New York: Russell, 1967.

General Introductions to and Reflections on Marxist Criticism

Bennett, Tony. *Formalism and Marxism.* London: Methuen, 1979.

Demetz, Peter. *Marx, Engels, and the Poets.* Chicago: U of Chicago P, 1967.

Eagleton, Terry. *Literary Theory: An Introduction.* Minneapolis: U of Minnesota P, 1983.

———. *Marxism and Literary Criticism.* Berkeley: U of California P, 1976.

Elster, Jon. *An Introduction to Karl Marx.* Cambridge: Cambridge UP, 1985.

———. *Nuts and Bolts for the Social Sciences.* Cambridge: Cambridge UP, 1989.

Fokkema, D. W., and Elrud Kunne-Ibsch. *Theories of Literature in the Twentieth Century: Structuralism, Marxism, Aesthetics of Reception, Semiotics.* New York: St. Martin's, 1977. See ch. 4, "Marxist Theories of Literature."

Frow, John. *Marxism and Literary History.* Cambridge: Harvard UP, 1986.

Jefferson, Ann, and David Robey. *Modern Literary Theory: A Critical Introduction.* Totowa: Barnes, 1982. See the essay "Marxist Literary Theories," by David Forgacs.

Laing, Dave. *The Marxist Theory of Art.* Brighton, Eng.: Harvester, 1978.

Selden, Raman. *A Readers' Guide to Contemporary Literary Theory.* Lexington: U of Kentucky P, 1985. See ch. 2, "Marxist Theories."

Slaughter, Cliff. *Marxism, Ideology, and Literature.* Atlantic Highlands: Humanities, 1980.

Some Classic Marxist Studies and Statements

Adorno, Théodor. *Prisms: Cultural Criticism and Society.* Trans. Samuel Weber and Sherry Weber. Cambridge: MIT P, 1982.

Althusser, Louis. *For Marx.* Trans. Ben Brewster. New York: Pantheon, 1969.

Althusser, Louis, and Étienne Balibar. *Reading Capital.* Trans. Ben Brewster. New York: Pantheon, 1971.

Bakhtin, Mikhail. *The Dialogic Imagination: Four Essays.* Ed. Michael Holquist. Trans. Caryl Emerson. Austin: U of Texas P, 1981.

———. *Rabelais and His World.* Trans. Hélène Iswolsky. Cambridge: MIT P, 1968.

Benjamin, Walter. *Illuminations.* Ed. with introd. by Hannah Arendt. Trans. H. Zohn. New York: Harcourt, 1968.

Caudwell, Christopher. *Illusion and Reality.* 1935. New York: Russell, 1955.

———. *Studies in a Dying Culture.* London: Lawrence, 1938.

Goldmann, Lucien. *The Hidden God.* New York: Humanities, 1964.

———. *Towards a Sociology of the Novel.* London: Tavistock, 1975.

Gramsci, Antonio. *Selections from the Prison Notebooks.* Ed. Quintin Hoare and Geoffrey Nowell Smith. New York: International UP, 1971.

Kettle, Arnold. *An Introduction to the English Novel.* New York: Harper, 1960.

Lukács, Georg. *The Historical Novel.* Trans. H. Mitchell and S. Mitchell. Boston: Beacon, 1963.

———. *Studies in European Realism.* New York: Grosset, 1964.

———. *The Theory of the Novel.* Cambridge: MIT P, 1971.

Marcuse, Herbert. *One-Dimensional Man.* Boston: Beacon, 1964.

Thompson, E. P. *The Making of the English Working Class*. New York: Pantheon, 1964.

———. *William Morris: Romantic to Revolutionary*. New York: Pantheon, 1977.

Williams, Raymond. *Culture and Society 1780–1950*. New York: Harper, 1958.

———. *The Long Revolution*. New York: Columbia UP, 1961.

———. *Marxism and Literature*. Oxford: Oxford UP, 1977.

Wilson, Edmund. *To the Finland Station*. Garden City: Doubleday, 1953.

Studies by and of Post-Althusserian Marxists

Dowling, William C. *Jameson, Althusser, Marx: An Introduction to "The Political Unconscious."* Ithaca: Cornell UP, 1984.

Eagleton, Terry. *Criticism and Ideology: A Study in Marxist Literary Theory*. London: Verso, 1978.

———. *Exiles and Émigrés*. New York: Schocken, 1970.

Goux, Jean-Joseph. *Symbolic Economies after Marx and Freud*. Trans. Jennifer Gage. Ithaca: Cornell UP, 1990.

Jameson, Fredric. *Marxism and Form: Twentieth-Century Dialectical Theories of Literature*. Princeton: Princeton UP, 1971.

———. *The Political Unconscious: Narrative as a Socially Symbolic Act*. Ithaca: Cornell UP, 1981.

Macherey, Pierre. *A Theory of Literary Production*. Trans. G. Wall. London: Routledge, 1978.

Marxist Approaches to Joyce

Cheng, Vincent. *Joyce, Race, and Empire*. Cambridge: Cambridge UP, 1995.

Deane, Seamus. *Celtic Revivals: Essays in Modern Irish Literature, 1880–1980*. London: Faber, 1985.

Duffy, Enda. *The Subaltern "Ulysses."* Minneapolis: U of Minnesota P, 1994.

Eagleton, Terry, Fredric Jameson, and Edward W. Said. *Nationalism, Colonialism, and Literature*. Minneapolis: U of Minnesota P, 1990.

Herr, Cheryl. *Joyce's Anatomy of Culture*. Urbana: U of Illinois P, 1986.

Manganiello, Dominic. *Joyce's Politics*. London: Routledge, 1980.

McCormack, W. J., and Alistair Stead, eds. *James Joyce and Modern Literature*. London: Routledge, 1982.

McGee, Patrick. *Paperspace: Style as Ideology in Joyce's "Ulysses."* Lincoln: U of Nebraska P, 1988.

Moretti, Franco. *Signs Taken for Wonders: Essays in the Sociology of Literary Forms*. Trans. Susan Fisher, David Forgacs, and David Miller. London: Verso, 1983.

Segall, Jeffrey. *Joyce in America: Cultural Politics and the Trials of "Ulysses."* Berkeley: U of California P, 1993.

A MARXIST PERSPECTIVE

PATRICK McGEE

"Heavenly Bodies": *Ulysses* and the Ethics of Marxism

In the spring of 1970, right after the Kent State debacle, I went to New York City as a member of a left-wing organization known as the Spartacist League. I thought I was a dedicated Marxist, a Trotskyite, and an almost fanatical believer in the injustice of the capitalist system. On a personal level, I blamed everything negative in my life—the violence I associated with my working-class background—on the system that I had every desire to change "by any means necessary." Once in New York, I did odd jobs, painted apartments, and eventually took a position at a post office in lower Manhattan that had just recently been the scene of a wildcat strike. I gave half of my salary to "the organization," as we called it, and I can't recall a moment's hesitation on that account. After some months, however, I began to have other doubts. Why was it that the daughter of a Fifth Avenue millionaire was the one member of our group entitled to earn a degree in comparative literature at New York University? Why was I, the son of a housepainter, discouraged from seeking more education and expected to become a foot soldier for the revolution? I must admit that I had no in-depth analysis of the gender relations in that organization, except for an utterly superficial commitment to women's liberation (as long as it did not conflict with the class struggle). When I finally left, I did so for many reasons, most of them having to do with my desire for an education. But one incident in particular has stuck in my memory.

From the late summer to the early fall of 1970, I read *Ulysses* for the first time. I could not possibly say what I got out of that book with the help of a Webster's dictionary, but my reading created an incident within the organization that certainly made me suspicious of my comrades' intentions with respect to my future. In a casual way, my roommate mentioned to the organization's head that I was reading Joyce; and the next thing you know I was called into the office for discussions of socialism and art, gentle admonitions about reading books that might be over my head, and not so subtle queries about whatever it was that might have leaked into my head from Joyce's writing. The word "bourgeois" was prominent in these discussions. Before long, one member of the group, the one I had already picked out as the future Stalin, wanted a list of every book I had read and every film I had seen for the last six months. Fortunately, shortly after this request was made, I started working the night shift at the post office and virtually dropped out of sight. A few months later, weary of dogmatism and illusions that did not know themselves as such, I left New York.

Many literary critics would probably question the purpose of the last two paragraphs. In my defense, I will quote this remark from the writing of Walter Benjamin: "Discretion concerning one's own existence, once an aristocratic virtue, has become more and more an affair of petty-bourgeois parvenus" (228). Benjamin probably would have thought twice about this statement in the age of Oprah and Donahue; but he nonetheless saw a link between a Marxist vision of the world and certain monumental acts of indiscretion, which he identified with the works of the surrealists. This view refers, I believe, to the tendency of such art to collapse the boundary between the personal and the social, the private and the public, the individual and the collective. In a sense, Marxism anticipated the feminist claim that the personal is political, though in this case the personal means the ideology of the bourgeois subject. Today indiscretions about class, race, gender, and sexual orientation threaten the stability of social institutions that thrive on the denial that such differences have any consequences for the quality of life and demand for social justice. Though "race," "gender," and "sexual orientation" have become key signifiers in the discourse of cultural difference (and the first two have entered into demands for economic justice under the rubric of affirmative action), wealth inequity as a system, which determines the specific attributes of these categories in any particular context, tends to undergo a "disavowal" as to its effects; it has even found a new source of legitimacy in the general distribution of tokens, who would seem to prove the overall justice of the claim that there is equal opportunity.

Still, I don't want to create the impression that my departure from New York was a simple move from illusion to truth. When I left behind one form of illusion in 1970, I knew perfectly well that I was probably going to dedicate my life to another form, to the study of those literary works and films that were also illusions, but with this difference: they knew it. I did not have any theory about that knowledge at the time, but I think I arrived at some elementary understanding of materialist art through Joyce. For me, *Ulysses* was the most monumental act of indiscretion I had ever come across. It was only later that I came to know how recklessly but ingeniously Joyce used the most minute details of his own life in *Ulysses* and in every other work that he wrote. He disclosed with shocking indifference the intimate secrets of his father and mother, his brothers and sisters, his wife and even (in *Finnegans Wake*) his children. He did not spare schoolmasters, friends, casual acquaintances, possible lovers, former students, and every conceivable representative of state authority. In a sense, everything in Joyce's books happened to Joyce.

But long before I knew enough about Joyce's life and historical context to appreciate his complete lack of discretion in the above respect, I was stunned by another indiscretion in his work. Leopold Bloom defecates in private and manages to masturbate in public without being completely visible (though I think at least one person sees what he is doing); Molly Bloom menstruates after recreating in her mind the intimate details of sexual intercourse with Blazes Boylan; Stephen Dedalus may masturbate while leaning against a rock on the beach (as some have argued, though I did not see that in 1970 and don't see it now) and certainly urinates on the beach and then picks his nose while looking around to see who has seen. In other words, Joyce's first indiscretion was the admission of the human body into literature—not the idealized body we get in the work of D. H. Lawrence but the "real" human body that is usually reduced to so many biological processes. Only the Marquis de Sade can be said to have fully anticipated Joyce, though Joyce evades the moral law that is the ironic condition of Sadean pleasure in cruelty. Joyce accepts the body as a thing that resists even as it shapes value and representation, and even morality.

When I later appreciated the extent of Joyce's indiscretions, I also realized that the body was the key to all of them. In *A Portrait of the Artist as a Young Man*, Stephen Dedalus picks lice off the back of his neck as a prelude to a long disquisition on art. The relation between Stephen's material poverty and his aesthetic idealizations lies in the Marxist term *mediation*, which sometimes carries some of the same value as the psychoanalytic term *sublimation*. If *Portrait* presents Stephen's theory as a distorted expression or disavowal of his material conditions, *Ulysses* could be said to demonstrate a more positive view of mediation as a process that does not hide but discloses the relationship between bodily social existence and aesthetic form. In the "Proteus" episode, Stephen's body is present by virtue of its absence from the language that articulates it. The body is like Proteus, the sea god who constantly changes his form, because its material reality can only reach us through the mediations of language and other forms of symbolic representation. Whatever the body may be as a thing-in-itself, as a construction of history it reaches Stephen as a linguistic representation (as opposed to Bloom's more visual imagination); and he can contact and possibly change it only through the same means: "His lips lipped and mouthed fleshless lips of air: mouth to her moomb. Oomb, allwombing tomb. His mouth moulded issuing breath, unspeeched: ooeeehah: roar of cataractic planets, globed, blazing, roaring wayaway-awayawayaway. Paper" (*U* 3.401–04). Stephen speaks and writes in an effort to rediscover the body as a thing-in-itself, a thing that would be the ground of social change and that he identifies with the mother's womb as its point of origin.

The reader should note that for Stephen speech, writing, and perception itself, though they are distinguishable, share a common structure, which he identifies with the curiously materialist idealism of the philosopher Berkeley: "The good bishop of Cloyne took the veil of the temple out of his shovel hat: veil of space with coloured emblems hatched on its field" (*U* 3.416–18). Though Berkeley was an idealist who saw nothing beyond the veil except the presence of God, for Joyce the veil is more like the trace of the body, its cultural form. Later Stephen fantasizes about the body of a man who drowned in Dublin Bay: "Bag of corpsegas sopping in foul brine. A quiver of minnows, fat of a spongy titbit, flash through the slits of his buttoned trouserfly. God becomes man becomes fish becomes barnacle goose becomes featherbed mountain" (*U* 3.476–79). Death is the most critical signifier of bodily existence because only in the destruction of the body do we become aware of something beyond our representations, something beyond death itself as a signifier that cannot be subjected to any cultural norm or value. Stephen's God, or the "Chewer of corpses" (*U* 1.278), is not so much death as the material process that concludes

life but the thing that lies beyond process, the thing to which we give
the name "matter" or "God" though it is really nothing in itself except the condition that we infer from its symbolic mediations in the
process of becoming or history. The body as thing is neither human
nor divine but the fundamental emptiness onto which those values can
be projected.

Joyce's exploration of the body through its symbolic mediations in
a particular historical location is the remarkable indiscretion that saves
him from being just another one of those "petty-bourgeois parvenus"
Benjamin refers to. It is not only Stephen's body that interests Joyce;
neither is it only the other prominent bodies in *Ulysses*. Leopold and
Molly Bloom, of course, and scores of minor characters, whose bodies
we come to know almost intimately. Blazes Boylan's genitals, Lydia
Douce's thigh, Simon Dedalus's thumbnail, Father Cowley's earlobes,
Gerty MacDowell's hair, Nosey Flynn's nose, and so forth: at every
turn in *Ulysses* the reader is confronted by the body and its processes,
including its pains and its pleasures. But underlying all these individual
bodies is the suggestion of the larger bodily formation that Joyce
hinted at in the schema he put together for Stuart Gilbert. Joyce suggested an organ or body part for each episode of *Ulysses* after "Proteus," which suggests that Stephen is in some sense absent from his
own body as the signifier of this larger social body, though he desperately seeks it somewhere in the vast network of symbolic forms that
constitute his social identity. Leopold Bloom, on the other hand,
though his body is no less mediated, takes it for granted and is much
more interested in experiencing its different pleasures than in knowing
its essence. One could argue, after Michel Foucault, that Stephen is
the prisoner of sex as a discursive formation. He is captured by

> this desirability of sex that attaches each one of us to the injunc-
> tion to know it, to reveal its law and its power; it is this desirability
> that makes us think we are affirming the rights of our sex against
> all power, when in fact we are fastened to the deployment of sexu-
> ality that has lifted up from deep within us a sort of mirage in
> which we think we see ourselves reflected—the dark shimmer of
> sex. (156–57)

Stephen stands in the tradition of D. H. Lawrence and the romantic
dream of sexual experience as a form of spiritual transfiguration.
Bloom, by contrast, anticipates Foucault's critique of the whole modern discourse of sex/desire (though later I will question this use of
the term *desire*): "The rallying point for the counterattack against the

deployment of sexuality ought not to be sex-desire, but bodies and pleasures" (157). Bloom does not seek so much to *know* the body in the manner of Stephen and Lawrence as to *experience* it through its multiple pleasures. He eats, defecates, masturbates, and voyeuristically devours the world with his eye (and, in this context, it is no accident that Stephen has broken his glasses and cannot see [*U* 15.3628–29]). Perhaps more important, though, Bloom never understands his body as something detached from the bodies that surround him; he never isolates his needs from the needs of the community of bodies through which he circulates like a blood cell through the human circulatory system (a metaphor made flesh in "Wandering Rocks"). *Ulysses* begins with a mock mass in which Buck Mulligan parodies the transubstantia-tion of "body and soul and blood and ouns," though he has a "little trouble about those white corpuscles" (*U* 1.21–23). Bloom repeats this gesture at the end of "Lotus-Eaters" with the simple phrase, "This is my body." Neither transubstantiation nor transfiguration is the issue in this case but the anticipation of bodily pleasure in bathing: "He foresaw his pale body reclined in it at full, naked, in a womb of warmth, oiled by scented melting soap, softly laved" (*U* 5.567–68).

I don't mean to imply, of course, that Bloom's relation to the body is natural, while Stephen's is unnatural or ideological. As literary constructions, both characters are deeply implicated in and determined by ideological structures or discourses. As Terry Eagleton demon-strates, however, the term *ideology* is notoriously difficult to get a handle on and cannot be pinned down to one meaning. He cites at least six possible definitions derived from the history of Western Marx-ism, and they all could have a bearing on our reading of *Ulysses*. First, ideology is the "general material process of production of ideas, beliefs and values in social life"; and as a character it is Bloom who most thor-oughly foregrounds this process as the very condition of what we call his endless and indiscriminate "stream of consciousness." Second, it is the system of ideas and beliefs of "a specific, socially significant group or class." From this perspective, every character in *Ulysses* represents a limited vision of the social totality, whether it takes the form of Bloom's utopian fantasies in "Circe" or Stephen's elitist disavowal of his sister's poverty in "Wandering Rocks." A third definition of ideol-ogy refers to "the *promotion* and *legitimation* of the interests of such social groups in the face of opposing interests," which includes a fourth meaning referring exclusively to "the activities of a dominant social power." Practically every page of *Ulysses* contains some symbol of the dominance of Britain over Ireland, including "His Majesty's

vermilion mailcars" at the opening of "Aeolus" (*U* 7.16). These symbols, along with the many signifiers of class distinction and power, reinforce forms of social dominance by virtue of their insertion into an
everyday reality that becomes a sort of second nature. The fifth definition involves the legitimation of such dominant interests explicitly by
"distortion and dissimulation." Sixth and finally, such "false or decep-
tive beliefs" can be defined as "arising . . . from the material structure
of society as a whole" (*Ideology: An Introduction* 28–30). *Ulysses* is almost an encyclopedia of the social distortions (of women, Jews, the
Irish, blacks, vagrants, revolutionaries, and so forth) that facilitate the
system of exclusions by which most societies tend to operate. Nevertheless, I believe that all of these meanings can be derived from a
broad interpretation of Louis Althusser's definition of ideology as "the
imaginary relation of . . . individuals to the real relations in which they
live" (*For Marx* 231). The use of this definition need not force one to
accept a rigid distinction between ideology and science, with which
many have faulted Althusser's structural Marxism, if one understands
the term "imaginary" in its psychoanalytic sense as one of three critical
registers: imaginary, real, and symbolic. The symbolic is the cultural
system with its storehouse of representations; the imaginary is how we
construct meanings out of those representations; and the real is what
every representation leaves behind as the remainder of its meaning, as
the impossibility of the absolute closure of the system.

In the work of Lacan, from which Althusser takes the term, the
imaginary is not the simple antithesis of the real but rather the realm
of meaning itself, which always requires the arbitrary closure of the
process of signification. At the risk of oversimplifying, one could think
of the symbolic as the material structure of language and everything
that can signify like a language, a structure that belies the term "structure" since it is in a state of constant flux or process. It is the material
condition of meaning, the potential for signification in the finite,
though always expanding, storehouse of sounds, graphic marks, and
visual images that are the traces of historical process itself. The imaginary is the arbitrary closure of that process, the means by which one
signifier is subordinated to another in the effort to pin down or
capture a piece of the real. If the symbolic is the historical chain of
signifiers, then the imaginary is the act of meaning–production that in-
terrupts or momentarily breaks that chain. Though the imaginary
closes in on the real as the object of its signification, it never reaches it
because the signifier never escapes its own historicity as a moment or
discrete unit in an open process. One could say that the signifier can

never make contact with the real as the absolute object of signification, that is, its absolute other, because it is also a piece of the real, a thing-in-itself. The real can only be known as that which the imaginary misses, as that which cannot be symbolized, as the historical limit of any possible meaning.

From these observations, it should be clear why the Joycean body is curiously present by virtue of its absence. There is no contradiction between Joyce's "naturalism," if you will, and his experiments with style. Joyce always insists on representing the unrepresentable, including the body's processes that have been disavowed by the norms of traditional literature and conventional culture. The reader can only approach the body as a thing-in-itself by deconstructing the signifiers that invest the body with meanings in a cultural context. In representing Bloom's act of defecation at the end of "Calypso," Joyce does not produce a naturalistic description of the process that would find its ideal version in a biology textbook. Rather, he represents the pleasure Bloom takes from the act, a pleasure that can never be fully anchored in the thing itself because it derives from the organization of signifiers into imaginary meanings and values. Of his bowel movement, Bloom thinks, "Life might be so. It did not move or touch him but it was something quick and neat" (U 4.511–12). Similarly, in "Nausicaa," Joyce does not try to efface the gap between language and Gerty's "real" orgasm (whatever that would be) in the manner of Lawrence. It isn't the orgasm that is Joyce's object of representation but the language that becomes charged with pleasure as its imaginary value. It is Gerty's (or this cultural symptom's) investment of imaginary value in the system of language that she inherits from her social context and that points toward something real, a thing in excess of meaning: "O so lovely, O, soft, sweet, soft!" (U 13.740).

None of the three terms I have discussed—imaginary, symbolic, real—is privileged over the others; rather, they are implicated in one another in the form of a knot. Consequently, the imaginary should be thought of as a "lived relation" to the real, as a historically determined construction of reality through a specific organization of the symbolic. It may be that Althusser understands by the term "real relations" the classical Marxist concept of the base as the relations of production that constitute "the economic structure of society, the real foundation," and by the term "imaginary relations" the concept of the superstructure, or the "social, political and intellectual life process in general" (Marx and Engels, 182). Still, he gives to the superstructure its own relative autonomy, which means that his concept of the social totality

tends to slide over into a formation resembling what the Italian Marxist, Antonio Gramsci, calls "hegemony." Raymond Williams has defined hegemony, in its broadest terms, as "a whole body of practices
and expectations" and "a lived system of meanings and values" that,
taken as a whole, constitute "a sense of reality for most people in
the society." It is "a 'culture,' but a culture which has also to be
seen as the lived dominance and subordination of particular classes."
From this perspective, concludes Williams, cultural practices and ideological systems are no longer a superstructure but "are among the
basic processes of the formation itself and, further, related to a much
wider area of reality than the abstractions of 'social' and 'economic'
experience" (110-11).

The concept of hegemony enables one to grasp the relation between base and superstructure as a whole process. Though the economy is crucial to the understanding of any society, it is not possible to
explain all forms of consciousness as expressions of economic interests.
Still, since Marx's critique of capitalism is historical, it necessarily
works on the assumption that capitalist hegemony identifies a particular economic structure as the privileged expression of human nature
and uses that claim to explain and justify capitalist social relations and
cultural values. For this reason, Althusser quite properly identifies the
economic mode of production as the "*determination in the last instance*" of an overdetermined capitalist culture (*For Marx* 111). But
the capitalist economy itself would not have been able to become the
hegemonic norm that it is without producing and colonizing ideologies and other forms of social practice. It follows that the real relations
of a society that in some sense exceed the imaginary or "lived" relations cannot be reduced to the economic structure but are the whole
material basis of culture. They are the body of culture that would include the real "bodies" of human beings and all the things that make
up culture but that we can only know by virtue of their absence, by the
failure of our representations to capture the real as a thing-in-itself.
This body is the open-ended and irreducible structure of capitalist society and of history itself as a "process without a subject or a *telos*" (Althusser, *Lenin and Philosophy* 162). One can say that the real relations
are the body of capitalist culture only if the "body" is understood as
the thing that resists symbolization, that exceeds every meaning or interpretation—in other words, as what Fredric Jameson calls, in an interpretation of Althusser's concept of structural causality, the "absent
cause" (Jameson, "On Interpretation"). This cause is absent, however,
only in the sense that it is irreducible. It is the absolute material limit

of any interpretation or construction of value. It is the limit that can be known only as a structural absence, as the historical finitude of any fixed meaning or lived relation to the world. In my view, this irreducible body is the object of Joyce's creation in *Ulysses* and the reason behind his insistence on the autonomy of the signifier, the privileging of style as ideology over any reductive view of the real as a simple given.

From this perspective, one can distinguish between Stephen's and Bloom's relations to the body without presuming that the difference in question is between a real and an ideological relation. Both viewpoints are ideological or imaginary relations to the real, but they nevertheless articulate a difference in the lived relation to the body that makes a difference. Bloom may represent the "petty-bourgeois" side of Joyce, but his relation to his own body figures a relation to the social body that presupposes the intersubjective ground of bodily existence. According to Eagleton, Marx believed "human powers and human society are an absolute end in themselves. To live well is to live in the free, many-sided realization of one's capacities, in reciprocal interaction with the similar self-expression of others" (*Ideology of the Aesthetic* 226). Still, the last part of this statement lays a restriction on human self-realization, which Eagleton identifies as the "foundation of a communist ethics": "The discriminatory norm in question is that we should foster only those particular powers which allow an individual to realize herself through and in terms of the similar free self-realization of others" (224). In Eagleton's view, this utopian vision is what Marxism owes to the aesthetic tradition going back to the eighteenth century and to Hegel in particular.

Joyce self-consciously participates in that tradition, though the difference between Stephen and Bloom points to a change in his own relation to the aesthetic between *Portrait* and *Ulysses*. For the melancholic Stephen, art centers on the ego and makes the body—in this case, Stephen's body—into a symptom, the signifier of what it lacks in order to be whole. The symptom articulates the demand for absolute meaning through the process of a compromise formation. In other words, the body as symptom is a compromise formation because it substitutes for the real an image of the body derived from ideology. As Lacan notes, "A symptom is the return by means of signifying substitution of that which is at the end of the drive in the form of an aim" (110). In *Ulysses*, the aim of Stephen's drive, the aim he will not surrender, is death; and the image of the body that dominates his consciousness, culminating in the image of his mother, is the body in death. Language as the material of art is the means by which he keeps this aim alive, though the aesthetic pleasure he takes from it depends on his ignorance, since, as Slavoj Žižek notes, "the subject can 'enjoy his symptom' only in so far as its logic escapes him" (21). In other words, the disinterested pleasure of the Kantian aesthetic, with which we can associate Stephen's aesthetic theory in *Portrait*, is simply the repression of the knowledge of desire. Though the image of Stephen's dead mother has become the articulation of his symptom, he projects onto her imaginary existence the repulsion that covers over and makes it possible for him to enjoy the real aim of his drive.

Bloom's mode of being in *Ulysses* suggests a relation to the aesthetic as a form of sublimation. For Lacan, sublimation is not, as it may have been for Freud, simply another kind of compromise formation. It refers to the "paradoxical fact that the drive is able to find its aim elsewhere than in that which is its aim—without its being a question of the signifying substitution that constitutes the overdetermined structure, the ambiguity, and the double causality, of the symptom as compromise formation" (110). Bloom may seem naive in his obsession with physical pleasure and in the utopian desires that emerge from his unconscious in the dream world of "Circe": "New worlds for old. Union of all, jew, moslem and gentile. . . . Free money, free rent, free love and a free lay church in a free lay state" (*U* 15.1685–93). In his more sober or conscious state of mind, he seems less optimistic about the future but no less concerned with the body of the other. Death may have its own attractions for Bloom, and the Circean unconscious spews out his fantasies of public immolation and private suicide (*U* 15.1930–37, 15.1964–68). In the context of a culture that is still dominated by Judeo-Christian values, death should be thought of as the aim of a collective drive; but the act of sublimation makes possible the ethical gesture of changing that aim, of surrendering the impossible demand for what calls itself love but secretly harbors the wish for the finality of death. In Lacanian terminology, demand is a symbolic articulation aimed at satisfying a need such as nourishment or sex, though we should not be led by this distinction into imagining that the need is transparent or self-evident. We can only infer the existence of needs through the representations of demands. As the demand is symbolic, something in it always exceeds the immediate necessities of the real and calls for the experience of absolute satisfaction. The only way to escape this absolute demand and satisfy an immediate need is to call up desire, which is a relation to the other, a compromise with reality that enables one to focus on a limited object that can never produce an absolute experience of satisfaction. Throughout *Ulysses*, Bloom subordinates his symbolic demand for love to his own physical needs and to the needs of those around him. Whether he feeds Molly or Stephen, the family cat or the stray dog; whether he contributes to the support of Paddy Dignam's widow or to the mental health of Mrs. Breen; whether he identifies with Mina Purefoy in labor or just helps the blind stripling across the street—in one way or another, Bloom is always thinking of the other's body and of the body as the other. Of course, Bloom also uses the other's body for his own pleasures; and, ideologically speaking, he is very much a creature of the world he lives in. Though he sees Dublin as the body of the other, it is a gendered body, "the womancity, nude, white, still, cool, in luxury"; and his utopia, or the "new Bloomusalem," takes the form of an animal body part with which he likes to satisfy his physical appetite, "a colossal edifice with crystal roof, built in the shape of a huge pork kidney" (*U* 15.1327–28, 1548–49). Even as he cares for the other, Bloom takes pleasure and pain from the other's body as from his own. It is as if these bodies were indistinguishable.

"Art," writes Eagleton, "is a form of creative surplus, a radical exceeding of necessity; in Lacanian terminology, it is what remains when need is subtracted from demand" (*Ideology of the Aesthetic* 204). In other words, art is the articulation of desire as the force that releases need from the tyranny of demand. Desire is something in excess of the body's needs, but it also protects the body from the destructive effects of the drive that translates physical need into symbolic demand. The drive is an absolute excess that could bring about total devastation since it seeks the final satisfaction of needs in their total extinction. The capitalist can never make too much profit, the consumer can never own too many goods, the politician can never have enough power, the philanderer can never have too many lovers, and so forth. The Lacanian terminology that Eagleton employs may not be transhistorical or universal, but it does seem to describe accurately enough the historical context from which it has emerged. It describes a capitalist system that has unleashed what Horkheimer and Adorno called instrumental reason as, if I may extrapolate, a form of reason fully in the service of an absolute demand for the domination of the physical world, even to the point of death. The only force that interferes with this process, that inhibits all the final solutions from the death camps to the nuclear arsenals, is desire as the absolute condition that can be laid upon unconditional demand. Demand destroys the other—including the body as an/other—because the other bars access to the experience of absolute satisfaction; desire, by contrast, gives ground to the other as the source of a compromise. Desire is never simply *my* desire but always the desire of the other. Unlike demand, which seeks an unmediated and absolute experience, desire is always mediated and substitutes for such an experience a socially determined goal. It comes from the other to the other; and one name for the other, in my view, is the body itself, not in its individuality but as a collective process. Thus, I would change Foucault's formulation of the "deployment of sexuality" as sex / desire in this way. It is not desire that fails to oppose the deployment of sexuality, for it is only desire that enables the body to experience pleasures that do not kill it. It is, rather, sex / demand, that is, sexual knowledge as the answer to the impossible demand of the drive. In *Ulysses*, Stephen makes a sexual demand that destroys the possibility of any relationship, sexual or otherwise, with a real person and drives him toward the place of his mother, the place of death. Bloom, on the other hand, evades demand by pursuing a series of objects and bodily pleasures that finally lead him back to his place with Molly. This is not the place of final satisfaction but, if you will, the place of the postponement of satisfaction, the suspension of demand in the vagaries of desire.

As a work of art, *Ulysses* is structured by the contradiction between the demand for absolute meaning and the desire that exceeds meaning as its material condition. It is a contradiction between the symptom as a compromise formation that keeps returning to the aim of the drive and the sublime object of desire that represents a change of aim as the possibility of ethical action. It is a contradiction between the ideology of the aesthetic and the ideology of the body. Formally, *Ulysses* is a pure expression of aesthetic ideology insofar as it posits itself as an autonomous work of art, what Adorno calls the "windowless monad." Its formal structure and the freedom of its stylistic play produces the illusion of historical transcendence, most profoundly registered in the systematic referencing of Homer's epic. The result, as Eagleton argues, is that "reality is coded to its roots, as the ephemeral working through of some deeper logic invisible to the naked eye, and randomness is accordingly banished" (*Ideology of the Aesthetic* 317). As such a reworking of the real, a process that reduces it to a totalized and universal meaning, *Ulysses* effectively becomes an aesthetic commodity, one that has erased the history of its production in a field of socially determined interests. It is a compromise formation or symptom of the real insofar as it posits itself as the imaginary resolution of the contradictions of real history. An Ireland colonized and dominated by an external power is transformed into a timeless present that transcends every historical specificity, including the language in which it is written. English is no longer the language of the colonizer but the neutral medium of a universal vision. Joyce proves that he can do anything with language as he proceeds to divorce the signifier from any necessary connection to the real. From this perspective, the work of art is what Bloom and Stephen become in "Ithaca": in Joyce's own words, they are "heavenly bodies, wanderers like the stars at which they gaze" (*Selected Letters* 278). *Ulysses* is such a heavenly or aesthetic body; and its language, like the stars, is "a mobility of illusory forms immobilised in space" (*U* 17.1143).

Yet, on this very note, the contradiction asserts itself. For it is precisely as an autonomous whole, as an aesthetic body, that *Ulysses* manifests its materiality and reveals its commodity form as the form of its historical existence. *Ulysses* is what Adorno would call an absolute commodity, a social product which "rids itself of the ideology inherent in the commodity form. The latter pretends that it is a being-for-other whereas in truth it is only for itself—that is, for the ruling interests of society" (336). In other words, as an absolute commodity, a work of art is always to some extent anti-art and subversive of its own relation to the order of aesthetic values. If I may rephrase Adorno's formulation, such art rids itself of the illusion that it expresses universal interests that lie beyond the particular interests of a social configuration of power. It discloses the institutional nature of art and its affirmative relation to hegemony, which would include "the lived dominance and subordination of particular classes" (Williams 110). Art can do this, ironically, because it never completely rids itself of ideology. As Adorno qualifies his own theory, "alas, even as an absolute commodity art has retained its commercial value, becoming a 'natural monopoly.' . . . It is possible that completely non-ideological art is entirely unfeasible" (336). Art never fully transcends its status as a commodity and a symptom of commodity culture. Yet, for that very reason, it is able to disclose the truth of the aesthetic commodity, its illusory form and the irreducible social body it reveals as the absent cause of its representations. Art rids itself of ideology by giving us a view of ideology that, in Althusser's words, "presupposes a *retreat*, an *internal distantiation*" (*Lenin and Philosophy* 204). Adorno takes one step beyond Althusser to recognize that this internal distance is art's self-contradiction.

"The collective," writes Benjamin, "is a body, too" (239). *Ulysses* posits that body as the absent cause of its exploration of style as ideology, as a mediation or lived relation to the real. But this body is absent not in the sense that it is somewhere else, an object external to language that language somehow represents. If understood in this way, such a sublime object of ideology, according to Žižek, would be "an embodiment of Nothing" (206). The real body—or rather the real itself—is not absent because it is elsewhere but because it is immanent to the thing itself. In other words, the styles of *Ulysses* and all of its technical innovations articulate the body not as something outside but immanent to representation. It is the material basis of representation, the fact that language and all other forms of representation are made up of something real, something in them more than them. Žižek describes "that strange body in my interior which is 'in me more than me,' which is radically interior and [at] the same time already exterior" (181). That strange body lies at the heart of Joyce's linguistic rearrangement of the world. It is the material force that connects the body of Joyce's text with the body of the world; and though it is nothing in itself, it is this collective body that must be liberated from the mode of production and all the ideological practices that enable the mode of production to become a cultural norm. It must be liberated from the tyranny of any single interpretation whether that interpretation takes the form of moral law, social convention, or human nature. It must be liberated not because in itself it embodies human freedom but because it is the condition of human freedom. It is the condition of those ideological practices that may be thought of as the practice of freedom. As Benjamin speculates about the collective body, "the *physis* that is being organized for it in technology can, through all its political and factual reality, only be produced in the image sphere to which profane illumination initiates us" (239). The image sphere is the realm of ideology, and only in ideology can the collective body, conditioned by technology, come to fruition as a new social reality. Joyce's *Ulysses* refuses to answer our demand for that new social reality even as it makes it possible to desire it. It does not substitute an imaginary for a historical reality, as some have argued, but insists that we confront the imaginary relation to the world, our interpretation of it, as a limit on the possibilities of human freedom, as a limit on our relation to the real.

As I argued earlier, for Stephen language as the material of art is the symptom of the body he misses. For Bloom, though he only has "a touch of the artist" (*U* 10.582), language is a function of the body itself. Stephen seeks an answer to his absolute demand for love from that mysterious feminine figure to whom he addresses this question in "Proteus": "What is that word known to all men?" (*U* 3.435). The answer to that question, though it may be "love," as some have argued, really signifies death. Stephen may begin to realize and resist this meaning in "Circe" when his mother becomes a green crab and "*sticks deep its grinning claws in Stephen's heart*" (*U* 15.4220–21). Stephen runs away from the image of his mother but cannot escape the death drive that brings him back to the place she occupies when he is knocked to the ground by a British soldier. To the imperialist system that the soldier represents, Stephen can only make the demand that the death drive compels him to make. In effect, Stephen imagines the object of love as a plenitude, a total fulfillment, and the absolute extinction of need and desire. It is as if Stephen did not know, first, that he is a body and, second, that a body can never know fulfillment before death except through an identification with the desire of the other. This identification is the key to Bloom and the ground of his ethical being. Though he knows that his wife has been unfaithful to him (however much he may exaggerate the degree of that infidelity), he does not act. He subordinates his own demand for love (which is always determined within the framework of culture by ideology) to the desire of the other as the structure of his own desire. As Eagleton summarizes the lessons of Freud for Marxist ethics:

> The one I love may not be able to give me the imaginary plenitude I seek, but she can at least give me the most real thing she has, namely her own desire for the same plenitude. We give each other our desire, which is to say exactly that which neither of us can fulfill in the other. To say "I love you" thus becomes equivalent to saying "It's *you* who can't satisfy me!" How privileged and unique I must be, to remind you that it isn't me you want . . .
> (*Ideology of the Aesthetic* 279)

I can think of nothing in literature that so powerfully exemplifies this economy of desire than the relationship between Leopold and Molly Bloom. They have not had complete carnal intercourse for "10 years, 5 months and 18 days" or complete mental intercourse since their daughter's "consummation of puberty" (*U* 17.2282–88). Their relationship is hardly ideal in the romantic sense or reciprocal in socioeconomic terms. Still, it could be taken as a model for a Marxist ethics of the body, not in the sense that it celebrates some sort of full self-realization of human powers but in the sense that it allows for the possibility of human freedom under the rule of desire as the absolute condition of unconditional demand. Such a freedom, of course, is relative to the desire of the other, which means that it is restricted by and limited to the necessity of compromise and negotiation as an ongoing political practice. It avoids the bad utopianism that, in Eagleton's view, "grabs instantly for a future, projecting itself by an act of will or imagination beyond the compromised political structures of the present." Without attending to these structures and what I would call the "real" body of the present, including the aesthetic bodies of works like *Ulysses*, such a bad utopianism "is in danger of persuading us to desire uselessly rather than feasibly, and so, like the neurotic, to fall ill with longing." Such utopianism answers to unconditional demand without the mediation of sublimated desire; and the same is true of that brand of social determinism that offers a future that is "inevitable but not necessarily desirable." Against both naive desire and political dogmatism, Eagleton suggests that "'value' must be somehow extrapolable from 'fact,' the outline of a future worth struggling for discerned within the practices of the degraded present" (*Ideology of the Aesthetic* 229). In my view, *Ulysses* aims at just this sort of "profane illumination" of the collective human body; it is what Stephen calls in the "Nestor" episode "an actuality of the possible as possible" (*U* 2.67).

It has been twenty-five years since I first read *Ulysses*, and I have become what no one in the political organization I referred to earlier either imagined or desired that I should become: a literary critic. I don't know if it is appropriate for me to call myself a Marxist critic, but I have tried to model my style of criticism on the work of two very problematic Marxists: Benjamin and Adorno. I don't mean that I emulate their styles (which I could not do), but I have tried to grasp within my own work the concept of constellation that governs their critical practices. That concept, according to Eagleton, posits

> a form of criticism so tenaciously immanent that it would remain entirely immersed in its object. The truth of that object would be disclosed not by referring it in rationalist style to a governing general idea, but by dismantling its component elements through the power of minutely particular concepts, then reconfigurating them in a pattern which redeemed the thing's meaning and value without ceasing to adhere to it. (*Ideology of the Aesthetic* 328)

This technique is not one that I can simply apply to Joyce, since I believe that the concept of constellation accurately describes Joyce's own approach to literary construction in *Ulysses* and *Finnegans Wake*. Joyce articulates the reality of colonial Ireland and the possibility of a postcolonial Ireland through the configuration of minute particulars, including those particulars that constitute the desires of the people. As a critic, I have never seen any *necessary* contradiction between this approach and the technique of deconstruction as it is practiced in the work of Jacques Derrida. As I suggested in my early work on Joyce, deconstruction and psychoanalysis should be considered advanced forms of ideology-critique, and I have always tried to incorporate them into that sort of analysis.

Marxist or any other form of political criticism is not a substitute for political action: *it is a form of political action*. But once this fact is recognized, it should become clear that no single form of political action is ever enough. Critical practice occupies a position in a historical constellation of forces that must involve many other political and social positions. Within that constellation, there are many forms of action in which decisions have to be made—political decisions with implications for the lives of "real" human beings. Even criticism requires a decision, and it is never simply an act of inconsequential free play. In every political act, there is a moment of commitment in which the political decision must be made; but there is also a responsibility that lies beyond commitment, an ethical responsibility to the desire of the other. This responsibility entails the refusal of dogmatism in every context, no matter how seductive, no matter how justified it may appear to be. In my view, it requires the refusal of a Manichean division of the world into the absolutely good and the absolutely evil. Today, after twenty-five years, I am as critical of the injustices of the capitalist system as I was in 1970. But I don't think the resolution of that injustice can be reduced to a simple formula. It will require, at the very least, the creation of a new socialist ethic as the foundation of a new collective social body that cannot be legislated or dynamited into existence. As Eagleton paraphrases the thought of Benjamin, in the production of this ethic and this body, "the function of the critic is to fashion those images by which humanity can assume this unfamiliar flesh" (336). For me, that "unfamiliar flesh" first made itself visible in the pages of *Ulysses*.

WORKS CITED

Adorno, Theodor. *Aesthetic Theory*. Trans. C. Lenhardt. Ed. Gretel Adorno and Rolf Tiedemann. London: Routledge, 1984.

Althusser, Louis. *For Marx*. Trans. Ben Brewster. New York: Pantheon, 1969.

————. *Lenin and Philosophy*. Trans. Ben Brewster. London: NLB, 1974.

Benjamin, Walter. "Surrealism: The Last Snapshot of the European Intelligentsia." *One-Way Street and Other Writings*. Trans. Edmund Jephcott and Kingsley Shorter. London: NLB, 1979. 225–239.

Eagleton, Terry. *The Ideology of the Aesthetic*. Oxford: Basil Blackwell, 1990.

————. *Ideology: An Introduction*. London: Verso, 1991.

Foucault, Michel. *The History of Sexuality*. Trans. Robert Hurley. Vol. 1. *An Introduction*. New York: Vintage, 1980.

Horkheimer, Max, and Theodor W. Adorno. *Dialectic of Enlightenment*. Trans. John Cumming. New York: Continuum, 1987.

Jameson, Fredric. "On Interpretation." *The Political Unconscious: Narrative as a Socially Symbolic Act*. Ithaca: Cornell UP, 1981.

Joyce, James. *Selected Letters*. Ed. Richard Ellmann. New York: Viking, 1975.

Lacan, Jacques. *The Ethics of Psychoanalysis 1959–1960*. Trans. Dennis Porter. New York: Norton, 1992. Book 7 of *The Seminar*.

Marx, Karl, and Frederick Engels. *Selected Works*. New York: International, 1968.

Williams, Raymond. *Marxism and Literature*. Oxford: Oxford UP, 1977.

Žižek, Slavoj. *The Sublime Object of Ideology*. London: Verso, 1989.

Glossary of Critical
and Theoretical Terms

Most terms have been glossed parenthetically where they first appear in the text. Mainly, the glossary lists terms that are too complex to define in a phrase or a sentence or two. A few of the terms listed are discussed at greater length elsewhere (*feminist criticism,* for instance); these terms are defined succinctly and a page reference to the longer discussion is provided.

AFFECTIVE FALLACY   First used by William K. Wimsatt and Monroe C. Beardsley to refer to what they regarded as the erroneous practice of interpreting texts according to the psychological responses of readers. "The Affective Fallacy," they wrote in a 1946 essay later republished in *The Verbal Icon* (1954), "is a confusion between the poem and its *results* (what it *is* and what it *does*). . . . It begins by trying to derive the standards of criticism from the psychological effects of a poem and ends in impressionism and relativism." The affective fallacy, like the intentional fallacy (confusing the meaning of a work with the author's expressly intended meaning), was one of the main tenets of the New Criticism, or formalism. The affective fallacy has recently been contested by reader-response critics, who have deliberately dedicated their efforts to describing the way individual readers and "interpretive communities" go about "making sense" of texts.

See also: Authorial Intention, Formalism, Reader-Response Criticism.

AUTHORIAL INTENTION   Defined narrowly, an author's intention in writing a work, as expressed in letters, diaries, interviews, and conversations. Defined more broadly, "intentionality" involves unexpressed motivations, designs, and purposes, some of which may have remained unconscious.

The debate over whether critics should try to discern an author's intentions (conscious or otherwise) is an old one. William K. Wimsatt and Monroe C. Beardsley, in an essay first published in the 1940s, coined the term "intentional fallacy" to refer to the practice of basing interpretations on the expressed or implied intentions of authors, a practice they judged to be erroneous. As proponents of the New Criticism, or formalism, they argued that a work of literature is an object in itself and should be studied as such. They believed that it is sometimes helpful to learn what an author intended, but the critic's real purpose is to show what is actually in the text, not what an author intended to put there.

See also: Affective Fallacy, Formalism.

BASE   *See* Marxist Criticism.

BINARY OPPOSITIONS   *See* Oppositions.

BLANKS   *See* Gaps.

CANON   Since the fourth century, used to refer to those books of the Bible that the Christian church accepts as being Holy Scripture. The term has come to be applied more generally to those literary works given special status, or "privileged," by a culture. Works we tend to think of as "classics" or the "Great Books" produced by Western culture—texts that are found in every anthology of American, British, and world literature—would be among those that constitute the canon.

Recently, Marxist, feminist, minority, and postcolonial critics have argued that, for political reasons, many excellent works never enter the canon. Canonized works, they claim, are those that reflect—and respect—the culture's dominant ideology and/or perform some socially acceptable or even necessary form of "cultural work." Attempts have been made to broaden or redefine the canon by discovering valuable texts, or versions of texts, that were repressed or ignored for political reasons. These have been published both in traditional and in nontraditional anthologies. The most outspoken critics of the canon, especially radical critics practicing cultural criticism, have called into question the whole concept of canon or "canonicity." Privileging no form of artistic expression that reflects and revises the culture, these critics treat cartoons, comics, and soap operas with the same cogency and respect they accord novels, poems, and plays.

See also: Cultural Criticism, Feminist Criticism, Ideology, Marxist Criticism.

CONFLICTS, CONTRADICTIONS   *See* Gaps.

CULTURAL CRITICISM   A critical approach that is sometimes referred to as "cultural studies" or "cultural critique." Practitioners of cultural criticism oppose "high" definitions of culture and take seriously popular cultural forms. Grounded in a variety of continental European influences, cultural criticism nonetheless gained institutional force in England, in 1964, with the founding of the Centre for Contemporary Cultural Studies at Birmingham University. Broadly interdisciplinary in its scope and approach, cultural criticism views the text as the locus and catalyst of a complex network of political and economic discourses. Cultural critics share with Marxist critics an interest in the ideological contexts of cultural forms.

DECONSTRUCTION A poststructuralist approach to literature that is strongly influenced by the writings of the French philosopher Jacques Derrida. Deconstruction, partly in response to structuralism and formalism, posits the undecidability of meaning for all texts. In fact, as the deconstructionist critic J. Hillis Miller points out, "deconstruction is not a dismantling of the structure of a text but a demonstration that it has already dismantled itself." *See* "What Is Deconstruction?" pp. 47–64.

DIALECTIC Originally developed by Greek philosophers, mainly Socrates and Plato, as a form and method of logical argumentation; the term later came to denote a philosophical notion of evolution. The German philosopher G. W. F. Hegel described dialectic as a process whereby a thesis, when countered by an antithesis, leads to the synthesis of a new idea. Karl Marx and Friedrich Engels, adapting Hegel's idealist theory, used the phrase "dialectical materialism" to discuss the way in which a revolutionary class war might lead to the synthesis of a new social economic order. The American Marxist critic Fredric Jameson has coined the phrase "dialectical criticism" to refer to a Marxist critical approach that synthesizes structuralist and poststructuralist methodologies.

See also: Marxist Criticism, Poststructuralism, Structuralism.

DIALOGIC *See* Discourse.

DISCOURSE Used specifically, can refer to (1) spoken or written discussion of a subject or area of knowledge; (2) the words in, or text of, a narrative as opposed to its story line; or (3) a "strand" within a given narrative that argues a certain point or defends a given value system.

More generally, "discourse" refers to the language in which a subject or area of knowledge is discussed or a certain kind of business is transacted. Human knowledge is collected and structured in discourses. Theology and medicine are defined by their discourses, as are politics, sexuality, and literary criticism.

A society is generally made up of a number of different discourses or "discourse communities," one or more of which may be dominant or serve the dominant ideology. Each discourse has its own vocabulary, concepts, and rules, knowledge of which constitutes power. The psychoanalyst and psychoanalytic critic Jacques Lacan has treated the unconscious as a form of discourse, the patterns of which are repeated in literature. Cultural critics, following Mikhail Bakhtin, use the word "dialogic" to discuss the dialogue *between* discourses that takes place within language or, more specifically, a literary text.

See also: Cultural Criticism, Ideology, Narrative, Psychoanalytic Criticism.

FEMINIST CRITICISM An aspect of the feminist movement whose primary goals include critiquing masculine-dominated language and literature by showing how they reflect a masculine ideology; writing the history of unknown or undervalued women writers, thereby earning them their rightful place in the literary canon; and helping create a climate in which women's creativity may be fully realized and appreciated. *See* "What Are Feminist and Gender Criticism?" pp. 129–43.

FIGURE *See* Metaphor, Metonymy, Symbol.

FORMALISM Also referred to as the New Criticism, formalism reached its height during the 1940s and 1950s, but it is still practiced today.

Formalists treat a work of literary art as if it were a self-contained, self-referential object. Rather than basing their interpretations of a text on the reader's response, the author's stated intentions, or parallels between the text and historical contexts (such as the author's life), formalists concentrate on the relationships *within* the text that give it its own distinctive character or form. Special attention is paid to repetition, particularly of images or symbols, but also of sound effects and rhythms in poetry.

Because of the importance placed on close analysis and the stress on the text as a carefully crafted, orderly object containing observable formal patterns, formalism has often been seen as an attack on Romanticism and impressionism, particularly impressionistic criticism. It has sometimes even been called an "objective" approach to literature. Formalists are more likely than certain other critics to believe and say that the meaning of a text can be known objectively. For instance, reader-response critics see meaning as a function either of each reader's experience or of the norms that govern a particular "interpretive community," and deconstructors argue that texts mean opposite things at the same time.

Formalism was originally based on essays written during the 1920s and 1930s by T. S. Eliot, I. A. Richards, and William Empson. It was significantly developed later by a group of American poets and critics, including R. P. Blackmur, Cleanth Brooks, John Crowe Ransom, Allen Tate, Robert Penn Warren, and William K. Wimsatt. Although we associate formalism with certain principles and terms (such as the "Affective Fallacy" and the "Intentional Fallacy" as defined by Wimsatt and Monroe C. Beardsley), formalists were trying to make a cultural statement rather than establish a critical dogma. Generally southern, religious, and culturally conservative, they advocated the inherent value of literary works (particularly of literary works regarded as beautiful art objects) because they were sick of the growing ugliness of modern life and contemporary events. Some recent theorists even suggest that the rising popularity of formalism after World War II was a feature of American isolationism, the formalist tendency to isolate literature from biography and history being a manifestation of the American fatigue with wider involvements.

See also: Affective Fallacy, Authorial Intention, Deconstruction, Reader-Response Criticism, Symbol.

GAPS   When used by reader-response critics familiar with the theories of Wolfgang Iser, refers to "blanks" in texts that must be filled in by readers. A gap may be said to exist whenever and wherever a reader perceives something to be missing between words, sentences, paragraphs, stanzas, or chapters. Readers respond to gaps actively and creatively, explaining apparent inconsistencies in point of view, accounting for jumps in chronology, speculatively supplying information missing from plots, and resolving problems or issues left ambiguous or "indeterminate" in the text.

Reader-response critics sometimes speak as if a gap actually exists in a text; a gap is, of course, to some extent a product of readers' perceptions. Different readers may find gaps in different texts, and different gaps in the same text. Furthermore, they may fill these gaps in different ways, which is why, a reader-response critic might argue, works are interpreted in different ways.

Although the concept of the gap has been used mainly by reader-response critics, it has also been used by critics taking other theoretical approaches.

Practitioners of deconstruction might use "gap" when speaking of the radical contradictoriness of a text. Marxists have used the term to speak of everything from the gap that opens up between economic base and cultural superstructure to the two kinds of conflicts or contradictions to be found in literary texts. The first of these, they would argue, results from the fact that texts reflect ideology, within which certain subjects cannot be covered, things cannot be said, contradictory views cannot be recognized as contradictory. The second kind of conflict, contradiction, or gap within a text results from the fact that works don't just reflect ideology; they are also fictions that, consciously or unconsciously, distance themselves from the same ideology.

See also: Deconstruction, Ideology, Marxist Criticism, Reader-Response Criticism.

GENDER CRITICISM   Developing out of feminist criticism in the mid-1980s, this fluid and inclusive movement by its nature defies neat definition. Its practitioners include, but are not limited to, self-identified feminists, gay and lesbian critics, queer and performance theorists, and poststructuralists interested in deconstructing oppositions such as masculine/feminine, heterosexual/homosexual. This diverse group of critics shares an interest in interrogating categories of gender and sexuality and exploring the relationships between them, though it does not necessarily share any central assumptions about the nature of these categories. For example, some gender critics insist that all gender identities are cultural constructions, but others have maintained a belief in essential gender identity. Often gender critics are more interested in examining gender issues through a literary text than a literary text through gender issues. *See* "What Are Feminist and Gender Criticism?" pp. 129–43.

GENRE   A French word referring to a kind or type of literature. Individual works within a genre may exhibit a distinctive form, be governed by certain conventions, and/or represent characteristic subjects. Tragedy, epic, and romance are all genres.

Perhaps inevitably, the term *genre* is used loosely. Lyric poetry is a genre, but so are characteristic *types* of the lyric, such as the sonnet, the ode, and the elegy. Fiction is a genre, as are detective fiction and science fiction. The list of genres grows constantly as critics establish new lines of connection between individual works and discern new categories of works with common characteristics. Moreover, some writers form hybrid genres by combining the characteristics of several in a single work. Knowledge of genres helps critics to understand and explain what is conventional and unconventional, borrowed and original, in a work.

HEGEMONY   Given intellectual currency by the Italian communist Antonio Gramsci, the word (a translation of *egemonia*) refers to the pervasive system of assumptions, meanings, and values—the web of ideologies, in other words—that shapes the way things look, what they mean, and therefore what reality *is* for the majority of people within a given culture.

See also: Ideology, Marxist Criticism.

IDEOLOGY   A set of beliefs underlying the customs, habits, and/or practices common to a given social group. To members of that group, the beliefs seem obviously true, natural, and even universally applicable. They may seem just as obviously arbitrary, idiosyncratic, and even false to outsiders or members of another group who adhere to another ideology. Within a society, several ideologies may coexist, or one or more may be dominant.

Ideologies may be forcefully imposed or willingly subscribed to. Their component beliefs may be held consciously or unconsciously. In either case, they come to form what Johanna M. Smith has called "the unexamined ground of our experience." Ideology governs our perceptions, judgments, and prejudices—our sense of what is acceptable, normal, and deviant. Ideology may cause a revolution; it may also allow discrimination and even exploitation.

Ideologies are of special interest to sociologically oriented critics of literature because of the way in which authors reflect or resist prevailing views in their texts. Some Marxist critics have argued that literary texts reflect and reproduce the ideologies that produced them; most, however, have shown how ideologies are riven with contradictions that works of literature manage to expose and widen. Still other Marxists have focused on the way in which texts themselves are characterized by gaps, conflicts, and contradictions between their ideological and anti-ideological functions.

Feminist critics have addressed the question of ideology by seeking to expose (and thereby call into question) the patriarchal ideology mirrored or inscribed in works written by men—even men who have sought to counter sexism and break down sexual stereotypes. New historicists have been interested in demonstrating the ideological underpinnings not only of literary representations but also of our interpretations of them. Fredric Jameson, an American Marxist critic, argues that all thought is ideological, but that ideological thought that knows itself as such stands the chance of seeing through and transcending ideology.

See also: Cultural Criticism, Feminist Criticism, Marxist Criticism, New Historicism.

IMAGINARY ORDER   One of the three essential orders of the psychoanalytic field (*see* Real and Symbolic Order), it is most closely associated with the senses (sight, sound, touch, taste, and smell). The infant, who by comparison to other animals is born premature and thus is wholly dependent on others for a prolonged period, enters the Imaginary order when it begins to experience a unity of body parts and motor control that is empowering. This usually occurs between six and eighteen months, and is called by Lacan the "mirror stage" or "mirror phase," in which the child anticipates mastery of its body. It does so by identifying with the *image* of wholeness (that is, seeing its own image in the mirror, experiencing its mother as a whole body, and so on). This sense of oneness, and also difference from others (especially the mother or primary caretaker), is established through an image or a vision of harmony that is both a mirroring and a "mirage of maturation" or false sense of individuality and independence. The Imaginary is a metaphor for unity, is related to the visual order, and is always part of human subjectivity. Because the subject is fundamentally separate from others and also internally divided (conscious/unconscious), the apparent coherence of the Imaginary, its fullness and grandiosity, is always false, a *mis*recognition that the ego (or "me") tries to deny by imagining itself as coherent and empowered. The Imaginary operates in conjunction with the Real and Symbolic and is not a "stage" of development equivalent to Freud's "pre-oedipal stage," nor is it prelinguistic.

See also: Psychoanalytic Criticism, Real, Symbolic Order.

IMPLIED READER A phrase used by some reader-response critics in place of the phrase "the reader." Whereas "the reader" could refer to any idiosyncratic individual who happens to have read or to be reading the text, "the implied reader" is *the* reader intended, even created, by the text. Other reader-response critics seeking to describe this more generally conceived reader have spoken of the "informed reader" or the "narratee," who is "the necessary counterpart of a given narrator."

See also: Reader-Response Criticism.

INTENTIONAL FALLACY *See* Authorial Intention.

INTENTIONALITY *See* Authorial Intention.

INTERTEXTUALITY The condition of interconnectedness among texts. Every author has been influenced by others, and every work contains explicit and implicit references to other works. Writers may consciously or unconsciously echo a predecessor or precursor; they may also consciously or unconsciously disguise their indebtedness, making intertextual relationships difficult for the critic to trace.

Reacting against the formalist tendency to view each work as a freestanding object, some poststructuralist critics suggested that the meaning of a work emerges only intertextually, that is, within the context provided by other works. But there has been a reaction, too, against this type of intertextual criticism. Some new historicist critics suggest that literary history is itself too narrow a context and that works should be interpreted in light of a larger set of cultural contexts.

There is, however, a broader definition of intertextuality, one that refers to the relationship between works of literature and a wide range of narratives and discourses that we don't usually consider literary. Thus defined, intertextuality could be used by a new historicist to refer to the significant interconnectedness between a literary text and nonliterary discussions of or discourses about contemporary culture. Or it could be used by a poststructuralist to suggest that a work can be recognized and read only within a vast field of signs and tropes that is *like* a text and that makes any single text self-contradictory and "undecidable."

See also: Discourse, Formalism, Narrative, New Historicism, Poststructuralism, Trope.

MARXIST CRITICISM An approach that treats literary texts as material products, describing them in broadly historical terms. In Marxist criticism, the text is viewed in terms of its production and consumption, as a product *of* work that does identifiable cultural work of its own. Following Karl Marx, the founder of communism, Marxist critics have used the terms *base* to refer to economic reality and *superstructure* to refer to the corresponding or "homologous" infrastructure consisting of politics, law, philosophy, religion, and the arts. Also following Marx, they have used the word *ideology* to refer to that set of cultural beliefs that literary works at once reproduce, resist, and revise.

See also: "What Is Marxist Criticism?" pp. 203–17.

METAPHOR The representation of one thing by another related or similar thing. The image (or activity or concept) used to represent or "figure" something else is known as the "vehicle" of the metaphor; the thing represented is called the "tenor." In other words, the vehicle is what we substitute for the tenor. The relationship between vehicle and tenor can provide much additional meaning. Thus, instead of saying, "Last night I read a book," we might say, "Last night I plowed through a book." "Plowed through" (or the activity of plowing) is the vehicle of our metaphor; "read" (or the act of reading) is the tenor, the thing being figured. The increment in meaning through metaphor is fairly obvious. Our audience knows not only *that* we read but also *how* we read, because to read a book in the way that a plow rips through earth is surely to read in a relentless, unreflective way. Note that in the sentence above, a new metaphor—"rips through"—has been used to explain an old one. This serves (which is a metaphor) as an example of just how thick (another metaphor) language is with metaphors!

Metaphor is a kind of "trope" (literally, a "turning," that is, a figure of speech that alters or "turns" the meaning of a word or phrase). Other tropes include allegory, conceit, metonymy, personification, simile, symbol, and synecdoche. Traditionally, metaphor and symbol have been viewed as the principal tropes; minor tropes have been categorized as *types* of these two major ones. Similes, for instance, are usually defined as simple metaphors that usually employ *like* or *as* and state the tenor outright, as in "My love is like a red, red rose." Synecdoche involves a vehicle that is a *part* of the tenor, as in "I see a sail" meaning "I see a boat." Metonymy is viewed as a metaphor involving two terms commonly if arbitrarily associated with (but not fundamentally or intrinsically related to) each other. Recently, however, deconstructors such as Paul de Man and J. Hillis Miller have questioned the "privilege" granted to metaphor and the metaphor/metonymy distinction or "opposition." They have suggested that all metaphors are really metonyms and that all figuration is arbitrary.

See also: Deconstruction, Metonymy, Oppositions, Symbol.

METONYMY   The representation of one thing by another that is commonly and often physically associated with it. To refer to a writer's handwriting as his or her "hand" is to use a metonymic "figure" or "trope." The image or thing used to represent something else is known as the "vehicle" of the metonym; the thing represented is called the "tenor."

Like other tropes (such as metaphor), metonymy involves the replacement of one word or phrase by another. Liquor may be referred to as "the bottle," a monarch as "the crown." Narrowly defined, the vehicle of a metonym is arbitrarily, not intrinsically, associated with the tenor. In other words, the bottle just happens to be what liquor is stored in and poured from in our culture. The hand may be involved in the production of handwriting, but so are the brain and the pen. There is no special, intrinsic likeness between a crown and a monarch; it's just that crowns traditionally sit on monarchs' heads and not on the heads of university professors. More broadly, *metonym* and *metonymy* have been used by recent critics to refer to a wide range of figures and tropes. Deconstructors have questioned the distinction between metaphor and metonymy.

See also: Deconstruction, Metaphor, Trope.

NARRATIVE   A story or a telling of a story, or an account of a situation or of events. A novel and a biography of a novelist are both narratives, as are Freud's case histories.

Some critics use the word *narrative* even more generally; Brook Thomas, a new historicist, has critiqued "narratives of human history that neglect the role human labor has played."

NEW CRITICISM *See* Formalism.

NEW HISTORICISM First practiced and articulated in the late 1970s and early 1980s in the work of critics such as Stephen Greenblatt—who named this movement in contemporary critical theory—and Louis Montrose, its practitioners share certain convictions, primarily that literary critics need to develop a high degree of historical consciousness and that literature should not be viewed apart from other human creations, artistic or otherwise. They share a belief in referentiality—a belief that literature refers to and is referred to by things outside itself—that is fainter in the works of formalist, poststructuralist, and even reader-response critics. Discarding old distinctions between literature, history, and the social sciences, new historicists agree with Greenblatt that the "central concerns" of criticism "should prevent it from permanently sealing off one type of discourse from another, or decisively separating works of art from the minds and lives of their creators and their audiences."

See also: Authorial Intention, Deconstruction, Formalism, Ideology, Poststructuralism, Psychoanalytic Criticism.

OPPOSITIONS A concept highly relevant to linguistics, inasmuch as linguists maintain that words (such as *black* and *death*) have meaning not in themselves but in relation to other words (*white* and *life*). Jacques Derrida, a poststructuralist philosopher of language, has suggested that in the West we think in terms of these "binary oppositions" or dichotomies, which on examination turn out to be evaluative hierarchies. In other words, each opposition—beginning/end, presence/absence, or consciousness/unconsciousness—contains one term that our culture views as superior and one term that we view as negative or inferior.

Derrida has "deconstructed" a number of these binary oppositions, including two—speech/writing and signifier/signified—that he believes to be central to linguistics in particular and Western culture in general. He has concurrently critiqued the "law" of noncontradiction, which is fundamental to Western logic. He and other deconstructors have argued that a text can contain opposed strands of discourse and, therefore, can mean opposite things: reason *and* passion, life *and* death, hope *and* despair, black *and* white. Traditionally, criticism has involved choosing between opposed or contradictory meanings and arguing that one is present in the text and the other absent.

French feminists have adopted the ideas of Derrida and other deconstructors, showing not only that we think in terms of such binary oppositions as male/female, reason/emotion, and active/passive, but that we also associate reason and activity with masculinity and emotion and passivity with femininity. Because of this, they have concluded that language is "phallocentric," or masculine-dominated.

See also: Deconstruction, Discourse, Feminist Criticism, Poststructuralism.

PHALLUS The symbolic value of the penis that organizes libidinal development and which Freud saw as a stage in the process of human subjectivity. Lacan viewed the Phallus as the representative of a fraudulent power (male over female) whose "Law" is a principle of psychic division (conscious/unconscious) and sexual difference (masculine/feminine). The Symbolic order (*see* Symbolic Order) is ruled by the Phallus, which of itself has no inherent meaning *apart from* the power and meaning given to it by individual cultures and societies, and represented by the name of the father as lawgiver and namer.

POSTSTRUCTURALISM The general attempt to contest and subvert structuralism initiated by deconstructors and certain other critics associated with psychoanalytic, Marxist, and feminist theory. Structuralists, using linguistics as a model and employing semiotic (sign) theory, posit the possibility of knowing a text systematically and revealing the "grammar" behind its form and meaning. Poststructuralists argue against the possibility of such knowledge and description. They counter that texts can be shown to contradict not only structuralist accounts of them but also themselves. In making their adversarial claims, they rely on close readings of texts and on the work of theorists such as Jacques Derrida and Jacques Lacan.

Poststructuralists have suggested that structuralism rests on distinctions between "signifier" and "signified" (signs and the things they point toward), "self" and "language" (or "text"), texts and other texts, and text and world that are overly simplistic, if not patently inaccurate. Poststructuralists have shown how all signifieds are also signifiers, and they have treated texts as "intertexts." They have viewed the world as if it *were* a text (we desire a certain car because it *symbolizes* achievement) and the self as the subject, as well as the user, of language; for example, we may shape and speak through language, but it also shapes and speaks through us.

See also: Deconstruction, Feminist Criticism, Intertextuality, Psychoanalytic Criticism, Semiotics, Structuralism.

PSYCHOANALYTIC CRITICISM Grounded in the psychoanalytic theories of Sigmund Freud, it is one of the oldest critical methodologies still in use. Freud's view that works of literature, like dreams, express secret, unconscious desires led to criticism and interpreted literary works as manifestations of the authors' neuroses. More recently, psychoanalytic critics have come to see literary works as skillfully crafted artifacts that may appeal to *our* neuroses by tapping into our repressed wishes and fantasies. Other forms of psychological criticism that diverge from Freud, although they ultimately derive from his insights, include those based on the theories of Carl Jung and Jacques Lacan. *See* "What Is Psychoanalytic Criticism?" pp. 169–81.

READER-RESPONSE CRITICISM An approach to literature that, as its name implies, considers the way readers respond to texts as they read. Stanley Fish describes the method by saying that it substitutes for one question, "What does this sentence mean?" a more operational question, "What does this sentence do?" Reader-response criticism shares with deconstruction a strong textual orientation and a reluctance to define a single meaning for a work. Along with psychoanalytic criticism, it shares an interest in the dynamics of mental response to textual cues. *See* "What Is Reader-Response Criticism?" pp. 91–103.

REAL One of the three orders of subjectivity (*see* Imaginary Order and Symbolic Order), the Real is the intractable and substantial world that resists and exceeds interpretation. The Real cannot be imagined, symbolized, or known directly. It constantly eludes our efforts to name it (death, gravity, the physicality of objects are examples of the Real), and thus challenges both the Imaginary and the Symbolic orders. The Real is fundamentally "Other," the mark of the divide between conscious and unconscious, and is signaled in language by gaps, slips, speechlessness, and the sense of the uncanny. The Real is not what we call "reality." It is the stumbling block of the Imaginary (which thinks it can "imagine" anything, including the Real) and of the Symbolic, which tries to bring the Real under its laws (the Real exposes the "phallacy" of the Law of the Phallus). The Real is frightening; we try to tame it with laws and language and call it "reality."

See also: Imaginary Order, Psychoanalytic Criticism, Symbolic Order.

SEMIOLOGY, SEMIOTIC   *See* Semiotics.

SEMIOTICS   The study of signs and sign systems and the way meaning is derived from them. Structuralist anthropologists, psychoanalysts, and literary critics developed semiotics during the decades following 1950, but much of the pioneering work had been done at the turn of the century by the founder of modern linguistics, Ferdinand de Saussure, and the American philosopher Charles Sanders Peirce.

Semiotics is based on several important distinctions, including the distinction between "signifier" and "signified" (the sign and what it points toward) and the distinction between "langue" and "parole." *Langue* (French for "tongue," as in "native tongue," meaning language) refers to the entire system within which individual utterances or usages of language have meaning; *parole* (French for "word") refers to the particular utterances or usages. A principal tenet of semiotics is that signs, like words, are not significant in themselves, but instead have meaning only in relation to other signs and the entire system of signs, or langue.

The affinity between semiotics and structuralist literary criticism derives from this emphasis placed on langue, or system. Structuralist critics, after all, were reacting against formalists and their procedure of focusing on individual words as if meanings didn't depend on anything external to the text.

Poststructuralists have used semiotics but questioned some of its underlying assumptions, including the opposition between signifier and signified. The feminist poststructuralist Julia Kristeva, for instance, has used the word *semiotic* to describe feminine language, a highly figurative, fluid form of discourse that she sets in opposition to rigid, symbolic masculine language.

See also: Deconstruction, Feminist Criticism, Formalism, Oppositions, Poststructuralism, Structuralism, Symbol.

SIMILE   *See* Metaphor.

SOCIOHISTORICAL CRITICISM   *See* New Historicism.

STRUCTURALISM   A science of humankind whose proponents attempted to show that all elements of human culture, including literature, may be understood as parts of a system of signs. Structuralism, according to Robert Scholes, was a reaction to "'modernist' alienation and despair."

Using Ferdinand de Saussure's linguistic theory, European structuralists such as Roman Jakobson, Claude Lévi-Strauss, and Roland Barthes (before his shift toward poststructuralism) attempted to develop a "semiology" or "semiotics" (science of signs). Barthes, among others, sought to recover literature and even language from the isolation in which they had been studied and to show that the laws that govern them govern all signs, from road signs to articles of clothing.

Particularly useful to structuralists were two of Saussure's concepts: the idea of "phoneme" in language and the idea that phonemes exist in two kinds of relationships: "synchronic" and "diachronic." A phoneme is the smallest consistently significant unit in language; thus, both "a" and "an" are phonemes, but "n" is not. A diachronic relationship is that which a phoneme has with those that have preceded it in time and those that will follow it. These "horizontal" relationships produce what we might call discourse or narrative and what Saussure called "parole." The synchronic relationship is the "vertical" one that a word has in a given instant with the entire system of language ("langue") in which it may generate meaning. "An" means what it means in English because those of us who speak the language are using it in the same way at a given time.

Following Saussure, Lévi-Strauss studied hundreds of myths, breaking them into their smallest meaningful units, which he called "mythemes." Removing each from its diachronic relations with other mythemes in a single myth (such as the myth of Oedipus and his mother), he vertically aligned those mythemes that he found to be homologous (structurally correspondent). He then studied the relationships within as well as between vertically aligned columns, in an attempt to understand scientifically, through ratios and proportions, those thoughts and processes that humankind has shared, both at one particular time and across time. One could say, then, that structuralists followed Saussure in preferring to think about the overriding langue or language of myth, in which each mytheme and mytheme-constituted myth fits meaningfully, rather than about isolated individual paroles or narratives. Structuralists followed Saussure's lead in believing what the poststructuralist Jacques Derrida later decided he could not subscribe to—that sign systems must be understood in terms of binary oppositions. In analyzing myths and texts to find basic structures, structuralists tended to find that opposite terms modulate until they are finally resolved or reconciled by some intermediary third term. Thus, a structuralist reading of *Paradise Lost* would show that the war between God and the bad angels becomes a rift between God and sinful, fallen man, the rift then being healed by the Son of God, the mediating third term.

See also: Deconstruction, Discourse, Narrative, Poststructuralism, Semiotics.

SUPERSTRUCTURE   *See* Marxist Criticism.

SYMBOL   A thing, image, or action that, although it is of interest in its own right, stands for or suggests something larger and more complex—often an idea or a range of interrelated ideas, attitudes, and practices.

Within a given culture, some things are understood to be symbols: the flag of the United States is an obvious example. More subtle cultural symbols might be the river as a symbol of time and the journey as a symbol of life and its manifold experiences.

Instead of appropriating symbols generally used and understood within their culture, writers often create symbols by setting up, in their works, a complex but identifiable web of associations. As a result, one object, image, or action suggests others, and often, ultimately, a range of ideas.

A symbol may thus be defined as a metaphor in which the "vehicle," the thing, image, or action used to represent something else, represents many related things (or "tenors") or is broadly suggestive. The urn in Keats's "Ode on a Grecian Urn" suggests many interrelated concepts, including art, truth, beauty, and timelessness.

Symbols have been of particular interest to formalists, who study how meanings emerge from the complex, patterned relationships between images in a work, and psychoanalytic critics, who are interested in how individual authors and the larger culture both disguise and reveal unconscious fears and desires through symbols. Recently, French feminists have also focused on the symbolic. They have suggested that, as wide-ranging as it seems, symbolic language is ultimately rigid and restrictive. They favor semiotic language and writing, which, they contend, is at once more rhythmic, unifying, and feminine.

See also: Feminist Criticism, Metaphor, Psychoanalytic Criticism, Trope.

SYMBOLIC ORDER One of the three orders of subjectivity (*see* Imaginary Order and Real), it is the realm of law, language, and society; it is the repository of generally held cultural beliefs. Its symbolic system is language, whose agent is the father or lawgiver, the one who has the power of naming. The human subject is commanded into this preestablished order by language (a process that begins long before a child can speak) and must submit to its orders of communication (grammar, syntax, and so on). Entrance into the Symbolic order determines subjectivity according to a primary law of referentiality that takes the male sign (phallus; *see* Phallus) as its ordering principle. Lacan states that both sexes submit to the Law of the Phallus (the law of order, language, and differentiation) but their individual relation to the law determines whether they see themselves as—and are seen by others to be—either "masculine" or "feminine." The Symbolic institutes repression (of the Imaginary), thus creating the unconscious, which itself is structured like the language of the symbolic. The unconscious, a timeless realm, cannot be known directly, but it can be understood by a kind of translation that takes place in language—psychoanalysis is the "talking cure." The Symbolic is not a "stage" of development (as is Freud's "oedipal stage"), nor is it set in place once and for all in human life. We constantly negotiate its threshold (in sleep, in drunkenness) and can "fall out" of it altogether in psychosis.

See also: Imaginary Order, Psychoanalytic Criticism, Real.

SYNECDOCHE *See* Metaphor, Metonymy.

TENOR *See* Metaphor, Metonymy, Symbol.

TROPE A figure, as in "figure of speech." Literally a "turning," that is, a turning or twisting of a word or phrase to make it mean something else. Principal tropes include metaphor, metonymy, personification, simile, and synecdoche.

See also: Metaphor, Metonymy.

VEHICLE *See* Metaphor, Metonymy, Symbol.

About the Contributors

THE VOLUME EDITOR

Margot Norris is professor of English and Comparative Literature at the University of California, Irvine. She is author of two books on Joyce, *The Decentered Universe of "Finnegans Wake"* (1976) and *Joyce's Web: The Social Unraveling of Modernism* (1992), and a book on modern intellectual history, *Beasts of the Modern Imagination: Darwin, Nietzsche, Kafka, Ernst, and Lawrence* (1985). Together with Vincent Cheng and Kimberly J. Devlin, she has edited a collection of essays called *Joycean Cultures: Culturing Joyces*, scheduled for publication in 1998. Margot Norris is currently working on two new book projects: one examining modern mass warfare and the second on Joyce's *Dubliners*.

THE CRITICS

Jacques Derrida is professor at the École des Hautes Études en Sciences Sociales, Paris, and since 1987, holds a visiting professorship at the University of California, Irvine. He is the author of over thirty books that have been translated into numerous languages, including landmark studies in philosophy and theory such as *Writing and Difference, Of Grammatology, Dissemination, Glas, Margins of Philosophy,*

Limited Inc, Positions, The Ear of the Other, The Truth in Painting,
Spurs: Nietzsche's Styles, and *Shibboleth: Pour Paul Celan.* His influential study *The Post Card: From Socrates to Freud and Beyond,* which appeared in a translation by Alan Bass in 1987, has particular relevance
for his essay on *Ulysses* in this volume. Books about Jacques Derrida
include studies by Christopher Norris (1987) and volumes of "Derrida-
Readers" by Peggy Kamuf (1992) and David Wood (1992).

Kimberly J. Devlin is associate professor of English at the University of California, Riverside. She is author of *Wandering and Return
in "Finnegans Wake"* (1991). With Marilyn Reizbaum, she has
coedited a forthcoming volume of new essays on the eighteen episodes
of *Ulysses* called *"Ulysses": (En)gendered Perspectives.* Devlin has published several articles on Joyce and, more recently, a Lacanian interpretation of Conrad's *Heart of Darkness.* She is presently at work on a
book entitled *Joycean Fraudstuff.*

Wolfgang Iser is professor emeritus in the Department of Literature of the University of Constance, Germany, and since 1978, holds
appointment at the University of California, Irvine. He has published
books on Edmund Spenser, William Shakespeare, Henry Fielding,
Laurence Sterne, Walter Pater, and Samuel Beckett but is best known
for his theoretical studies on reader-response, *The Implied Reader:
Patterns of Communication in Prose Fiction from Bunyan to Beckett*
(1974) and *The Act of Reading: A Theory of Aesthetic Response* (1978).
More recently he has published *Prospecting: From Reader Response to
Literary Anthropology* (1989) and *The Fictive and the Imaginary:
Charting Literary Anthropology* (1993).

Vicki Mahaffey is associate professor of English at the University
of Pennsylvania, where she teaches modernism, Irish literature, and
women's studies. She is author of *Reauthorizing Joyce* (1988) and a
book on experimentation and desire in the works of Oscar Wilde,
W. B. Yeats, and James Joyce that will be published in 1997. She is
currently working on a feminist introduction to modernist literature.

Patrick McGee teaches at Louisiana State University. He has published articles on Joyce, Faulkner, Woolf, postcolonial African fiction,
pedagogy, and cultural theory. He is the author of *Paperspace: Style as
Ideology in Joyce's "Ulysses"* (1988) and *Telling the Other: The Question
of Value in Modern and Postcolonial Writing* (1992). He has two

works forthcoming: *Cinema, Theory, and Political Responsibility in Contemporary Culture* and *Ishmael Reed and the Ends of Race.*

THE SERIES EDITOR

Ross C Murfin, general editor of Case Studies in Contemporary Criticism, and volume editor of Conrad's *Heart of Darkness* and Hawthorne's *The Scarlet Letter* in the series, is provost and vice president for Academic Affairs at Southern Methodist University. He has taught at the University of Miami, Yale University, and the University of Virginia and has published scholarly studies on Joseph Conrad, Thomas Hardy, and D. H. Lawrence.